FROM INTERNET PICS TO THE BUSINESS GRIND

From Internet Pics to the Business Grind

Paisley Miller

First Printing, 2025

CONTENTS

ONE

UNDERSTANDING YOUR ENTREPRENEURIAL FOUNDATION

Before starting a new conventional business, it's essential to assess your existing digital assets and online presence. Many entrepreneurs, especially those with large followings on platforms like OnlyFans, have significant untapped potential in their current online footprint. This section focuses on evaluating this digital real estate. Think of it as an audit of your online empire, not to duplicate it, but to extract foundational elements that can be repurposed and enhanced. The goal is to shift your perspective from specific platform limitations to underlying, transferable strengths that form a robust digital business.

The first critical step is to meticulously inventory your audience. This goes beyond follower count; it's about understanding the individuals behind the numbers. Delve into your existing analytics: What are the demographics of your most engaged followers (age, location, interests, etc.)? Beyond basic demographics, explore psychographics: what are their motivations, values, and aspirations? Which content consistently generates the highest engagement (likes, comments, shares, direct messages)? Identifying these patterns reveals what truly resonates with your audience, offering valuable insights into their preferences and needs, which can be directly applied to understanding potential customer segments for your new venture. For example, if fitness and wellness content consistently garners significant attention, it indicates a strong interest in that sector within your follower base, signaling a potential health and wellness product or service. Conversely, if your audience prefers behind-the-scenes glimpses into your creative process, it suggests an appreciation for authenticity and "how-to" content, which can be translated into educational content or consulting services.

Engagement metrics are a goldmine. Don't just focus on vanity metrics; analyze the depth of interaction. Which posts spark conversations? Which types of content lead to direct inquiries or purchases? Understanding these engagement drivers will inform your content strategy for your new business. For instance, if Q&A sessions consistently drive high interaction, it suggests your audience values direct communication and problem-solving. This can be leveraged by offering live Q&A webinars or a dedicated customer support chat for your new business. Similarly, if your audience responds enthusiastically to exclusive content or early access, it indicates a readiness for loyalty programs or tiered service offerings in your future business. The key is to understand your audience's behavior and its drivers. This analysis moves beyond superficial engagement to reveal genuine interest and potential purchasing intent. Consider the difference between a passive like and a thoughtful comment or a direct message seeking advice; the latter represents a much deeper level of engagement and a stronger indicator of potential customer value.

To effectively transition your online presence into a thriving business, a thorough assessment of your existing digital footprint is crucial. This involves deconstructing your current online assets into fundamental, transferable components, providing a clear roadmap for success in a more traditional business context. This exercise highlights the inherent value you've already created and leverages established foundations to build something new and enduring.

1. **Content Analysis:**

- **Successful Formats:** Identify which content formats—short-form video, long-form written content, live streams, or interactive polls—have resonated most with your audience. Each format engages differently, speaking to varied communication preferences.
- **Audience Preference:** If instructional videos consistently receive high engagement, prioritize visual learning content like video tutorials or product demonstrations for your new e-commerce store or service. If personal stories and narratives perform well, integrate storytelling into your marketing to foster brand loyalty. This analysis reveals not only what resonates, but also how, guiding you to create engaging and effective content that conveys your new business's value proposition.

2. **Community Dynamics:**

- **Fostered Community:** Assess if you've cultivated a sense of community and established interaction norms among your followers.

Understanding audience interaction provides critical insights for building and managing a customer base.

- **Leveraging Community:** If your community is characterized by supportive exchanges, leverage this for your new venture by creating forums, dedicated social media groups, or exclusive customer communities. This fosters belonging and encourages peer-to-peer interaction, serving as a powerful differentiator and a source of ongoing engagement and feedback.
- **Transferable Skills:** Your experience in managing discussions, responding to comments, and fostering a positive environment translates directly to valuable customer relations and community management skills for any business.

3. Brand Perception (Brand Equity):

- **Audience Association:** Document what people associate with you—expertise, creativity, authenticity, lifestyle, or values. This represents your current brand equity.
- **Professional Identity:** Understanding current brand perception is crucial for evolving into a professional business identity. Identify core elements that have resonated and that you

wish to carry forward. For example, trustworthiness and reliability are invaluable assets for building customer confidence.

- **Strategic Reframing:** If certain aspects of your current brand might be perceived negatively in a conventional business context, strategically address and reframe them. This could involve moderating language, adjusting visual presentation, or focusing public communications on professional aspects of your skillset.

4. Audience Loyalty:

- **Drivers of Loyalty:** Determine why people consistently follow you—content quality, personality, value, or connection. Understanding these drivers informs strategies for customer retention in your new business.
- **Building Enduring Relationships:** High audience loyalty indicates your capacity to build enduring customer relationships, which can be a powerful catalyst for growth through repeat purchases, positive reviews, and word-of-mouth marketing.
- **Replicating Loyalty:** Recognize the trust and rapport you've built and channel it into your new context by identifying and replicating

specific actions or qualities that fostered this loyalty.

5. Communication Channels:

- **Effective Pathways:** Examine which communication channels—email newsletters, direct messages, specific social media platforms, or private communities—have been most successful.
- **Targeted Engagement:** Identifying effective pathways is essential for planning how to reach and engage your new audience. If email marketing yielded high conversion rates, prioritize building an email list. If direct messaging built personal connections, integrate personalized communication into customer service or sales.
- **Strategic Adaptation:** Understand audience preferences to allocate marketing resources effectively and ensure timely messaging. This isn't about abandoning what worked, but strategically adapting it. Leverage existing strong engagement on professional social media platforms, or cultivate new, more appropriate channels if current platforms aren't conducive to a professional business.

Conclusion:

This deep dive into your digital footprint is an assessment of your current intangible assets, providing a more robust starting point than many new entrepreneurs possess. The skills you've honed—understanding audience behavior, crafting engaging content, building relationships, and managing an online presence—are core entrepreneurial competencies. By meticulously mapping these existing online assets, you lay the groundwork for a strategic business transition, armed with a deep understanding of your core value proposition and transferable elements that will drive future success. This is the critical first step in transforming your established digital influence into a legitimate, sustainable entrepreneurial enterprise, seeing your existing platform as a launchpad for a more diversified and professional business future. This unique competitive advantage, when strategically leveraged, can significantly accelerate your path to success in traditional business arenas.

The skills you've developed by building and managing an online presence, especially on platforms that allow direct monetization, are far more extensive than they might first appear. These are not merely "social media skills" but deeply ingrained entrepreneurial competencies highly valued in traditional business. It's crucial to see your past endeavors as a rigorous, hands-on training ground for building and operating a legitimate business—a comprehensive apprenticeship that has equipped you with a unique and valuable skillset.

One significant area of expertise you've honed is digital marketing and audience acquisition. Through trial and error, you've learned to attract attention, create compelling hooks, and nurture interest into a committed following. This involves understanding platform algorithms, employing effective keyword strategies, and crafting visible, shareable content. You've experimented with various content formats (videos, images, written posts, live streams) to resonate with specific audience segments, thereby developing your ability to segment audiences, understand their needs, and tailor your messaging. The skills in creating effective calls to action, understanding conversion funnels, and driving engagement are directly applicable to any business seeking to grow its customer base. Crafting compelling captions or visually appealing thumbnails are micro-lessons in persuasive communication and brand visibility. You've become adept at identifying trends and adapting your approach, making your adaptability and market awareness invaluable.

Beyond acquisition, you've mastered direct-to-consumer (DTC) sales and monetization strategies. On platforms where income is tied to engagement, you've become an expert at presenting value and facilitating transactions. This includes understanding pricing strategies, creating tiered offerings, and communicating the benefits of premium content. You've learned to manage customer expectations, deliver on promises, and handle financial aspects from pricing to payouts. This direct line to the consumer has given you a keen understanding of customer lifetime value and the importance of repeat business. You've seen firsthand how customer satisfaction impacts revenue and have optimized offerings based on direct feedback. This practical experience in driving revenue through digital channels is a core competency for modern businesses, especially in e-commerce and subscription models. Experimenting with pricing tiers or bundled packages is essentially running a small-scale e-commerce operation, honing skills in product development, pricing, and sales strategy.

Customer relationship management (CRM) is another area where you've likely gained significant expertise. Managing a large following involves handling a high volume of direct messages, comments, and inquiries. You've learned to respond to feedback, address concerns, manage fan interactions, and build a sense of community and loyalty. This requires excellent communication skills, empathy, patience, and the ability to set boundaries. You've likely developed informal systems for managing these interactions, learning to prioritize, delegate, and ensure consistent engagement. The ability to maintain positive customer relationships, handle complaints gracefully, and foster connection is critical for retention and brand advocacy. Crafting thoughtful replies or engaging in direct conversations to resolve issues are the essence of good customer service and relationship building. You've become adept at understanding audience psychology, anticipating needs, and responding in ways that strengthen their connection to you and your brand.

You've demonstrated exceptional skill in brand building and management, cultivating a personal brand that clearly defines your image, values, and unique selling proposition. This involves deliberate choices about your content, communication style, and online persona, ensuring consistent messaging and a cohesive, recognizable identity. This experience in brand creation and maintenance is essential for establishing a credible and trustworthy business. You've navigated public perception, managed your reputation, and ensured your brand effectively communicates its intended message. This hands-on experience in shaping public perception is a powerful asset for transitioning to a formal business structure, as you understand the importance of authenticity, consistency, and a clear value proposition in building a resonant brand.

Your journey has also required strong development in content strategy and creation. Beyond simply posting, you've strategically planned what content to create, when to release it, and how to maximize its impact. This includes understanding content pillars, implicitly planning editorial calendars, and analyzing content performance to refine your approach. You've developed a keen eye for what captures attention, educates, entertains, and drives action. The ability to consistently produce high-quality, engaging content is a cornerstone of modern marketing and business communication. Your adaptability in tailoring content for different platforms and audience preferences is crucial in a dynamic market; for instance, recognizing that short-form video drives initial attraction, while longer content builds authority, demonstrates strategic thinking.

A significant, often undervalued, skill you possess is analytics interpretation and data-driven decision-making. You've likely sifted through platform data on audience engagement, content performance, and demographics to understand what's working and what isn't, using this information to adjust your strategy. This provides you with a practical understanding of key performance indicators (KPIs) and how to use them to inform business decisions. The ability to analyze data, identify trends, and translate insights into actionable steps is critical for any business leader.

You've learned to look beyond surface-level numbers to understand underlying behaviors and preferences, allowing you to be agile and responsive to market changes and customer feedback—a crucial advantage. Whether understanding post shares, video watch times, or peak engagement hours, you've been conducting continuous market research.

Finally, and perhaps most importantly, you've cultivated immense self-discipline, resilience, and entrepreneurial drive. Building and maintaining an online presence, especially one that generates income, demands significant dedication, self-motivation, and the ability to overcome setbacks. You've likely faced periods of low engagement, criticism, and the inherent unpredictability of online content creation, yet you've persevered. This resilience, coupled with the drive to create and monetize your efforts, is the very essence of entrepreneurship. You understand the importance of goal setting, effective time management, and commitment, even when immediate results are not apparent. This internal locus of control and willingness to put in the hard work are foundational qualities for any business venture. You've learned to manage your own workflow without external oversight, a hallmark of successful independent professionals and business owners. This ability to self-start, self-manage, and self-motivate is an invaluable intangible asset.

When cataloging these skills, it's essential to reframe them in conventional business language. "Managing my DMs" becomes "customer service and relationship management." "Making TikToks" transforms into "short-form video content creation and social media marketing." "Getting subscribers" is rephrased as "acquiring and retaining customers through targeted digital strategies." This translation is vital for articulating your value proposition to potential investors, partners, or even in a job search. You are not merely someone who was popular online; you are a skilled digital marketer, a direct-to-consumer sales professional, a brand builder, and a data-savvy operator with a proven track record of audience engagement and revenue generation. Recognizing the depth and breadth of these transferable competencies is the critical next step in confidently transitioning your entrepreneurial spirit from specialized platforms to the broader opportunities of the conventional business world. You possess a real-world business education that many formal programs struggle to replicate.

The evolution from creator to CEO involves a profound mental shift, far beyond a mere change in title or duties. For those whose careers are rooted in digital platforms, the initial focus is on their craft, content, and audience connection. This creator-centric approach, crucial for building a following and personal brand, differs significantly from the principles that drive scalable, sustainable businesses. To successfully transition into a more robust entrepreneurial role, a deliberate shift from a creator's mindset to a CEO's is essential.

This psychological transformation entails re-evaluating one's purpose, priorities, and operational framework. Creators are often driven by expression, engagement, or sharing, measuring success by likes, shares, comments, and subscriber growth. While these metrics remain important, for a CEO, they become inputs rather than the ultimate output. A CEO's perspective is market-oriented and internally focused on the business's operational health, emphasizing profitability, scalability, strategic growth, and long-term viability. Creators channel their energy into immediate content creation and distribution, whereas CEOs focus on building systems, managing resources, and navigating the complex economic landscape.

A key aspect of this mindset shift is embracing strategic planning. Creators often rely on intuition and timely relevance, reacting to trends and audience demands. While agility is valuable, a CEO must adopt a more deliberate, forward-looking approach. This means moving beyond daily or weekly content calendars to develop a comprehensive business plan.

This plan should clearly articulate the company's vision, mission, and values, define target markets, set achievable financial goals, and map out strategies for success. It involves thorough market research, competitor analysis, and understanding broader economic and industry trends. For those accustomed to the fluid nature of content creation, this transition requires discipline in formalizing ideas, setting measurable objectives (KPIs beyond engagement metrics), and establishing accountability. It's about creating a roadmap that guides every decision, aligning actions with overarching strategic objectives.

Financial management is another crucial area that demands an evolved mindset. Many creators, while aware of their income, may not have operated with rigorous financial oversight. As a CEO, understanding and managing finances becomes paramount. This includes tracking revenue and expenses, budgeting, forecasting, managing cash flow, understanding profitability drivers, and potentially dealing with investments, loans, or equity. Creators might see income as a direct reward for effort; CEOs view it as the lifeblood of an enterprise requiring prudent management for survival and growth. This necessitates a deeper understanding of accounting principles, tax regulations, and financial planning tools. It means transitioning from simply "earning money" to "managing capital" and making informed decisions about resource allocation. The ability to read financial statements, understand balance sheets, and analyze a business's financial health is no longer optional but a core CEO competency.

The concept of the "grind" also transforms. For many creators, the grind involves relentless content production, the constant need for relevance, and significant personal investment in building a following. While commendable, a CEO's grind differs. It's about working smarter and more strategically, focusing on disciplined execution of the business plan, meticulous attention to operational details, and proactive problem-solving. It means directing efforts towards activities that significantly impact business goals, rather than merely being busy. Resilience remains vital, but it's now resilience in the face of market challenges, strategic pivots, and operational hurdles, not solely audience reception fluctuations. It requires a commitment to continuous learning, adaptability, and the willingness to make difficult decisions. While a creator's personal brand is often intertwined with their output, a CEO's focus is on building a robust, independent business, necessitating a more detached and objective approach to decision-making.

From Creator to CEO: A Mindset Shift for Sustainable Entrepreneurship

The shift from creator to CEO signifies a profound change in professional identity, essential for establishing a lasting and impactful business. This evolution necessitates a new approach, moving from individual output to strategic business leadership.

Embracing the CEO Mindset

Adopting a CEO perspective fosters the confidence needed to navigate entrepreneurial challenges. This reframes problem-solving, making complexities manageable within a structured operational framework. While the fear of failure persists, it is mitigated by a strategic understanding of risk management and conviction in your plan. This empowerment enables calculated risks, stronger negotiations, and the cultivation of vital stakeholder relationships. It's about recognizing that your creative experiences have equipped you with unique and relevant skills for the business world, and having the belief to leverage them effectively.

Building Scalable Systems and Processes

A core aspect of the CEO mindset is the commitment to building scalable systems and processes. Unlike creators who often rely on personal energy, a CEO understands that business growth beyond a single individual requires robust infrastructure. This includes defining workflows, standardizing operations, implementing quality control, and potentially building a team. The aim is to transition from a model where everything depends on you to one where the business operates efficiently even in your absence. This requires delegation, trust in others, and empowering a team to execute the vision, alongside a commitment to continuous improvement and efficiency optimization.

Legal Acumen and Responsibility

This transition also brings a heightened awareness of legal and compliance requirements. While creators might operate informally, a CEO must understand and adhere to business laws, contracts, intellectual property rights, and regulatory frameworks. This often involves engaging legal counsel, establishing appropriate business structures, and ensuring all operations are compliant. This proactive approach to legal matters is essential for professionalism, risk mitigation, and is a hallmark of a responsible business leader.

The Brand Evolution: From Personal to Corporate

A creator's personal brand often centers on individual output, whereas a CEO's brand focuses on the company's offerings and how it serves its customers. This signifies a move from self-expression to a broader economic creation, delivering value to customers and generating sustainable profit through the intricate machinery of a business.

Defining Your Entrepreneurial Vision Beyond the Platform

Your journey as a creator has provided a strong foundation in audience engagement, content creation, community building, and understanding digital trends. Now, the crucial step is to consciously articulate a future for your enterprise that aligns with an evolved purpose, leverages your unique capabilities, and addresses a tangible market need. The critical question is: What is your entrepreneurial vision beyond the platform?

This necessitates a strategic re-evaluation of your aspirations, essentially crafting a new operating system for your professional life that supports growth, scalability, and lasting impact. Your past success offers invaluable insights into audience desires and content effectiveness. It's time to channel this knowledge into a more structured and ambitious framework. Consider possibilities like an e-commerce empire, a consulting or coaching business, or scalable digital products such as online courses, software, or templates. Each path offers a unique way to translate your influence and skills into a sustainable and impactful business.

Aligning Values, Skills, and Market Opportunity

To effectively define this vision, introspection into your core values and long-term aspirations is crucial. Beyond engagement metrics, what impact do you want to make? What problems are you most passionate about solving? Identifying these pain points within your community or market forms the bedrock of creating genuine business value. When your personal values, inherent skills, and a clear market opportunity converge, you create a powerful engine for entrepreneurial success. For example, a platform focused on sustainable living could evolve into an eco-friendly e-commerce business, a consulting service for sustainable practices, or a digital product educating consumers on environmental footprint reduction. Aligning these options with your deepest motivations ensures a business that is both personally fulfilling and commercially viable.

Exploring Entrepreneurial Paths for Creators

Many creators can naturally transition into e-commerce, especially if they have a dedicated audience around a specific niche. This can involve launching an online store to sell curated products that with their audience's interests, like a fitness influencer selling athletic wear or an artist selling prints. The key is to build on established trust and understanding of your audience to offer authentic and desirable products. This requires careful management of supply chains, inventory, customer service, and a seamless online store experience from product selection to delivery.

Alternatively, if your platform has established you as an expert, a consulting or service-based business can be a logical next step. For example, if you excel at social media strategy, you can offer your expertise directly to individuals or businesses through coaching, agency services, workshops, or advisory roles. Service-based businesses offer the potential for high profit margins and direct client relationships, allowing for tailored solutions. Success depends on clearly articulating your value, demonstrating tangible results, and building strong client testimonials, along with disciplined time management and robust systems for client onboarding, project management, and billing. A podcaster who is a thought leader in leadership development could offer executive coaching to

CEOs, leveraging their influence into a valuable, premium service.

Digital products offer another powerful and scalable avenue, often providing passive income potential. Online courses, e-books, templates, software, or membership sites can be developed once and sold repeatedly to a global audience without the logistical complexities of physical products. If your platform provides knowledge, an online course or e-book could be a natural fit. For those skilled in organization or design, selling templates for social media graphics or business planning can be lucrative. Membership sites can foster deep engagement and recurring revenue through exclusive content and community access. The challenge lies in the initial investment of time, expertise, and production quality for creation, along with effective marketing and distribution strategies to reach the right audience. Consider a travel vlogger creating an online course on budget travel planning with downloadable itineraries.

When defining your entrepreneurial vision, it's crucial to consider your business structure and long-term goals. Do you envision a lean, solo operation or a larger organization with a team? If you aim for a business that operates independently, prioritize building scalable systems, investing in technology, automating workflows, and planning for future hiring from the outset. If your focus is on your personal brand and direct client interaction, a service-based model might be more appropriate, even with a smaller operational footprint. Your vision should also align with your desired lifestyle. Be honest about your priorities to ensure your business supports your life goals rather than compromising them.

Defining your entrepreneurial vision is an iterative process. As you explore avenues, engage with your audience, and gather market feedback, your vision will evolve. Be open to new possibilities and willing to adapt your strategy. Consider your existing skills, what you enjoy, and consistent audience feedback about your strengths. These insights are invaluable in shaping a successful and sustainable business. For instance, if your audience consistently praises your ability to simplify complex topics, this strength could be leveraged in a consulting or educational product business.

Developing a Professional Identity

Finally, this evolution demands developing a professional identity that commands respect in broader business circles. While a strong personal brand as a creator is an asset, a CEO role requires projecting a different kind of authority and credibility. This involves communicating with a more formal and professional demeanor, understanding business etiquette, and demonstrating a command of business principles. It means clearly and confidently articulating the business's vision, strategy, and value proposition to investors, partners, suppliers, and employees. A creator's authenticity and personality are important, but they must be balanced with professional gravitas that inspires trust and signals competence. This may involve executive presence coaching, refining communication skills, and seeking opportunities to learn from experienced business leaders. The goal is to be recognized not just as a talented individual, but as a capable and trustworthy business owner leading an organization.

Ultimately, the mindset shift from creator to CEO is about embracing responsibility on a grander scale. It's about building a lasting and impactful enterprise founded on strategic planning, sound financial management, disciplined execution, and a professional commitment to excellence, moving from personal expression to enduring economic creation. This internal transformation empowers you to approach the complexities of the business world with a clear vision, a strategic plan, and the unwavering determination of a true CEO.

Defining your entrepreneurial vision is a powerful journey. It involves transforming your existing influence as a creator into a focused, strategic direction that yields lasting value. This means moving beyond immediate content creation to embrace a broader, more ambitious perspective. By carefully considering various entrepreneurial paths, aligning them with your personal values and skills, and identifying genuine market needs, you establish the foundation for a business that is both successful and deeply meaningful.

This clear vision will serve as your compass, guiding decisions, motivating actions, and ultimately shaping your entrepreneurial future. It's the crucial next step in evolving your platform presence into a powerful, purpose-driven business. Remember, the most impactful ventures arise from a clear understanding of purpose and a well-defined vision for the future, ensuring a chapter of calculated growth and enduring success. This strategic clarity turns potential into tangible reality, laying the groundwork for the robust business you are destined to build.

Your existing audience is more than just followers; it's a finely tuned ecosystem of individuals who have actively engaged with your content and invested their time and emotional energy into your persona and purpose. This engaged community is your most immediate and valuable asset as you transition from a platform-centric creator to a multifaceted entrepreneur. Underestimating this audience means overlooking your most potent resource. The strategic art lies in understanding how to ethically and effectively leverage this existing community as the foundational bedrock for your burgeoning customer base. This is not exploitation; it's intelligent cultivation and a natural progression that honors the relationship you've already built.

The first and most critical step is to move beyond simply knowing your audience to truly understanding them on a deeper, more nuanced level through deliberate audience segmentation. Your followers are rarely a single entity. Within your broad follower base, there are likely distinct subgroups, each with unique interests, pain points, and purchasing behaviors. For example, a fitness influencer might have segments focused on weight loss, muscle building, athletic performance, or simply a healthier lifestyle. Similarly, a finance educator might have segments interested in cryptocurrency, long-term investing, personal budgeting, or early retirement strategies.

Identifying these distinct segments is paramount. This can be achieved through various methods: analyzing your platform analytics to understand demographics, engagement patterns, and content preferences; conducting surveys and polls to directly solicit feedback; and actively observing conversations within your community, noting recurring questions and expressed desires. The more granular your understanding of these segments, the more effectively you can tailor your offerings and communication.

Once you've identified these segments, the next crucial phase is to understand their needs and desires beyond your current platform. While they engage with your platform content, what are the latent needs that your entrepreneurial vision can address? This requires a shift in perspective from what you create to what your audience needs. For instance, a fashion influencer who primarily posts outfit inspiration might discover through surveys that a significant portion of their audience struggles with finding sustainable and ethically produced clothing within their budget. This insight reveals a potential market gap that your new venture could fill, perhaps through a curated online store featuring such items or a guide to conscious consumption.

The key is to listen actively and ask probing questions. What challenges do they face that your skills or products could alleviate? What aspirations do they hold that your business could help them achieve? This investigative approach transforms your audience from passive consumers into active participants in shaping your entrepreneurial direction.

Furthermore, consider the market landscape. Are there unmet needs in your niche? What are your competitors doing, and where are the opportunities for differentiation? Researching market trends, analyzing the competitive landscape, and understanding customer pain points will help you identify a clear path forward. Your unique perspective as a creator who has already built an audience is a significant advantage. You have a direct channel to potential customers and a level of trust that is difficult for new businesses to establish. Use this advantage wisely by seeking to solve genuine problems for your audience. This alignment between your strengths, your values, and market demand is the trifecta of a compelling entrepreneurial vision.

When articulating your business vision, begin by addressing these core questions:

- What specific problem will your business solve for customers?
- Who is your ideal customer, and what are their unique needs and desires?
- What is your business's unique value proposition?
- What are your financial goals, including key milestones for the first year, three years, and five years?

Detailed answers provide a clear roadmap. For instance, rather than a general "selling products," a focused vision might be: "To be the leading e-commerce provider of ethically sourced activewear for women aged 25-40, known for superior quality, sustainable practices, and exceptional customer service." This level of detail guides all subsequent decisions, from product sourcing to marketing.

Introducing New Offerings to Your Audience

Introducing new products or services requires balancing anticipation with trust. Instead of a sudden launch, adopt a transparent, phased approach.

Building Anticipation with Transparency:

- **Share Your Journey:** Detail your thought process, the problems you're addressing, and the solutions you're developing. This could involve behind-the-scenes content, blog posts on market research, or private Q&A sessions for feedback. For an e-commerce store, share the process of sourcing suppliers, designing your logo, or selecting initial products.
- **Gather Pre-Launch Feedback:** This strategy not only generates excitement but also pro-

vides invaluable pre-launch feedback, essentially creating a built-in focus group.

Cultivating Trust and Aligning Values:

Maintaining audience loyalty during a transition is crucial, as trust is earned through authenticity and consistent value.

- **Articulate the "Why":** Clearly explain how your new venture aligns with your core values and your audience's perception of your purpose. If your brand has a strong ethical foundation, ensure your new business reflects that commitment.
- **Avoid Dissonance:** For example, if your following is built on mindfulness, launching a fast-fashion line without addressing potential conflicts would be a misstep. Instead, explain the rationale, research, and intention behind every decision to deepen your connection and turn your audience into partners in your entrepreneurial journey.

Practical Introduction Strategies:

Consider these steps for introducing new offerings:

- **Exclusive Access:** Create a dedicated email list for early access or exclusive updates, fostering direct and personal communication.
- **Social Media Teasers:** Use social media to tease developments, share testimonials from early testers, or run limited-time pre-order campaigns.
- **Inner Circle Experience:** The aim is to make your audience feel like an exclusive "inner circle," privy to exciting developments before the general public. This exclusivity, combined with genuine value, can drive early sales and momentum. An author, for instance, might offer email subscribers early access to new chapters or exclusive character interviews.

Leveraging Your Audience for Market Research:

Your community is a valuable resource for market research. Engage them in conversations about their needs, challenges, and aspirations through various methods:

- **Surveys and Polls:** Use platforms like SurveyMonkey, Google Forms, or social media polls to gather data on purchasing preferences, price sensitivity, desired product features, or unmet needs.

- **Focus Groups (Virtual or In-Person):** Host virtual focus groups with engaged followers to discuss product ideas, pricing strategies, or brand messaging for richer, qualitative data.
- **Community Forums or Groups:** Utilize dedicated forums or private social media groups for ongoing dialogue and feedback on emerging business ideas.
- **Direct Outreach:** Connect with highly engaged individuals or those representing key customer segments. Frame these conversations as seeking their expert opinion and valuing their perspective.

Refinement and Optimization:

The information gathered from these research activities is crucial for refinement, helping you to:

- **Pivot Strategy:** Adjust your strategy if initial ideas don't resonate.
- **Optimize Product Features:** Refine product features based on user feedback.
- **Develop Targeted Marketing:** Create marketing messages that directly address your audience's pain points and desires. For example, if durability is a key concern, emphasize that aspect in your marketing and product development.

Bridging Existing Content with New Ventures:

Your existing platform content can serve as a bridge to your new venture.

- **Repurpose and Update:** Repurpose or update historically high-performing content to subtly introduce your new business.
- **Seamless Narrative:** If past content focused on problem-solving, create new content that highlights how your new product or service provides those solutions, ensuring a natural evolution. A content creator sharing productivity tips, for instance, could launch a planner that incorporates those very techniques, making the transition feel organic.

Thoughtful Monetization Strategies:

Integrate your monetization strategy with your audience's capacity and willingness to pay.

- **Understand Perceived Value:** Determine if you're positioning yourself as a premium provider, an accessible option, or somewhere in between. Historical engagement, purchasing behavior, and direct feedback can inform these decisions. A student-focused audience might prefer an affordable digital product, while professionals might invest in higher-ticket services.

- **Range of Entry Points:** Offer a range of entry points, such as a "low-barrier" product (downloadable guide, short workshop, basic membership) to allow your audience to experience your new business without a significant financial commitment. This tiered approach respects different budgets and commitment levels.

Respectful Communication:

Crucially, ensure your communication about new ventures is always respectful of the relationship you've built.

- **Authentic Tone:** Avoid aggressive sales tactics or manipulative language. Maintain an authentic, informative, and appreciative tone.
- **Collaborative Language:** Use phrases like "I'm excited to share a new project inspired by our conversations about X," or "Many of you have asked about Y, so I've developed Z to help with that," to reinforce a collaborative and audience-centric approach. This emphasizes that you are building with them, not just for them.

The transition to a diversified business model also presents an opportunity to refine your brand identity. As you move beyond a single platform, your brand needs to be adaptable and encompass the broader scope of your entrepreneurial ambitions. This might involve creating a new brand name or evolving your existing brand to reflect your expanded mission. Ensure that your visual identity, messaging, and overall brand experience are consistent across all touchpoints, from your social media presence to your website and any new products or services you launch. This consistency is vital for building a strong, recognizable brand that resonates with your audience.

Ultimately, leveraging your audience as the foundation of your customer base is an exercise in trust, transparency, and genuine value creation. It's about recognizing the immense power of a community that has already connected with your vision and channeling that connection into a mutually beneficial business relationship. By understanding their needs, building anticipation ethically, and communicating with honesty, you can transform your loyal following into your most dedicated and valuable customers, setting the stage for a truly sustainable and impactful entrepreneurial venture. This strategic approach ensures that your growth is not just about acquiring new customers, but about deepening relationships with those who have already invested in your journey.

TWO

FROM ONLINE PERSONA TO PROFESSIONAL BRAND

Evolving an online persona into a professional brand is not about demolition, but a sophisticated process of deconstruction, analysis, and strategic adaptation. Your existing online presence, built and validated by audience engagement, serves as the foundation.

Deconstructing Your Persona: Uncovering the Architecture of Appeal

The first crucial step is a thorough deconstruction of your persona to understand its underlying architecture. This involves:

- **Revisiting Genesis:** Identify the initial spark, purpose, and core values that drove your early online presence. What problem were you solving, passion expressing, or unique perspective offering?
- **Analyzing Appeal Elements:** Go beyond superficial traits to identify content pillars and specific topics that consistently resonated with your audience. These reveal what your audience values most.
- **Examining Communication Style:** Understand how you spoke to your audience – your tone, language, and the feedback received. This provides crucial data about what resonated effectively.
- **Fostering Emotional Connection:** Identify the emotions your content evoked (inspiration, comfort, curiosity) to ensure your professional brand continues to connect on a deeper level.
- **Identifying the Authentic Core:** Determine the genuine aspects of your persona—your non-negotiable beliefs, principles, and passions. This authentic core must be preserved and strengthened in your professional brand.

Strategically Adapting for Your Professional Brand

Once deconstruction is complete, the next phase is to strategically adapt these core elements:

- **Reframing Messaging:** Translate your expertise, passion, and values into a compelling narrative that aligns with business objectives and resonates with a commercially oriented audience. This may involve shifting from informal advice to a more structured, authoritative tone while retaining approachability.
- **Evolving Visual Identity:** Ensure your visual identity is cohesive, polished, and reflective of your industry and target market. This means adopting a more refined look while still incorporating unique design elements that nod to your original style.
- **Shifting the Narrative:** Focus your professional brand's narrative on solving problems and delivering value for your target audience, shifting the spotlight from yourself to the client or customer.
- **Maintaining Authenticity:** Throughout this adaptation, ensure your core values and genuine aspects are not compromised. The aim is a professional brand that is credible, deeply rooted in who you truly are, and serves your new business goals as a natural extension of your established online presence.

A thorough analysis of your online persona's structure is crucial for a meaningful professional brand evolution, not just a superficial makeover. By understanding what initially drew your audience, you can pinpoint transferable strengths that will form the foundation of your new business identity. This involves identifying the core values, unique perspective, and communication style that fostered engagement, then strategically applying these to a professional context. For example, if your persona excelled at simplifying complex issues, this problem-solving ability should be central to your professional brand. While the presentation might shift from casual advice to structured case studies or white papers, the underlying skill remains a consistent thread, now demonstrating professional expertise and business value.

Analyze content that garnered strong reactions, as these indicate what truly resonates with your audience. High engagement on posts about overcoming procrastination, for instance, signals a demand for productivity solutions and an appreciation for your empathetic, actionable approach. This insight can then be leveraged when rebranding by developing productivity tools, coaching programs, or workshops tailored to this identified need. This deconstruction transforms engagement metrics into strategic business intelligence, showing what your audience already values.

The "voice" of your online persona is another critical element. Whether it was encouraging, witty, analytical, or empathetic, these vocal qualities significantly shape audience perception. As you transition to a professional brand, carefully consider this voice. It's not about eliminating personality, but ensuring the tone aligns with your new professional context and target market. A bubbly lifestyle blogger, for example, might adopt a more polished yet approachable tone for a B2B consulting brand. The goal is to find a professional equivalent of your authentic voice that conveys authority and expertise while maintaining connection.

Understanding the emotional drivers behind your online persona's success is also paramount. Did your content inspire confidence, foster community, or evoke curiosity? These emotional connections are powerful brand assets. Your professional brand should aim to elicit similar, though perhaps more sophisticated, emotional responses. If your persona built trust through vulnerability, your professional brand can build on this by demonstrating unwavering integrity and transparent communication. If it inspired aspiration, showcase client success stories and tangible results.

This deconstruction process also involves identifying elements of your online persona that might hinder a professional brand. This self-editing phase requires evaluating informalities, slang, or visual elements that, while endearing to your current audience, could undermine credibility in a new professional context. This isn't about purging personality but making conscious decisions about what supports or detracts from your new brand objectives. It's about understanding your desired perception and ensuring every element aligns with that vision.

Consider this deconstruction a rigorous audit of your digital self. What assets will you carry forward? What needs refinement, updating, or even strategic retirement to align with your new professional aspirations? This requires objective self-assessment, perhaps even seeking feedback from trusted mentors or colleagues. The goal is to isolate the core strengths and authentic qualities that made your online persona compelling and translate them into a credible and captivating professional brand. The transition should be a deliberate elevation of your most valuable attributes, not a departure from your true self.

This meticulous analysis of your existing online persona is a strategic imperative for successful professional rebranding. By dissecting the components that contributed to audience engagement, you uncover foundational elements that can be repurposed and elevated for a more sophisticated business identity. This granular examination covers everything from your core values to your specific communication styles that fostered connection, identifying authentic threads that can be recontextualized to build trust and credibility in a professional arena. For instance, if your online persona was known for a deep passion for problem-solving, demonstrated through detailed explanations and tutorials, this is a powerful asset. For a professional brand, this passion needs to be framed within a business context, showcasing how your problem-solving acumen provides tangible client solutions. This might involve repackaging informal advice into structured methodologies, comprehensive service offerings, or expert consulting packages, all while retaining the core of your problem-solving approach.

The effectiveness of your online persona likely stemmed from a specific content strategy, including topics, formats, and frequencies. A crucial part of deconstruction is identifying which content elements had the most significant impact and why. For example, if vlogs offering behind-the-scenes glimpses into your creative process garnered high engagement, it indicates your audience values transparency and a direct connection to your work. For a professional brand, this insight can inform a content strategy that incorporates "behind-the-scenes" visibility, perhaps through client testimonials or case study narratives. The objective is not to replicate the exact format, but to translate the underlying value proposition—authenticity and insight into your process—into a professional context.

Furthermore, critically assess the nuances of your communication style—the "voice" that connected with your audience. Was it informal and relatable, or authoritative and clear? Identify the qualities of this voice that fostered trust and resonance. When adapting this for a professional brand, aim for a voice that balances professionalism with approachability, conveying authority without being distant. A creator known for a witty and conversational tone might adopt a more polished and articulate voice for business communications, incorporating more formal language while retaining warmth and personality. This careful calibration ensures your professional brand's voice is both credible and captivating, resonating with a business-oriented audience while remaining authentically you.

The Strategic Evolution from Online Persona to Professional Brand

The journey from an online persona to a robust professional brand necessitates a deliberate and thoughtful approach. This transformation isn't about discarding your past, but rather strategically reframing it to align with your professional aspirations and target audience.

Deconstructing Your Online Persona

A critical first step involves a thorough deconstruction of your existing online persona. This self-assessment should delve into both the tangible and intangible aspects:

- **Emotional Resonance:** Analyze the emotional impact of your content. Did it inspire, build community, or offer comfort? Identifying these consistent emotional connections is key, as they foster loyalty. For a professional brand, these drivers can translate into trust, confidence, and partnership. If your online persona cultivated community, your professional brand can replicate this through exclusive client forums or personalized communication. The ultimate goal is to deliver not only tangible value but also a positive and supportive emotional experience.
- **Alignment with Professional Goals:** Critically evaluate elements of your online persona that might not align with your professional rebranding objectives. This requires honest self-assessment. Are there specific con-

tent types, informal language, or outdated visual aesthetics that could undermine your credibility or appeal to a new market? For instance, a playful approach suitable for a personal brand might need to evolve into a more sophisticated, results-oriented tone for corporate clients. This isn't about abandoning your personality but making strategic choices to present the most compelling and relevant version of yourself. Identify universally appealing aspects and those requiring adaptation for professional endeavors.

The insights gained from this deconstruction serve as a strategic roadmap. They highlight core strengths, authentic values, and audience-driven preferences that will form the bedrock of your new brand identity. Understanding the genesis and evolution of your online persona empowers you to make informed decisions about messaging, visual identity, content strategy, and overall brand narrative. This ensures your professional brand is a natural, authentic, and powerful evolution, resonating with both existing and new professional clientele, built on genuine appeal and strategic foresight.

Constructing Your New Professional Narrative

The evolution into a professional brand is fundamentally about artfully constructing a new narrative. This narrative is your meticulously woven story, drawing from past experiences, highlighting honed skills, and projecting towards future ambitions.

- **Reframing Your History:** It's not about rewriting your past, but reframing it through a lens of professional purpose and demonstrable value. Consider it a compelling executive summary of your journey, tailored for your desired professional audience. Articulate not just *what* you've done, but *why* it matters, *how* it has prepared you, and the *unique perspective* you bring.
- **Strategic Authenticity:** While your online persona was likely an unfiltered expression of your genuine self, your professional narrative requires strategically deployed authenticity. Identify the core truths of that persona – your innate values, passions, and unique thinking – and present them in a manner aligned with professional expectations.
- **Demonstrating Transferable Skills:** Clearly articulate your transferable skills. For example, if your online persona excelled at breaking down complex topics, highlight this in a professional context: "My experience in creating accessible content for diverse online audiences has honed my ability to distill complex

technical information into clear, actionable strategies for business stakeholders, leading to improved understanding and faster decision-making."

- **Emphasizing Growth and Learning:** The professional world values adaptability and continuous improvement. Frame your journey as an ongoing process of development, not a static achievement. Highlight instances where you've sought new knowledge, adapted to change, or enhanced your skill set through courses, workshops, or mentorship. These learning experiences are crucial chapters in your professional story, demonstrating your commitment to staying relevant and effective.

Developing a Professional Narrative from Your Online Persona

Transitioning from a hobbyist or online persona to a professional requires crafting a compelling narrative that highlights your dedication to professional development. This involves showcasing how you've invested in skills, education, and sought feedback to enhance your capabilities. For instance, a photographer moving into professional services might emphasize advanced lighting courses, business management studies, and client interaction feedback.

Articulating Your Vision

A crucial element of this professional narrative is a clear, concise, and compelling vision. What are your aspirations and the impact you aim to make in your new professional landscape? This demonstrates a strategic outlook and purpose beyond simply engaging an online audience. If your previous persona focused on personal journeys, your professional narrative should pivot to how those lessons can benefit clients, customers, or collaborators. A travel blogger, for example, might become a destination marketing consultant, focusing their narrative on helping regions attract tourism by leveraging their firsthand knowledge of traveler psychology and storytelling abilities.

Building Credibility and Trust

Your narrative is the primary vehicle for establishing credibility and trust. It must speak the language of conventional business environments, demonstrating an understanding of business acumen—whether through market trends, project management skills, or financial principles relevant to your field. If your online persona was primarily about personal expression, your professional narrative needs to highlight cultivated business-savvy aspects. This could involve referencing successful collaborations, revenue generated from online activities (if appropriate), or efficient business operations. A writer who gained a following through personal essays and is now building a freelance copywriting business would focus their narrative on understanding client briefs, meeting deadlines, industry experience, and delivering results-oriented copy.

The Importance of Professional Language

The language used in your professional narrative is paramount. While authenticity is important, it must be tempered with professionalism. Avoid overly casual language, slang, or inside jokes that might alienate a business-oriented audience. Instead, opt for clear, precise, and confident language, using industry-standard terminology where appropriate, ensuring clarity. The tone should be assured, respectful, and forward-looking, conveying purpose and professional intent. For example, instead of "I'm just messing around with this idea," say, "I am exploring innovative strategies for X, leveraging my experience in Y."

Showcasing Tangible Results and Impact

It's vital to showcase the tangible results and impact of your work, even if initial metrics were likes, shares, or community growth. In a professional context, these must be translated into business outcomes. Consistent online engagement can be reframed as an ability to capture and hold audience attention—a critical skill for marketing and sales. Building a community highlights expertise in fostering engagement and cultivating loyalty. A social media influencer transitioning to brand ambassadorship might emphasize their proven ability to connect with specific demographics, drive product awareness, and influence purchasing decisions, backed by data from their online presence. They might articulate this by saying, "My track record of consistently achieving high engagement rates and cultivating a loyal community demonstrates my capacity to effectively connect brands with their target audiences, driving significant measurable outcomes."

Self-Discovery and Refinement

Crafting this new professional narrative is also an exercise in self-discovery and refinement. As you explore how your online persona translates into professional value, you gain a deeper understanding of your strengths and weaknesses. This introspective process helps identify areas for further development to align with professional goals, forming a continuous loop of action, reflection, and adaptation. For instance, a visual artist with a unique style might realize a need to strengthen business management skills. Their narrative would then include proactive steps to learn about project management software, client invoicing, and contract negotiation, positioning them as a well-rounded professional ready for client projects.

A compelling professional narrative, much like any good story, requires a clear beginning, middle, and end. This structure provides clarity and helps your audience understand your progression.

- **Beginning:** Detail your foundational experiences and the origins of your interest in your field.
- **Middle:** Showcase your journey of skill development, challenges overcome, and key accomplishments.
- **End/Future Outlook:** Articulate your current professional standing and future aspirations.

Consistency Across Platforms

Whether on a resume, LinkedIn, an elevator pitch, or a formal presentation, maintaining consistency in your narrative is crucial. Every touchpoint should reinforce your core message, building a strong and recognizable professional identity. This ensures that your online presence aligns with your in-person professional capabilities, fostering trust and minimizing disconnect.

The "Why" Behind Your Pursuits

Your passion is a powerful narrative element. If your past online presence was driven by genuine passion, make this intrinsic motivation a central theme. It demonstrates a commitment beyond mere obligation, speaking to a deeper drive for excellence. For example, an environmental activist transitioning to sustainability consulting can highlight their lifelong commitment to environmental stewardship as a driver for their expertise.

Bridging the Gap: Crafting Your Narrative

Creating a new professional narrative involves strategically bridging your authentic self with professional expectations. This means:

- Distilling experiences.
- Highlighting transferable skills.
- Demonstrating commitment to growth.
- Articulating a clear future vision.

By combining these elements with a professional tone and a focus on tangible value, you build credibility, captivate your audience, and position yourself for success. This strategic storytelling ensures your professional brand is an authentic extension of who you are, presented for a business-oriented audience.

Intentional Storytelling and Proof Points

Constructing a professional narrative is an act of intentional storytelling, making you the architect of your own professional biography. It's about curating and articulating relevant aspects of your authentic self, showcasing capabilities and potential, rather than fabricating a persona. When transitioning from an informal online presence to a professional brand, you present a refined story that resonates with a business audience seeking value, expertise, and reliability.

Proof points are specific examples, achievements, or experiences that serve as tangible evidence of your skills. If your online persona highlighted creative problem-solving, your professional narrative should include concrete examples: detail a challenge, your innovative approach, and the positive outcome. For instance, a developer who shared coding tutorials online could highlight a project where they streamlined a client's workflow with a custom application, detailing the problem, solution, and quantifiable impact.

Understanding the Professional Ecosystem

Your narrative must reflect an understanding of your target professional ecosystem, including industry trends, market demands, and client challenges. Your personal journey should be contextualized within this broader landscape. If entering a new industry, articulate how existing skills are transferable and how you've actively sought to understand the new field's nuances (e.g., certifications, industry publications, networking). A teacher becoming a corporate trainer, for example, could highlight curriculum development skills while demonstrating an understanding of corporate training objectives and measurable learning outcomes.

Developing a compelling professional narrative requires a critical assessment of your communication style in relation to your career aspirations. While your online persona may have embraced informality or unique quirks, a professional narrative demands a more refined and universally understood approach. This doesn't mean sacrificing your personality, but rather adapting its expression for a business audience. The goal is to convey your enthusiasm, dedication, or collaborative spirit in a manner that is both professional and relatable. For instance, a musician known for energetic live performances might translate that energy into engaging teaching methods and dynamic workshops as a music educator, fostering a love for music while maintaining a professional demeanor.

Crucially, your professional narrative should also demonstrate resilience and adaptability. The professional world is constantly evolving, requiring individuals who can navigate challenges, learn from setbacks, and adjust to changing circumstances. Subtly weave in examples of these qualities. Perhaps your online journey involved overcoming technical difficulties, adapting to algorithm changes, or pivoting your content strategy based on audience feedback. When framed correctly, these experiences highlight your capacity to persevere and evolve – qualities highly valued in any professional setting. If your online business faced a market downturn, your narrative could detail how you analyzed the situation, adapted your offerings, and successfully navigated the challenge, showcasing your business acumen and resilience.

Ultimately, translating your online presence into a professional brand is about solidifying your identity as a professional. It involves presenting a cohesive and compelling case for your value proposition, ensuring that your audience (potential clients, employers, or investors) understands not only what you do but also who you are and why they should trust you.

This demands a deliberate and strategic approach to storytelling, leveraging your past experiences, highlighting acquired skills, and clearly articulating future aspirations, all while maintaining authenticity and professionalism. It serves as the bridge connecting your established digital presence to your future professional success.Constructing Your Digital Infrastructure

The transition from a dynamic online persona to a robust professional brand necessitates the deliberate construction of a digital infrastructure that not only mirrors but elevates your new business identity. This infrastructure forms the bedrock of your brand's credibility, professionalism, and operational efficiency, ensuring seamless and impactful engagement with clients, partners, and the wider professional community. It's about establishing a tangible, accessible, and polished presence that clearly differentiates your business from any previous, more informal, digital footprint, thereby signaling a clear commitment to a professional trajectory.

1. Professional Website: Your Digital Headquarters

At the forefront of this endeavor is the creation of a professional website, which is no longer just an online brochure; it's your digital headquarters. This central hub is where your brand narrative, services, and value proposition converge. The design and functionality of your website create critical first impressions. It must be aesthetically aligned with your brand's visual identity, employing a clean, modern design that conveys professionalism and trustworthiness. Navigation should be intuitive, allowing visitors to easily find information about your offerings, expertise, and how to engage your services. High-quality imagery, clear calls to action, and well-written content are paramount.

For example, a creative consulting brand should showcase visually engaging case studies and client testimonials to demonstrate impact. Conversely, a financial advisory service website should exude stability, clarity, and data-driven insights, perhaps featuring detailed service descriptions, team biographies, and relevant regulatory information.

Beyond aesthetics and user experience, your website must be optimized for search engines (SEO) to ensure discoverability. This includes strategic keyword research, on-page optimization, and mobile responsiveness, ensuring potential clients can find you when searching for the solutions you provide. Furthermore, essential business pages are vital components:

- **"About Us" section:** Elaborates on your journey and expertise.
- **"Services" or "Products" page:** Details your offerings.
- **"Contact Us" page:** Provides clear contact information and potentially a contact form.
- **"Testimonials" or "Portfolio" section:** Showcases social proof.

Finally, ensuring your website is secure with an SSL certificate reinforces trust and data protection, a non-negotiable aspect of a professional online presence.

2. Professional Business Email Addresses: Enhancing Credibility

Parallel to establishing your website, implementing professional business email addresses is a fundamental step. Moving away from personal email accounts (e.g., @gmail.com or @yahoo.com) to domain-specific addresses (e.g., yourname@yourbusiness.com) signifies a commitment to your venture and instills greater credibility in client communications. This simple yet impactful change immediately elevates your perceived professionalism.

When a client receives an email from a dedicated business address, it communicates that you are a serious entity operating with a structured approach. This is particularly crucial when dealing with sensitive information, contracts, or formal inquiries. The use of a professional email address also facilitates better organization of business communications, allowing you to create specific inboxes for different aspects of your business, such as sales, support, or general inquiries, further enhancing operational efficiency. For example, an invoice or proposal from "accounts@yourbusiness.com" carries more weight than one from a generic personal account, reassuring stakeholders of the sender's legitimacy and professionalism. It's not just about the address itself, but about the message it sends: you are invested, organized, and take your business seriously.

Building a Robust Digital Foundation for Your Professional Brand

Establishing a strong professional brand in the digital landscape requires a well-structured and consistent online presence. This involves three key components: a professional website, branded email addresses, and strategic social media management.

Your Website: The Online Anchor

Your website serves as your 24/7 digital storefront and information hub. It needs to be a dynamic reflection of your business, values, and offerings, meticulously planned in both design and functionality.

- **Hosting and CMS:** Choose a reliable hosting provider and a user-friendly website builder or Content Management System (CMS) like WordPress, Squarespace, or Wix that aligns with your technical expertise and long-term business goals.
- **Visual Design:** The visual design is crucial for communicating your brand's essence. Select a color palette, typography, and imagery that resonate with your industry and target audience. For instance, a financial advisor might opt for a clean, minimalist design with blues and grays to convey trust, while a creative agency could use vibrant colors and bold typography to reflect innovation.
- **User Experience (UX):** Ensure effortless navigation. Visitors should easily find information on services, your team, portfolio, and contact details. Clear Calls to Action (CTAs) should guide them towards desired outcomes, such as booking a consultation, requesting a quote, or subscribing to a newsletter.
- **Content:** Your website content must be professional, informative, and engaging. Include well-written service descriptions highlighting benefits, compelling "About Us" narratives

showcasing expertise, and authentic client testimonials for social proof.

- **Search Engine Optimization (SEO):** Integrate SEO from the outset. Conduct keyword research, optimize page titles and meta descriptions, use header tags effectively, and ensure your website is mobile-responsive and loads quickly to improve search engine rankings and deter visitors from leaving.

Professional Email Addresses: Credibility and Efficiency

Moving from personal email accounts (e.g., @gmail.com) to branded email addresses (e.g., [yourname]@[yourbusiness.com]) is a fundamental step in projecting credibility.

- **Trust and Legitimacy:** Branded emails immediately signal a professional identity, fostering trust and reassuring prospective clients that they are dealing with a legitimate business.
- **Enhanced Features:** Professional email accounts often offer increased storage, better security, and the ability to create aliases or group addresses (e.g., sales@[yourbusiness.com]), which are invaluable for efficient communication management.

- **Streamlined Workflows:** A structured approach to communication, such as directing inquiries to dedicated 'info' or 'support' addresses, ensures prompt delivery to the appropriate person or department, leading to faster response times and improved customer service.

Social Media: Consistency and Engagement

Securing relevant social media handles and maintaining consistency across platforms is vital, as these are often the first point of contact for potential clients.

- **Handle Alignment:** Ideally, your social media handles (e.g., @InnovateSolutions) should align with your business name to minimize confusion and reinforce brand recognition.
- **Optimized Profiles:** Optimize your profiles with high-quality pictures or logos, compelling bios stating your mission and offerings, and links to your website.
- **Strategic Content:** Social media platforms serve as extensions of your brand's personality. Content should be strategically curated to appeal to your target audience and support business objectives. For example, a graphic design

agency might use Instagram for visual work and LinkedIn for thought leadership.

- **Consolidating Online Presence:** Ensure all digital touchpoints – website, email, and social media – are consistent in messaging, visual branding, and tone. If your previous online persona was personal, pivot to showcasing business expertise and client-centric approaches. This might involve rebranding profiles with new logos, updating bios, and ensuring all shared content aligns with your professional brand's mission.

Ongoing Maintenance: A Dynamic Ecosystem

Developing this professional digital infrastructure is an ongoing process, not a one-time task. Regularly update your website with new content, testimonials, and case studies. Monitor social media engagement and ensure all digital assets are functioning correctly to maintain a polished and professional image. This deliberate and strategic approach ensures your professional brand is not only established but also robustly supported, ready to attract and serve your target audience effectively.

Building a Robust Professional Digital Infrastructure

In today's digital landscape, a strong online presence is paramount for brand visibility, engagement, and reputation management. This involves strategically building and maintaining a professional digital infrastructure that effectively communicates your value and fosters trust.

1. Strategic Social Media Presence:

- **Consistent Handles:** Secure consistent and relevant social media handles across all key platforms (LinkedIn, X, Instagram, Facebook, Pinterest, TikTok, etc.). Ideally, these should mirror your business name to reinforce brand recognition. If your exact name is unavailable, opt for the closest professional variation (e.g., "AcmeInnovate" instead of "Acme Innovations").
- **Optimized Profiles:** Meticulously optimize each profile with a high-quality, professional logo or brand image, and a compelling cover photo that visually represents your business. Your bio should concisely communicate your value proposition, mission, and expertise, including a direct link to your professional website.
- **Strategic Content & Engagement:** Share strategic content that aligns with your brand's voice and objectives. Focus on industry in-

sights, valuable content, service highlights, client success stories, and active participation in relevant conversations. Consistent posting and engagement are crucial for building a strong social media presence.

2. Cohesive Online Presence:

- **Unified Brand Identity:** All your digital touchpoints, including your website, social media, online directories, and professional networking sites, must reflect a unified brand identity and professional ethos. Consistency in your brand name, logo, messaging, and tone of voice is vital.
- **Curated Professional Presentation:** If your previous online persona was informal, carefully curate and refine your presentation for a professional audience. Select relevant aspects of your past online presence and reframe them to enhance credibility. Repurpose or adapt past content (e.g., industry trend analyses from a personal blog can become thought leadership posts on LinkedIn).
- **Clear Differentiation:** Present a polished, credible image that differentiates your new venture from past activities. Clearly articulate your business's focus and the value it delivers to

build a distinct professional identity that is easily recognizable and trustworthy.

3. Essential Business Tools and Services:

- **Operational Efficiency:** Integrate essential business tools and services to enhance operational efficiency. This includes setting up a professional CRM system (e.g., HubSpot, Salesforce) to manage client interactions, implementing project management software (e.g., Asana, Trello) to track projects and deadlines, and securing cloud storage for business documents.
- **Professional Approach:** These tools, though not directly client-facing, demonstrate a systematic and responsive approach to business, contributing to client satisfaction and reinforcing reliability.

4. Digital Security Best Practices:

- **Non-Negotiable Element:** Embracing digital security best practices is a non-negotiable aspect of building a professional digital infrastructure.
- **Protecting Your Reputation:** Implement strong passwords, enable two-factor authentication, and secure your website with an SSL cer-

tificate to encrypt data. Protecting client data and maintaining the integrity of your online presence are paramount to building and sustaining trust. Cybersecurity is a foundational element of your digital strategy, as a data breach can severely damage your professional reputation.

5. Comprehensive Website Content and Functionality:

- **Dedicated Blog Section:** Beyond basic pages, a professional website benefits from a dedicated blog section. This allows you to share expertise, provide valuable industry insights, and engage with your audience on a deeper level.
- **Thought Leadership & Lead Generation:** Consistent blog content drives traffic through SEO and positions you as a thought leader in your field. Examples include marketing consultants writing on digital marketing trends or legal professionals sharing articles on common legal questions. This content acts as a powerful lead-generation tool, attracting individuals seeking information and solutions you can provide.

The ultimate objective of this professional digital infrastructure is to create a seamless and compelling online experience for your target audience, presenting your business as credible, reliable, and capable. This investment lays the groundwork for sustained business success, providing a scalable platform for future growth and ensuring your online identity is a powerful asset.

Demonstrating Expertise and Building Trust:

- **Professional Portfolio/Case Studies:** Instead of just listing services, showcase your capabilities through real-world examples. For designers, this means high-quality visuals and project descriptions (client needs, solutions). For service providers (consultants, coaches), detail client challenges, implemented strategies, and quantifiable outcomes (e.g., 20% sales increase, 15% cost reduction, 30% improved engagement). Tangible proofs of success build confidence and differentiate you.

Optimizing Client Communication and Engagement:

- **"Contact Us" Page:** Go beyond a simple email. Offer multiple contact avenues (phone, physical address, embedded form). Design the contact form to collect specific information (inquiry nature, industry, budget) for effective lead qualification. Include business hours and expected response times, and specify your time zone for global businesses.

- **Social Media Strategy:** Active engagement and strategic content distribution are crucial. Understand each platform: LinkedIn for B2B networking and professional articles; Instagram/Pinterest for visual showcases; X (formerly Twitter) for real-time updates and customer service; Facebook for community building. Develop a content calendar with a mix of promotional, educational, behind-the-scenes, testimonial, and interactive posts. Respond promptly and professionally to all comments, messages, and reviews; handling negative feedback gracefully can even build trust.

Enhancing Online Visibility and Credibility:

- **Online Directories and Review Sites:** Ensure consistent and accurate listings (NAP – Name, Address, Phone) on platforms like Google My Business, Yelp, and industry-specific directories. Encourage satisfied clients to leave reviews to boost social proof and online visibility.

Securing and Maintaining Your Digital Infrastructure:

- **Website Technical Aspects:** Implement a reliable backup system to prevent data loss and minimize downtime. Prioritize ongoing website security by staying updated on best practices, using security plugins, regularly scanning for vulnerabilities, and keeping your CMS, themes, and plugins updated.

Transforming Your Online Presence to a Professional Brand:

- **Strategic Content Evolution:** Shift from personal interests to content that educates, showcases expertise, demonstrates value, and drives business growth. Focus on informative, valuable, and relevant content that addresses prospective clients' needs and challenges.
- **Business Blog for Authority:** Establish a dedicated business blog as a hub for industry insights, practical advice, and thought leadership. For example, a cybersecurity firm might blog about emerging threats or data protection, while a financial planner could cover retirement

strategies or tax regulations. Identify audience pain points and provide clear, actionable answers. High-quality, consistent blog content improves SEO, drives organic traffic, and establishes you as a go-to resource. Research, write well, format for readability, and incorporate relevant keywords.

Overall Investment in Professionalism:

Establishing a professional digital infrastructure is an investment in your business's credibility, reach, and efficiency. It creates a polished, unified, and secure online environment that reflects the quality of your offerings. By meticulously building a robust website, branded email, consistent social media, and strong cybersecurity, you create a powerful foundation for growth, attracting your target audience, and instilling confidence. This deliberate construction signals a serious, professional business entity, embodying your brand's promise of excellence and value.

Beyond written content, video is a highly engaging way to connect with your audience and showcase expertise, offering a personal and dynamic presentation of your brand. Consider creating explainer videos, product demonstrations, or client testimonials. For instance, a software company could demonstrate app functionality, while a health coach might share workout tutorials. Platforms like YouTube and Vimeo are ideal for hosting; embedding these videos on your website and social media will boost engagement. Focus on clear audio and visuals, concise messaging, and professional presentation that aligns with your brand. A series of videos addressing common questions can build a valuable resource library, positioning you as a knowledgeable expert. Authenticity and clarity often resonate more than overly polished content; a simple setup with good lighting, a decent microphone, and a clear script can be highly effective.

Case studies are a critical component of a business content strategy, providing powerful evidence of your capabilities and tangible results. These in-depth analyses, detailing how you helped clients overcome challenges and achieve goals, are invaluable for building trust and credibility. A well-crafted case study typically outlines the client's problem, your solution, and measurable outcomes. For example, a marketing agency could show a 50% increase in online leads from a social media campaign. Include client testimonials for added authenticity. Aim for variety in client types and challenges to demonstrate broad expertise. Always obtain explicit client permission before sharing details, and consider anonymizing sensitive information. Displaying case studies prominently on your website (e.g., in a "Case Studies" or "Portfolio" section) allows potential clients to see the impact of your work and envision similar success. They offer concrete proof of your value proposition.

Engaging on professional networking platforms, especially LinkedIn, is essential for B2B or professional services audiences. LinkedIn is a dynamic platform for building your professional brand, connecting with peers, and engaging with potential clients. Regularly share blog posts, articles, and industry insights. Participate in relevant groups and discussions, offering expertise and answering questions, which increases visibility and establishes you as a knowledgeable professional. Tailor content for LinkedIn's professional audience, using compelling headlines and engaging summaries. Sharing personal reflections on industry trends can add a human element. Actively connect with individuals in your target market, sending personalized requests and engaging with their content to build a valuable network. Consistent activity and engagement are key for LinkedIn's algorithm. Other professional platforms or industry-specific forums can also be valuable for reaching niche audiences.

The overarching goal of your content strategy should be to provide value and solve problems for your target audience. Consistently delivering high-quality, relevant content attracts potential customers and builds loyalty and trust. View your content as an ongoing conversation, offering helpful insights and solutions rather than direct sales pitches, nurturing relationships and positioning you as a trusted advisor. For example, a graphic designer could offer free downloadable templates, or a business coach a free webinar on goal setting. These "lead magnets" provide immediate value and allow you to collect contact information (with consent) for email lists and lead nurturing.

Furthermore, repurpose your content to maximize reach and impact. A comprehensive blog post can be broken into social media updates, a video script, or an e-book. A webinar can be transcribed into blog posts or key segments extracted for social media clips. This ensures fresh material across channels. For instance, an in-depth SEO guide can become a LinkedIn carousel, an Instagram story statistic, and a downloadable resource. Strategic reuse saves time and resources while amplifying your brand's message.

The tone and voice of your content are crucial. While your online persona might have been informal, your professional brand content should be authoritative, knowledgeable, and approachable. This means being clear, confident, and consistent, reflecting your brand's personality (e.g., innovative and energetic, or calm and reassuring). A tech company might use dynamic language, while a financial firm opts for stability and clarity.

Beyond publishing your own content, curating and sharing relevant industry news and insights from reputable sources is also valuable. This demonstrates you are well-informed and engaged, providing additional value by filtering important information. When sharing curated content, always add your own commentary to explain its significance and relevance to your audience. This content curation builds authority and network simultaneously. Always credit original sources and add unique insights.

Optimizing Your Content Strategy

Continuously measure your content strategy's performance using analytics tools from your website, blog, and social media. Track metrics like website traffic, engagement, lead generation, and conversion rates. Understanding which content resonates most, which channels drive traffic, and what topics generate interest will help you refine your approach. For example, if blog posts on a specific topic consistently show high engagement and lead to inquiries, produce more content on that theme. Similarly, if video content outperforms written posts on social media, allocate more resources to video production. This data-driven approach ensures your content strategy remains effective and aligns with business objectives, continuously optimizing efforts to build a strong professional brand.

The Enduring Power of Conventional Networking

While the digital realm has transformed connections, traditional networking and relationship building remain crucial for professional success. Transitioning from an online persona to a robust professional brand necessitates active engagement in traditional business environments. Industry conferences, chamber of commerce meetings, and specialized workshops offer unparalleled opportunities for deeper, more meaningful connections than online interactions alone. Approach these interactions with intention, a clear understanding of your value proposition, and a genuine desire to foster mutually beneficial relationships.

Maximizing Industry Events

Industry events like trade shows, conferences, and seminars are ideal for expanding your professional network. These gatherings unite like-minded individuals, potential collaborators, mentors, and future clients who share an interest in a specific field.

Preparation is key:

- **Research:** Before attending, review the event agenda to identify speakers, panel discussions, and workshops that align with your business goals and expertise.
- **Identify Key Individuals:** Many events provide attendee lists or networking apps to help you identify people you want to connect with.
- **Craft an Elevator Pitch:** Develop a concise and compelling pitch that clearly states who you are, what you do, and the value you offer. This aims to spark interest and open dialogue, not to hard sell.
- **Engage Thoughtfully:** Listen more than you speak. Ask open-ended questions about their challenges, industry insights, and professional aspirations. This demonstrates genuine interest and provides valuable information to tailor your responses and identify areas of synergy.
- **Focus on Mutual Benefit:** Remember that networking is a two-way street. Focus on how you can assist others or introduce them to help-

ful contacts, rather than solely on what you can gain.

Joining Professional Organizations

Becoming a member of professional organizations and associations is an effective way to integrate into the conventional business landscape and build a sustainable network. These groups typically consist of individuals who share a common profession, industry, or interest. Membership often provides access to exclusive events, educational resources, and a built-in community of peers.

When choosing organizations:

- **Relevance:** Select those most relevant to your industry and target audience.
- **Activity and Reputation:** Look for active, well-regarded associations that offer engagement opportunities beyond annual meetings.
- **Active Participation:** Volunteer for committees, join special interest groups, or contribute to industry publications. Active participation signals commitment and creates more avenues for relationship building.
- **Connect Broadly:** Make an effort to connect with individuals at various career stages, not just high-profile members. Everyone offers

unique experiences and perspectives, and valuable connections can emerge unexpectedly.

- **Mentorship:** Consider seeking a mentor or offering mentorship to someone earlier in their career. These relationships provide invaluable guidance, support, and fresh perspectives, strengthening your personal brand and expanding your professional circle.

Cultivating Genuine Connections

Building relationships in conventional settings is about cultivating genuine connections, not just collecting business cards.

- **Prompt Follow-Up:** After an event or meeting, follow up promptly and personally. Reference a specific point of conversation to reinforce the connection.
- **Personalized Communication:** Send a personalized email, a LinkedIn connection request with a tailored message, or a brief phone call. Avoid generic follow-ups.
- **Suggest Next Steps:** Suggest a specific next step, such as a coffee meeting, an introduction to someone in your network, or an offer to share a relevant article or resource. The goal is to move the relationship beyond a single interaction into sustained engagement.

- **Provide Value:** Think about how you can provide value to your new connections. Share insights, offer feedback, or introduce them to potential clients or partners. Proactive value-adding solidifies relationships and builds trust.

Consistency and Authenticity for Long-Term Success

Long-term networking success hinges on consistency and authenticity. Building a strong professional network requires time and consistent effort; it's an ongoing process of nurturing relationships. Be yourself, be transparent, and be reliable. People are more likely to connect with and support individuals they trust and who demonstrate integrity.

Your network is a resource that offers more than just business opportunities; it provides advice, support, and shared learning. Don't hesitate to reach out to your network for insights when facing challenges or to share your successes. This mutual exchange strengthens bonds and fosters a supportive professional community.

Networking events require a clear objective. Instead of broadly "meeting people," define specific types of individuals you aim to connect with and why. For example, your goal might be to meet three early-stage tech founders to discuss funding or two senior retail marketing managers to review campaign strategies. This focused approach makes interactions more purposeful and increases the chances of meaningful connections. Prepare open-ended questions tailored to your objectives to guide conversations and gather valuable information. For instance, if you're interested in marketing strategies, ask, "What's your biggest marketing challenge and how are you addressing it?" or "What emerging digital marketing trends excite you most?"

Beyond formal events, actively seek opportunities within your existing professional network. Engage with current and former colleagues, classmates, university alumni, and project collaborators. These accessible connections often provide fertile ground for building strong, trusting relationships due to shared experiences. Don't underestimate the power of casual coffee catch-ups; these informal interactions can rekindle connections and uncover new opportunities.

The "giving before you get" principle is crucial in conventional networking. Offer assistance, share knowledge, or make introductions without expecting immediate returns. This generosity builds goodwill and positions you as a valuable community member. For example, if you overhear a problem you have expertise in, offer a brief suggestion or resource. If you know two people who would benefit from meeting, make a thoughtful introduction. These genuine acts of kindness create strong impressions and foster reciprocal relationships.

Understanding networking etiquette and unspoken rules is another vital aspect of conventional spaces. This varies by industry and event but generally involves respecting others' time, listening attentively, maintaining eye contact, and projecting professionalism. Avoid dominating conversations, interrupting, or talking excessively about yourself. The goal is to create a comfortable and engaging interaction for everyone. When exchanging contact information, ensure the other person is open to it with a simple, "Would you be open to connecting on LinkedIn?" or "May I have your business card?"

Transitioning from online engagement to offline relationship building requires consciously translating your digital brand into tangible interactions. If your online brand is characterized by insightful articles and helpful advice, bring that knowledgeable and helpful persona to in-person conversations. If your brand emphasizes innovation, let that enthusiasm and forward-thinking mindset shine through. Your offline interactions should naturally extend your digital presence, reinforcing your cultivated online identity. This consistency is vital for building a cohesive and credible professional brand. For example, if you've positioned yourself as a sustainable business practices expert online, be prepared to discuss these topics with insight and passion, referencing recent articles or studies at an industry conference.

Leveraging professional organizations also involves active participation in committees or working groups. This allows you to embed yourself within the industry, contributing to its development and gaining a deeper understanding of its challenges and opportunities. Taking on responsibilities demonstrates commitment and builds stronger relationships with other dedicated professionals. For instance, joining a membership committee might involve welcoming new members and ensuring their integration, allowing you to build rapport and understand diverse professional needs.

Consider attending local meetups or smaller, niche industry gatherings. These events often foster a more intimate networking environment, making it easier to strike up conversations and build deeper connections. They are excellent for gaining specific insights into local market trends or connecting with specialists within your broader industry. The informality of many meetups can also reduce intimidation for those new to larger, more formal conferences.

At events, don't hesitate to approach approachable individuals, even without a pre-arranged connection. A simple icebreaker like, "Hi, I'm [Your Name]. I noticed you were [mention something specific, e.g., at the session on AI in marketing], what did you think?" works well. People are generally receptive to genuine curiosity and shared interests. Be confident, polite, and prepared to offer something of value, even if it's just an interesting perspective or a listening ear.

Finally, nurturing these relationships is an ongoing commitment. Regularly check in with your network, share relevant information, and offer support. The strength of your professional brand is built not just on what you say or do, but on the quality of relationships you cultivate and the community you build. When approached strategically and authentically, conventional networking spaces are invaluable for developing a well-rounded and influential professional brand that extends beyond the digital realm. They provide the human element, tangible connections, and deep insights essential for sustained growth and impact in any industry. By actively engaging in these environments, you transform your professional identity from a digital avatar into a recognized and respected contributor within your field, fostering a supportive and instrumental network for long-term success.

THREE

MARKET RESEARCH AND OPPORTUNITY IDENTIFICATION

The journey of entrepreneurship often sparks from a deeply held interest, a burning passion, or a diligently honed skill. While this enthusiasm is a powerful motivator, the crucial next step is to bridge the gap between personal enjoyment and tangible business opportunity. This process isn't about abandoning your passion, but rather channeling it into a commercially viable endeavor. By deconstructing your interests, you can unearth their hidden potential, transforming a hobby into a sustainable and rewarding business. This requires a blend of introspection and objective analysis—a vital phase for any entrepreneur aiming to build a thriving business that resonates with their personal drive.

1. Self-Assessment: Uncovering the Core of Your Interests

To begin this deconstruction, start with a thorough self-assessment. Take time to understand the specific aspects of your interests that truly captivate you. Is it the creative process, problem-solving, intellectual challenge, the opportunity to help others, or the tangible outcome?

For instance, if you're passionate about cooking, pinpoint what specifically ignites your enthusiasm: experimentation with flavors, the precision of baking, the art of presentation, or the joy of bringing people together through food? Understanding these granular details is crucial. Instead of a general passion for "food," identifying a love for "artisanal bread making" or "creating elaborate vegetarian dishes" provides a much more focused starting point. Similarly, a broad passion for "helping people" can be narrowed down to "empowering small businesses with effective digital marketing strategies" or "providing accessible mental health resources for young adults," creating a clearer business direction.

2. Problem-Solving: How Your Passion Can Serve Others

Once you've identified the specific facets of your interests, ask a crucial question: What problems can this passion solve for others? Every successful business addresses a need or a pain point in the market. Your passion serves as a lens through which you can identify these unmet needs, transforming your interests into potential solutions.

If you're passionate about sustainable living, what environmental challenges concern you most—plastic waste, inefficient energy consumption, or the lack of access to eco-friendly products? Your passion for sustainability can then be translated into a business offering biodegradable packaging solutions, home energy audit services, or a marketplace for ethical goods. Consider the frustrations you or others experience related to your interests. What inconveniences exist? What could be done better, faster, cheaper, or more effectively?

3. Leveraging Skills and Knowledge: Your Inherent Assets

Deep engagement with an interest often leads to the development of specialized skills, expertise, and a unique perspective—these are your inherent assets. If you've spent years perfecting a craft like woodworking, you've likely developed dexterity, an eye for detail, and an understanding of materials and techniques. These skills can form the foundation of a custom furniture business, a woodworking workshop, or even a consultancy on wood selection. Recognize that your passion is not just about enjoyment; it's fertile ground for developing valuable competencies that others may lack or seek.

4. Structured Inventory: Uncovering Business Potential

To effectively uncover business potential, create a structured inventory of your passions and interests. Dedicate a notebook or digital document to this exercise. List every hobby, interest, subject you enjoy learning about, or activity that brings you satisfaction. Don't censor yourself—list everything that comes to mind.

For each item, jot down:

- **Specific aspects you enjoy:** What specifically do you love about it?
- **Skills you've developed:** What competencies have you gained?
- **Observed problems:** What frustrations or unmet needs have you noticed within this domain?

To identify viable business opportunities from your passions, deconstruct your interests and systematically connect them to market needs.

First, thoroughly analyze each of your passions. For instance, if you love hiking, delve into its various aspects: the enjoyment of endurance, the appreciation for detailed trail maps, the first-aid skills you've acquired, and even frustrations like unreliable weather forecasts. This detailed examination helps uncover specific knowledge, skills, and pain points within your interests.

Next, cross-reference your passions with potential market demands. This involves bridging your personal interests with the commercial world. Look for clear intersections. Consider your passion for technology alongside the observation that many seniors struggle with digital devices; this could lead to a business offering tech support and training for the elderly. Similarly, a love for vintage clothing combined with tailoring skills might suggest a business in reselling and upcycling garments. The key is to determine what others would pay for, as external demand is crucial for any product or service.

An effective technique to discover these intersections is to brainstorm "what if" scenarios. If gardening is your passion, ask "What if I could offer a subscription box for rare heirloom seeds?" or "What if I could design and install custom urban gardens for apartment dwellers?" For music enthusiasts, questions like "What if I could create an online platform for independent musicians to collaborate?" or "What if I could offer specialized music therapy sessions?" can reveal innovative business ideas beyond obvious applications.

It's also important to consider the potential scale of your ventures. Some passions might suit small, lifestyle businesses, while others could form the basis for larger, scalable enterprises. Your personal goals and lifestyle aspirations should guide how you frame your business. Do you desire flexibility and creative control, or rapid growth and market dominance?

Consider your unique "value proposition" rooted in your passions and skills. This differentiates you in the marketplace. If artisanal coffee is your passion, your value proposition might be sourcing rare beans, offering expert brewing techniques, or creating a unique café atmosphere. For graphic design, it could be highly responsive service, a distinct artistic style, or niche expertise in branding for tech startups. Clearly articulating this value proposition is vital for business development.

To further refine your understanding, engage with others who share your interests and those who represent your potential customer base. Discuss your ideas, asking about their needs, challenges, and current solutions. Actively listen to their feedback, as potential customers often articulate problems or desires you haven't considered. For example, if you're creating educational apps for children, speaking with parents and teachers will offer invaluable insights into needed content and effective features. This feedback loop is essential for validating assumptions and shaping your business concept.

Thoroughly researching existing businesses in your areas of interest is crucial. Analyze their strengths and weaknesses and pinpoint market gaps. Understanding your competitive landscape enables you to develop a distinct offering. Perhaps current businesses are too generic or expensive, or they lack a personal touch. Your unique selling points could be your attention to detail, commitment to quality, or a personalized approach.

Ultimately, reflect on the "why" behind your passion. Is it about creativity, connection, problem-solving, or making a difference? Understanding these deeper motivations ensures your business is not only commercially viable but also deeply meaningful. This intrinsic motivation provides resilience during challenges and sustains your commitment, preventing your venture from becoming a chore rather than a calling.

Consider someone passionate about vintage motorcycles. While they might initially enjoy restoring and riding classic bikes, deconstructing this passion could reveal several business avenues:

1. **Restoration Services:** Leveraging mechanical skills and historical knowledge to restore vintage motorcycles for other enthusiasts, solving the problem of finding reliable restoration experts.
2. **Customization and Modification:** Offering bespoke customization services, transforming classic bikes into unique works of art or performance machines, creating one-of-a-kind pieces that reflect individual taste.
3. **Specialized Parts and Accessories:** Identifying gaps in parts availability through restoration work, then sourcing or manufacturing these parts to serve a niche market.
4. **Curated Sales and Brokering:** Developing an eye for identifying well-maintained or rare vintage motorcycles, acting as a broker or retailer for these sought-after items.
5. **Educational Content and Workshops:** Sharing expertise through online tutorials, ar-

ticles, or in-person workshops on motorcycle restoration and maintenance.

Each of these potential businesses directly stems from the initial passion but addresses different market needs and leverages different entrepreneurial skills. The key is to approach your passions with a curious and analytical mindset, constantly asking: "Who needs this? What problem does it solve? What makes my approach unique?" This systematic deconstruction forms the bedrock of a successful and fulfilling entrepreneurial venture, ensuring your business is an authentic expression of your deepest interests and capabilities. It transforms the abstract idea of "doing what you love" into a concrete plan for creating value.

While deconstructing your passions and interests lays a strong foundation for identifying viable business opportunities, passion and identified needs alone don't guarantee success. A critical, often challenging, step is to meticulously analyze the existing market and competitive landscape. This requires moving beyond personal enthusiasm to objectively evaluate the broader ecosystem in which your business would operate. Without this rigorous examination, even the most inspired idea can falter against established players or overlooked market dynamics. This section explores essential market research practices, focusing on dissecting the competitive arena to help you carve out your unique space.

To begin this crucial analysis, first identify your direct and indirect competitors. Direct competitors offer similar products or services to the same target audience. For example, if your passion for artisanal coffee leads you to open a specialty coffee shop, your direct competitors would be other independent coffee houses nearby, as well as larger chains offering similar high-quality beverages. Indirect competitors, however, may not offer the exact same product but satisfy the same customer need or solve the same problem. In our coffee shop example, indirect competitors could include cafes serving pastries and light meals alongside coffee, fast-food restaurants with coffee, or even supermarkets selling premium coffee beans for home brewing. Considering both types is vital, as customers often have multiple options to fulfill a particular need.

Once competitors are identified, the next step is to gather intelligence on their operations through a multi-faceted approach, using both publicly available information and direct observation. Start with their online presence: scrutinize their websites for product portfolios, pricing strategies, customer testimonials, and overall brand messaging. What tone do they use? What values do they emphasize? Social media platforms are also rich in information. Observe their engagement levels, content types, audience interaction, and customer comments. Are they responsive to feedback? Are there recurring complaints or praises? Understanding their digital footprint offers significant insight into their strategy and customer perception.

Beyond the digital realm, conduct "on-the-ground" research. For a physical business, visit competitors' locations. Observe their store layout, customer service quality, pricing, and general atmosphere. When are they busiest? What types of customers do they attract? This firsthand experience can reveal crucial operational details and customer preferences not always apparent online. For service-based businesses, consider engaging their services as a customer. This allows you to experience their product or service delivery firsthand, providing invaluable insights into their strengths and weaknesses from a user's perspective. For instance, if you're interested in a web design business, hiring a competitor for a small project can reveal their project management style, communication efficiency, and final output quality.

A critical component of competitive analysis is understanding your competitors' strengths and weaknesses. What do they do exceptionally well? What are their unique selling propositions (USPs)?

Are they known for superior quality, lower prices, exceptional customer service, innovative product features, or a strong brand reputation? Conversely, where do they fall short? Are their prices too high for the perceived value? Is their customer service lacking? Are their products outdated or of poor quality? Identifying these aspects will help you pinpoint opportunities to differentiate your offering. For example, if all local bakeries focus on traditional pastries, your strength might be offering innovative vegan or gluten-free options, addressing an unmet dietary need.

Furthermore, analyzing their marketing and sales strategies is essential. How do they acquire customers? Do they rely heavily on advertising, content marketing, social media campaigns, partnerships, or word-of-mouth referrals? Understanding their customer acquisition channels can inform your own marketing efforts. For example, if competitors are heavily investing in paid social media ads with limited organic reach, you might explore a content marketing strategy focused on search engine optimization (SEO) to attract customers searching for solutions you provide. Examining their sales processes – from initial contact to closing the deal – can also reveal best practices or areas for improvement.

Understanding the Competitive Landscape: A Comprehensive Guide

To thrive in any market, a thorough understanding of the competitive landscape is paramount. This involves a multi-faceted approach, analyzing market dynamics, economic influences, and your own unique position.

1. Market Trends and Dynamics:

- **Industry Trends:** Research broader industry trends, technological advancements, and evolving consumer preferences. For example, the rise of e-commerce has transformed retail, making online presence and efficient logistics vital.
- **Sustainability:** Growing consumer awareness around sustainability drives demand for eco-friendly products and practices across various sectors.
- **Proactive Positioning:** Identifying these trends allows you to anticipate market shifts and proactively position your business. Consider emerging technologies that could disrupt your industry or underserved consumer segments.

2. Economic Factors:

- **Economic Health:** Analyze the overall health of the economy, including inflation rates, consumer spending power, and government regulations.
- **Impact on Business:** A recession, for instance, might reduce discretionary spending, affecting luxury goods. Conversely, government incentives can create a favorable environment for new entrants.
- **Realistic Planning:** Understanding macroeconomic influences is crucial for realistic business planning and financial forecasting. Consider the impact of interest rates on loans or trade policies on material costs.

3. Identifying Market Gaps and Unique Selling Proposition (USP):

- **Market Gaps:** Research should identify market gaps—areas where existing offerings are insufficient or absent. These represent significant opportunities for differentiation and market entry. For example, a local need for specialized pet grooming for exotic animals, if currently unmet, is a clear market gap.
- **Unique Selling Proposition (USP):** Your USP is what makes your business stand out. It's the compelling reason customers choose you over competitors. Craft your USP based on

competitor analysis, leveraging your strengths, addressing weaknesses, or filling identified market gaps. This could involve higher quality, personalized customer experience, niche specialization, or unique features (e.g., a customizable service).

4. Barriers to Entry:

- **Obstacles:** These are obstacles that hinder new businesses from entering a market. Examples include high startup costs, strong brand loyalty, complex regulations, proprietary technology, and established distribution networks.
- **Feasibility Assessment:** Understanding these barriers is essential for assessing your business idea's feasibility. High barriers may necessitate innovative strategies, significant funding, or strategic partnerships. For example, entering the airline industry requires immense capital and regulatory approvals.

5. Systematic Research Methodologies:

- **Quantitative Data:** Use surveys and questionnaires to gather data on customer preferences, price sensitivity, and satisfaction with existing offerings.

- **Qualitative Insights:** Focus groups provide qualitative insights into customer opinions, attitudes, and unmet needs, exploring the "why" behind consumer behavior.
- **Expert Perspectives:** Interviews with industry experts, potential customers, and even former employees of competitors offer invaluable perspectives.
- **Secondary Data:** Data analysis of industry reports, market research databases, and government statistics provides a broader understanding of market size, growth potential, and consumer demographics.

6. SWOT Analysis:

- **Framework:** A SWOT analysis (Strengths, Weaknesses, Opportunities, Threats) synthesizes research findings. Apply this to both your potential business and key competitors.
- **Comprehensive View:** Understanding internal strengths and weaknesses in relation to external market opportunities and threats offers a comprehensive view of the competitive landscape. For example, a competitor's weakness in online customer service coupled with growing online shopping presents an opportunity for your business.

7. Competitive Intensity:

- **Market Saturation:** Consider the market's competitive intensity. Is it saturated with many players, or a growing market with room for new entrants?
- **Strategic Implications:** Highly intense markets often require aggressive differentiation, lower initial profit margins, and a strong focus on customer retention. Lower intensity markets may offer easier entry but could also indicate a lack of significant demand.

Understanding competitors' pricing strategies is crucial. Do they offer the lowest cost, or are they premium providers justifying higher prices through quality, brand, or unique features? Analyzing their pricing models (cost-plus, value-based, or competitive) will help you determine your own optimal strategy. If your cost structure is lower, you might undercut them; if your offering provides superior value, you can justify a premium price.

The ultimate goal of this market research is to identify a clear and defensible market niche. This niche should be large enough to support your business but small enough for you to effectively serve and differentiate yourself from larger competitors.

It's about finding the sweet spot where your passion meets a genuine, unmet market need.

In essence, understanding the competitive landscape is fundamental for entrepreneurial success. It requires a deep dive into who your competitors are, what they offer, how they operate, and what drives their success or failure. By meticulously gathering and analyzing this information, you gain critical insights to develop a compelling value proposition, identify market gaps, formulate effective strategies, and position your venture for sustainable growth and a competitive edge. This analytical rigor transforms a passionate idea into a strategically sound business plan.

After dissecting the competitive arena, the next crucial step is to focus intensely on your target audience—the individuals who will drive your venture's success. While understanding competitors helps you position yourself, understanding your audience reveals why your business should exist and to whom you should offer your solution. This section delves into understanding prospective customers beyond basic demographics, uncovering their lives, motivations, and challenges.

Demographics provide a foundational understanding of your customer base (age, gender, income, education, location). For example, knowing your target audience for sustainable fashion is primarily women aged 25-45 in urban areas with disposable income gives you a general direction. However, this alone doesn't explain their interest in sustainable fashion, their values, daily routines, or purchasing motivations. To build a thriving business, you need to enrich this demographic framework with qualitative understanding: their psychographics, behaviors, pain points, and aspirations.

To achieve this depth, a multi-pronged research approach is essential. Surveys and questionnaires are invaluable for gathering quantitative and qualitative data from a broad audience. Move beyond simple multiple-choice questions; incorporate open-ended prompts that encourage detailed responses. For instance, instead of asking "Do you buy sustainable clothing?", ask "What factors influence your clothing purchase decisions, and how important are sustainability and ethical production?" or "Describe your typical apparel shopping experience, including highlights and frustrations." Platforms like SurveyMonkey, Google Forms, or Typeform can distribute these surveys efficiently. The key is to craft questions that elicit genuine insights, and then analyze responses for recurring themes, frustrations, and desires.

Direct interviews are a powerful method for deeper audience understanding. These guided conversations with potential customers are opportunities to listen, learn, and empathize. Prepare open-ended questions probing their daily lives, challenges, aspirations, and their relationship with your product or service category. For a plant-based meal delivery service for busy professionals, you might ask: "Walk me through a typical weekday evening. What are your biggest challenges in preparing or acquiring dinner?" or "What are your health and diet goals, and what obstacles prevent you from achieving them?" Also, ask about their current solutions, what they like or dislike about them, and their biggest frustrations. These conversations provide invaluable qualitative data, revealing nuances and emotional drivers that quantitative data often misses. Focus on their broader lifestyle and how your offering might fit in, as significant insights can come from problems you hadn't considered.

Analyzing online behavior offers another potent avenue for understanding your target audience. People leave digital trails of their interests, needs, and interactions. Social media listening is paramount: monitor relevant hashtags, join industry-specific groups, and observe discussions on platforms like Reddit, Facebook, LinkedIn, and Twitter. What questions are people asking? What problems are they solving? What are they complaining about, recommending, or criticizing? Tools like Hootsuite, Sprout Social, or advanced searches can track these conversations. Beyond social media, analyze online forums, blog comments, and product reviews for existing solutions. For a service targeting freelancers, discussions on platforms like Upwork or Fiverr, or within freelance communities, can reveal common pain points regarding client acquisition, payment issues, or project management.

Understanding Your Audience: The Key to Business Success

To truly connect with your target audience and develop a successful business, a deep understanding of their needs, behaviors, and aspirations is essential. This goes beyond basic demographics to encompass a comprehensive view of who they are and what drives them.

1. Leveraging Search Engine Data for Audience Insights

Search engine data offers invaluable insights into what your audience is actively seeking. By analyzing keywords used in searches related to your business idea, you can identify demand and the specific language your audience uses to articulate their needs.

Tools like Google Keyword Planner, Ahrefs, and SEMrush reveal search volumes and related terms. For example, if you're considering a productivity app, keywords like "time management techniques," "how to focus," or "task prioritization tools" highlight specific needs within your potential user base.

2. Creating Detailed Customer Personas

A crucial outcome of this research is the development of detailed customer personas. These semi-fictional representations of your ideal customers are brought to life by the data you gather. More than just demographics, a persona is a narrative encompassing their motivations, goals, challenges, values, daily routines, and preferred communication channels. Each persona should have a name, a visual representation, a backstory, and a comprehensive profile.

Example: Personas for an Artisan Platform

Consider an online platform connecting local artisans with consumers of unique, handcrafted goods:

- **Persona 1: "Conscious Carol"**
    - **Demographics:** Female, 38, Marketing Manager, married with two children, sub-

urban, $120,000/year household income, Bachelor's degree.

- **Psychographics:** Values authenticity, craftsmanship, sustainability, supports small businesses, appreciates unique items with stories, believes in ethical consumption, concerned about environmental impact.
- **Pain Points:** Struggles to find unique, high-quality, non-generic gifts; feels guilty about mass production; time-consuming to find ethical local artisans; worries about quality of online handmade items.
- **Aspirations:** Wants meaningful home decor; desires to instill conscious consumption values in children; seeks beautiful, durable goods reflecting personal style and values; wants to feel good about purchases.
- **Behaviors:** Browses Instagram for home decor and gifts; reads sustainable living blogs; attends craft fairs; prefers online shopping but wary of quality; willing to pay premium for ethical, high-quality items; reads reviews carefully.
- **Goals for the Platform:** Find unique, high-quality, ethically made home decor and gifts; discover artisan stories; easily

verify authenticity and quality; feel confident in purchases.

- **Persona 2: "Creative Chris"**
    - **Demographics:** Male, 29, Graphic Designer, single, downtown city apartment, $75,000/year income, Master's degree in Fine Arts.
    - **Psychographics:** Passionate about art, design, creative expression; appreciates unique aesthetics and innovative craftsmanship; enjoys discovering emerging artists and supporting fellow creatives; values good aesthetics and quality materials.
    - **Pain Points:** Difficulty finding unique art or handcrafted items aligning with modern, minimalist aesthetic; finds many handmade items too rustic; seeks affordable, high-quality decor expressing personality.
    - **Aspirations:** Curate a living space reflecting artistic sensibilities; find distinctive conversation pieces; discover new artists and potential collaborators.
    - **Behaviors:** Follows design influencers and art galleries on social media; subscribes to design magazines; visits art exhibitions and galleries; browses online

marketplaces like Etsy but finds it overwhelming; buys inspiring art and decor, often impulsively for the right aesthetic.
    - **Goals for the Platform:** Discover artisans with modern and minimalist aesthetics; find unique art pieces and handcrafted objects; easily filter by style and material; support independent artists.

3. Guiding Business Decisions with Personas

These detailed personas act as a constant compass for your business. They inform:

- **Product Development:** What features, materials, and aesthetics will appeal to your audience?
- **Marketing and Messaging:** What language, visual style, advertising channels, and benefits will resonate with each persona? You may need to tailor your approach to cater to distinct, yet sometimes overlapping, needs.

4. The Importance of Psychographics and Behavioral Analysis

- **Psychographics:** Understanding attitudes, values, interests, lifestyles, and opinions is paramount. Knowing Carol's value for authenticity and ethical consumption, for example, is more impactful than just her age. This suggests marketing should highlight product stories, ethical sourcing, and positive impact, with pricing justified by quality and ethical production.

- **Behavioral Analysis:** How do your target customers behave in relation to your product category? Are they extensive researchers or impulse buyers? Brand loyal or frequent switchers? Online, in-store, or subscription purchasers? For the artisan platform, knowing Carol researches thoroughly while Chris buys impulsively based on aesthetics has distinct implications. Carol needs detailed product descriptions, artisan bios, and customer reviews, while Chris benefits more from visually appealing photography and clear stylistic categorization.

5. Identifying Pain Points and Aspirations for Innovation

- **Pain Points:** These are the problems, frustrations, and unmet needs your audience experiences. Every successful business solves a problem or fulfills a desire. By understanding pain points, you can develop solutions that are more effective than existing options. For a meal delivery service, the pain point might be lack of time for healthy cooking after work; the solution offers peace of mind, saved time, and improved well-being.

- **Aspirations:** Connecting with your audience on an emotional level means understanding their dreams and goals. How can your business help them achieve these? If your audience aspires to a minimalist lifestyle, multifunctional furniture or organizational solutions tap into that directly. Marketing can then focus on how your products enable their desired lifestyle, not just their functional aspects.

Understanding your target audience is an ongoing process, not a one-time event. As your business and market evolve, so too will your audience's needs. Continuous feedback, market trend monitoring, and refining your customer understanding are essential to remain relevant, competitive, and deeply connected to your customers. This iterative process allows you to create products and services that truly resonate, fostering loyalty and sustainable success, transforming generic offerings into precisely tailored solutions.

With a deep understanding of your target audience established, the next crucial step is to rigorously validate your business idea. This phase tests assumptions against real-world demand, moving from "I think this will work" to "I know this will work" based on proven interest and willingness to engage or pay. Validation involves observing actions and gathering concrete evidence of market viability, not just asking if people like your idea. Without it, you risk investing significant resources into a concept that may never gain traction. This is your opportunity to de-risk your venture before full-scale development.

A powerful validation method is creating a Minimum Viable Product (MVP). An MVP delivers core value to early customers with just enough features, then gathers feedback to guide future development. It strips away non-essential features, focusing solely on solving the core problem. For example, project management software's MVP might only include task creation, assignment, and basic tracking, omitting advanced reporting initially. The goal is to get this simplified version to real users quickly.

Building an MVP involves identifying the core value proposition and then defining the minimum features needed to deliver it. This requires prioritizing features, asking if each is absolutely necessary for the primary benefit. Non-essential features can be added later based on feedback.

MVP development varies by business. For software, it might be a functional prototype; for physical products, a basic model; for services, offering the core service to a small group for feedback, possibly at a discount. The key is functionality for user interaction and value, with iteration in mind.

Once developed, getting the MVP to your target audience initiates the validation feedback loop. Early adopters, who actively seek solutions to your problem, are valuable allies. They are more forgiving of imperfections and eager to offer constructive criticism. Recruit them through your network, online communities, social media, or early sign-up lists.

Feedback from MVP users is invaluable and should be structured. Implement mechanisms for bug reports, feature suggestions, and general impressions, such as in-app forms, dedicated email, or interviews. Ask specific questions about their experience: what they liked, found confusing, how it met expectations, missing features, and if it solved their problem. Be ready for honest, critical feedback, as it's vital for improvement.

MVP usage data and insights directly inform the next product iteration, embodying the build-measure-learn loop of lean startup methodology. Feedback might lead to refining existing features, adding new ones, removing unused ones, or even pivoting if initial assumptions are incorrect. For instance, if a meal delivery MVP shows interest in meal kits over prepared meals, it could lead to a pivot. This iterative process, based on empirical evidence, significantly reduces the risk of building something unwanted.

Another effective validation method is a pilot program. Similar to an MVP, it often tests operational and customer service aspects in addition to the product or service itself. It's a scaled-down, real-world test of your entire business model. For a subscription coffee box, a pilot might involve a small group of subscribers, limited roasters, in-house fulfillment, and personal customer service.

Pilot programs offer multifaceted benefits. They test logistics and operational efficiency: reliable sourcing, accurate and timely order fulfillment, and efficient customer support. They also provide insights into live customer behavior and satisfaction, such as renewal rates, common questions, and brand interaction.

A well-designed pilot program needs clear objectives and Key Performance Indicators (KPIs) like customer acquisition cost, retention rate, satisfaction scores, order accuracy, and delivery times. Tracking these metrics helps identify bottlenecks and areas for improvement before a full launch. Feedback should cover the entire customer journey, not just the product.

Pilot program duration varies but must be long enough for meaningful data and behavioral patterns. It's an intense learning and adjustment period. Insights gained refine pricing, marketing, operations, and customer service protocols. Essentially, it's a dress rehearsal, ironing out kinks in a controlled environment.

Leveraging Landing Page Tests for Business Idea Validation

Landing page tests are a highly effective and economical method for assessing interest in a business idea, especially for digital products and services. This approach involves creating a web page that clearly outlines your product or service's value proposition, mimicking a real sales page, even if the product isn't ready. Essential components of such a page include a compelling headline, a description of benefits, and a clear call to action (e.g., "Sign up for early access," "Join our waiting list," or "Pre-order now").

The strength of landing page tests lies in their ability to measure genuine user intent. By directing targeted traffic to your landing page via various marketing channels (e.g., social media ads, search engine marketing, email campaigns), you can observe how many people are motivated enough to complete your desired action. The conversion rate—the percentage of visitors who perform the call to action—directly indicates market demand. A high conversion rate suggests strong resonance with your target audience and genuine interest in your offering.

Key Strategies for Effective Landing Page Tests:

- **Specificity is Crucial:** When setting up a test, clearly define your offering and target audience. Vague messages lead to inconclusive results. For example, a productivity app's landing page should detail unique benefits (e.g., AI-powered task prioritization, seamless cross-device syncing) and target specific segments (e.g., freelance creatives, remote teams). A call to action could be "Get notified when we launch and receive a 20% discount."
- **A/B Testing for Optimization:** To maximize effectiveness, A/B test different page elements. Create two versions with a single variation (e.g., different headlines, calls to action, or images) and direct half your traffic to each. Comparing conversion rates helps identify the most effective elements for attracting

interest and driving conversions, enabling data-driven optimization of your messaging and presentation.

- **Testing Pricing and Features:** Landing page tests can also validate different pricing models or feature sets. Create multiple landing pages, each highlighting a distinct pricing tier or specific premium features, and drive traffic to assess which offering garners the most interest. This granular testing provides invaluable insights into market willingness to pay and feature valuation.

Beyond Structured Testing: Gathering Customer Feedback

Beyond structured tests, actively collecting early customer feedback is paramount throughout the validation process. This goes beyond observing behavior; it involves direct engagement and conversation.

- **Encourage Dialogue:** Encourage users to share thoughts, opinions, and suggestions at every touchpoint through surveys, interviews, focus groups, or by being accessible and responsive to inquiries. The goal is to establish a dialogue with potential customers, understanding their evolving needs and perceptions.

- **Ask Open-Ended Questions:** When seeking feedback, ask open-ended questions that elicit detailed responses. Instead of "Did you like the feature?", ask "What did you think of the feature, and how could it be improved?" or "How did this feature help you accomplish your goal?" Listen actively and empathetically, probing deeper to uncover underlying motivations and pain points. Remember, feedback refines your business, not validates your ego.
- **Usability Testing:** This effective technique involves observing individuals interacting with your product or prototype, in person or remotely. Assign specific tasks and note difficulties or hesitations. This hands-on observation can reveal usability issues that might not be articulated in surveys or interviews (e.g., users consistently struggling to find a button or understand an instruction signals a need for UI or messaging improvement).
- **Build a Community:** Fostering a community around your nascent business, even pre-launch, is beneficial. This could be a private Facebook group, Slack channel, or email list for interested individuals to connect with you and each other. Within these communities, share updates, solicit opinions on design choices, and cultivate a sense of belonging. Engaged community members are often enthusiastic early

adopters and valuable sources of ongoing feedback, feeling invested in your success.

Remaining Objective and Data-Driven

Throughout the validation process, objectivity and a data-driven approach are crucial. Personal attachment to an idea can cloud judgment. Rely on evidence—conversion rates, feedback scores, usage statistics, interview transcripts—to make informed decisions. If data suggests initial assumptions were incorrect or demand is insufficient, be willing to adapt, pivot, or even abandon the idea if necessary. This willingness to be guided by market reality characterizes a resilient and successful entrepreneur. The validation phase is about discovering what truly works in the marketplace, not proving yourself right. Rigorously testing assumptions and gathering concrete evidence of demand significantly increases your chances of building an innovative, sustainable, and profitable business.

Identifying Niche Opportunities and Crafting a Unique Selling Proposition (USP)

In today's dynamic entrepreneurial landscape, a good idea alone rarely guarantees success. The marketplace is saturated, with products and services vying for consumer attention. To thrive, a business must not only offer value but also differentiate itself from competitors. This is where identifying niche opportunities and crafting a compelling Unique Selling Proposition (USP) become paramount. These two elements define your business's identity, attract your ideal customer, and build a sustainable competitive advantage. Without a clear understanding of your specific market position and unique value, you risk being lost in the noise, struggling to connect with a truly receptive audience.

Identifying Your Niche: Uncovering Underserved Markets

The journey to a successful business begins with thorough market research. This isn't just about understanding an industry broadly, but about delving into the specifics to pinpoint "underserved segments"—or niches. These are groups of customers whose needs aren't being fully met by current offerings. Imagine a vast forest: instead of trying to appeal to every tree, you focus on a particularly fertile grove where your unique skills can yield the most impactful results. Niches often emerge from overlooked customer demographics, specialized needs, or new trends that larger businesses haven't yet recognized or addressed effectively.

Strategies for Niche Identification:

- **Look Beyond the Obvious:** Identifying niches demands a keen eye for detail. Analyze broader market trends and then consider how specific demographics, psychographics, or behavioral patterns within those trends might reveal unmet needs. For example, within the broad wellness industry, a niche could be busy professionals seeking convenient, plant-based meals prepared in under 15 minutes, or older adults looking for gentle, low-impact fitness classes tailored to age-related conditions. These are not just broad categories, but specific combinations of needs, preferences, and limitations that can form the foundation of a successful niche business.
- **Leverage Your Personal Expertise:** Your own background, experiences, and skills are invaluable tools. What problems have you personally encountered that were poorly solved? Which industries do you know intimately through your career or passions? Often, the most insightful niche opportunities lie where you possess a unique perspective or a specific skillset that others lack. An engineer passionate about sustainable living might find a niche in developing eco-friendly home automation solutions. A former teacher with early childhood development expertise could create specialized educational toys or online learning platforms

for preschoolers. Utilizing your existing strengths provides a natural head start, offering a level of understanding and credibility that newcomers struggle to match.

- **Case Study: The Pet Care Industry:** Consider the massive pet care industry. Within it, numerous niches exist: premium organic dog food for specific breed sensitivities, specialized grooming for exotic pets, or technology solutions like smart feeders with health monitoring or GPS trackers for adventurous canines. Each caters to distinct needs, preferences, and price points, allowing businesses to focus their efforts for maximum impact.

Developing a Distinct Unique Selling Proposition (USP)

Once a potential niche is identified, the next crucial step is to develop a distinct Unique Selling Proposition (USP). This is a concise statement articulating what makes your business different and why customers should choose you over competitors—the answer to "Why you?" A strong USP is more than a tagline; it embodies your business's core value and competitive edge, and should be clear, memorable, and directly relevant to your target niche.

Crafting a Powerful USP:

- **Highlight Differentiators:** A powerful USP often dissects what truly sets your offering apart. Is it a unique product feature, superior customer service, a more convenient delivery method, a competitive pricing structure, or a unique brand story that resonates with your audience? The key is to identify a benefit that is both meaningful to customers and difficult for competitors to replicate.
- **Examples of Effective USPs:**
    - A local bakery's USP isn't just "freshly baked bread." A stronger USP might be: "Artisan sourdough bread made with locally sourced organic flour, delivered warm to your doorstep within two hours." This highlights quality ingredients, a specialized product, a unique process, and a significant convenience factor.
    - If you're a professional chef specializing in vegan cuisine, your restaurant's USP could be: "Authentic, globally-inspired vegan dishes crafted by a former Michelin-starred chef, offering an unparalleled fine-dining experience for plant-based connoisseurs." This leverages personal expertise and perceived prestige.
- **Address Pain Points:** Another approach is to identify a pain point your niche experiences

and position your offering as the definitive solution. For small business owners struggling with complex accounting software, a USP could be: "Intuitive, AI-powered accounting software designed for entrepreneurs—simplify your finances in minutes, not hours, with personalized support from former small business accountants." This directly addresses a common frustration and offers clear benefits and credible support.

- **Deliver on Your Promise:** Crucially, your USP must be a promise your business can consistently deliver upon. An over-promised and under-delivered USP will quickly erode customer trust and brand reputation. The validation steps discussed previously are vital here; ensure that the features, processes, or benefits highlighted in your USP are real, demonstrable, and valued by your target niche.

To ensure a Unique Selling Proposition (USP) remains effective, it must evolve with your business and the market. Gaining customer insights and adapting to competitive changes are not weaknesses, but rather indicators of agility and a commitment to relevance. Regularly refining your USP based on customer feedback and market dynamics keeps it a powerful tool for differentiation.

Discovering Lucrative Niches

Several practical methods can help uncover profitable niches:

- **Analyze Online Communities:** Platforms like Reddit, specialized Facebook groups, and industry-specific forums are rich sources of information. By observing discussions, you can identify recurring questions, common complaints, and unmet needs that traditional market research might miss. For example, a recurring concern on a gardening forum about sustainable pest control for urban balcony gardens could reveal a niche.
- **Leverage Keyword Research Tools:** Tools such as Google Keyword Planner, SEMrush, or Ahrefs show what terms people are actively searching for online. Identifying "long-tail keywords"—more specific, multi-word phrases—can uncover highly specific needs. For instance, instead of the broad "vegan skincare," a search for "vegan skincare for sensitive, acne-prone skin with rosacea" reveals a very specific, potentially underserved niche. Even with lower search volumes, such terms indicate a dedicated audience willing to pay for tailored solutions.

- **Draw on Your Background:** Your expertise can guide your niche pursuit. A deep understanding of technology might lead to AI-powered tools for artists or blockchain platforms for verifying collectibles. A healthcare background could inspire personalized nutrition plans based on genetic testing or wearable health device data integration. The synergy between your expertise and an identified market gap often leads to entrepreneurial success.

Assessing Niche Viability

Once a niche is identified, it's crucial to assess its viability:

- **Profitability and Growth:** Is the niche large enough to be profitable, and is it growing or shrinking?
- **Customer Willingness to Pay:** Are customers in this niche willing and able to spend money on solutions?
- **Competitive Landscape:** Are there existing competitors? If so, how are they serving the niche? Competitive analysis is vital; competition can validate a market. Focus on how to differentiate your offering and provide superior value.

The USP as a Strategic Advantage

A strong USP serves as both a defensive and offensive strategy. It creates a "moat" around your niche business, deterring competitors and attracting customers specifically looking for what you offer, reducing reliance on broad, expensive marketing. For example, a USP centered on ethical sourcing and sustainability will naturally attract customers who prioritize these values, leading to more efficient marketing and stronger customer relationships.

Developing and Implementing Your USP

Consider a hypothetical scenario: With a background in product design and a passion for sustainable living, you notice a trend towards reducing plastic waste in personal care. Identifying a niche within this—zero-waste, refillable personal care products specifically for travel—you craft a USP: "The only travel-sized, zero-waste personal care system featuring elegant, durable, and leak-proof refillable containers with organic, ethically sourced solid toiletries, designed for the conscious globetrotter." This USP targets a specific user and need, highlighting unique features and values.

Developing a USP involves understanding its implications for your entire business. If your USP promises unparalleled customer service, your operations—from hiring and training to feedback and problem resolution—must support it. If rapid delivery is your USP, your logistics and supply chain must be optimized for speed. Every aspect of your business should reinforce your USP.

Niche Evolution and Expansion

A niche is not necessarily small forever; many significant market segments, like online retail or electric vehicles, started as niches. By excelling in a specific niche, you can build a strong brand and loyal customer base, serving as a springboard for expansion into adjacent niches or broader markets. However, the initial focus on a well-defined niche and a clear USP is crucial for establishing this foundation.

The rise of specialized coffee shops illustrates this: from "coffee" to "espresso-based drinks" and then to "single-origin pour-overs," "cold brew specialists," or shops focusing exclusively on plant-based milks and vegan pastries. Each caters to a specific segment, with USPs clearly defining their differentiation. A shop advertising "ethically sourced, single-origin beans roasted in-house daily, prepared using artisanal pour-over methods" clearly targets a discerning coffee enthusiast.

Identifying niche opportunities and developing a USP is an ongoing process of discovery and refinement. It demands market analysis, self-awareness, creativity, and a deep understanding of customer needs. By diligently carving out your specific market corner and clearly articulating why you are the best choice for that segment, you create a business that is not only viable but also resilient, memorable, and ultimately successful. The goal is to become the *only* option for a particular group of people, rather than just another choice.

FOUR

CRAFTING YOUR BUSINESS PLAN

A business plan serves as the architectural blueprint for transforming a new business idea into a thriving enterprise. It meticulously details every structural element, operational system, and financial forecast. While previous sections focused on refining your vision, identifying your unique selling proposition, and understanding your market, this section explores the fundamental components of a formal business plan. This document is crucial not only for securing funding but also for guiding strategic decisions and ensuring accountability as your business expands. A well-crafted business plan acts as a compass, keeping your venture on track through all entrepreneurial challenges.

Executive Summary

Positioned at the very beginning of your business plan, the Executive Summary is often the final section written. It provides a concise distillation of the entire document, designed to immediately capture the reader's attention and encourage them to delve deeper. This critical summary should encapsulate the essence of your business: the problem you solve, your proposed solution, your target market, your competitive advantage, and your financial projections. For potential investors or lenders, the executive summary frequently determines whether they will dedicate further time to your proposal. It must be persuasive, clear, and to the point, typically spanning one to two pages. It should highlight the most attractive aspects of your business, such as market opportunity, the experience of your management team, and projected profitability, painting a picture of a strong, viable, and potentially lucrative venture.

Company Description

Following the executive summary, the Company Description provides comprehensive background information about your business. This section outlines your company's mission statement—the fundamental purpose and values driving your organization. What problem are you aiming to solve, and what societal or customer need are you fulfilling? It also details your company's vision, a forward-looking statement of your aspirations. Beyond these foundational statements, you will describe your legal structure (e.g., sole proprietorship, partnership, LLC, or corporation). Include information regarding your company's history, location, and any key milestones achieved. For new ventures, this section will focus on the core concept, foundational principles, and long-term aspirations. For example, a sustainable fashion brand would articulate its commitment to ethical sourcing, fair labor practices, and minimizing environmental impact, alongside details about apparel types and target demographics.

Market Analysis

The Market Analysis section demonstrates a deep understanding of your chosen industry and specific market segment. This requires thorough research into the size of your target market, its growth potential, and prevailing trends. You will identify your ideal customer profile, examining their demographics, psychographics, purchasing habits, and pain points. This section also includes a comprehensive competitive analysis, identifying direct and indirect competitors, their strengths and weaknesses, their product/service comparisons, and their market share. Understanding the competitive landscape helps you identify differentiation opportunities and effectively position your business. For instance, in the plant-based food market, an analysis would detail the growth of vegan/vegetarian consumers, identify key players like Beyond Meat and Impossible Foods, analyze their offerings and pricing, and pinpoint emerging trends like specific protein sources or allergen-free options. This analysis would then inform how your own plant-based product can carve out a unique space.

Organization and Management

Finally, the Organization and Management section details your company's structure and the expertise of your leadership team. This section is vital for investors who are evaluating the people behind the business as much as the idea itself. You will outline your organizational chart, defining the roles and responsibilities of key personnel. Include brief biographies of your management team, highlighting their relevant experience, skills, and track records of success. If you have an advisory board, detail their expertise and contributions. For a startup, this might involve showcasing the founders' complementary skill sets and prior entrepreneurial experience. If your business relies on specialized expertise (e.g., biotech or advanced software), demonstrating the qualifications of your scientific or technical leads is paramount. The goal is to instill confidence in your reader by presenting a capable and well-structured team equipped to execute the business plan.

Product/Service Line

This section thoroughly describes your offerings. Detail the features and benefits, highlighting what makes your product or service unique and how it addresses customer needs. If you have multiple offerings, describe each one clearly. For physical products, include details on design, materials, manufacturing, and intellectual property (e.g., patents, trademarks). For services, explain the delivery process, key differentiators, and unique methodologies. Visual aids like prototypes, diagrams, or mockups can be beneficial. For example, a sustainable packaging company might discuss material composition, biodegradability, cost-effectiveness, and a scalable manufacturing process.

Marketing and Sales Strategy

Outline your approach to reaching and converting customers. Translate your market analysis into actionable plans. This includes your pricing strategy (how you determined it and how it aligns with your market position and target customers) and your promotional strategy (how you will communicate your value proposition through advertising, PR, social media, content marketing, etc.). Describe your sales process, including lead generation, prospect qualification, and closing sales. Detail your distribution channels (direct-to-consumer, retail partners, online marketplaces). A SaaS company, for instance, might use SEO, targeted LinkedIn ads, blog posts, white papers, and a freemium or free trial model, followed by tiered subscriptions.

Financial Projections

This essential section quantifies your business strategy and demonstrates its financial viability. Include projected income statements, cash flow statements, and balance sheets for three to five years, based on realistic assumptions from your market analysis and sales forecasts. Key metrics to include are revenue growth, gross profit margins, operating expenses, net profit, and break-even analysis. Detail your funding requirements, how funds will be used, and expected ROI for investors. Sensitivity analysis (exploring how assumption changes affect financial outcomes) adds credibility. A restaurant startup's projections, for example, would include detailed forecasts for food, labor, rent, marketing, and sales based on seating, average check, and anticipated customer traffic, demonstrating profitability.

Appendices

Beyond the core components, you might include appendices depending on your business and audience. These can house supporting documents such as resumes of key personnel, market research data, permits and licenses, letters of intent from customers, or detailed financial statements.

Overall Goal

The business plan aims to present a cohesive, well-researched, and persuasive case for your business's potential success, acting as a roadmap for execution and a compelling argument for support. Each section should flow logically, building a complete and credible picture of your venture. While the level of detail will vary, the overarching objective is to clearly articulate your business idea, strategy, and expected outcomes to instill confidence and secure commitment.

Market Analysis - Deeper Dive

It's crucial to go beyond simply identifying a market and perform granular segmentation and targeting. A broad market like "online retail" is too vast. Identify specific sub-segments or niches, such as "artisanal, sustainably sourced coffee beans sold online to home baristas in urban areas." This specificity allows for more targeted marketing and product development. Further segmentation can occur based on customer loyalty programs, subscription models, or specialized brewing preferences (e.g., cold brew vs. pour-over). Understanding the size of these specific segments is vital: are there enough potential customers to sustain profitability? Tools like Google Trends, industry reports (e.g., Statista, IBISWorld), and analyzing niche keyword search volume provide valuable insights into market size and growth potential.

Market Analysis: Competitive Landscape

A thorough competitive analysis goes beyond simply listing competitors. It requires a strategic approach, examining each competitor's value proposition, pricing strategies, marketing channels, strengths (e.g., established brand, customer base, proprietary technology), and weaknesses (e.g., poor customer service, outdated products, high prices). Integrating a SWOT analysis (Strengths, Weaknesses, Opportunities, Threats) for your own business within this competitive context is invaluable.

For example, a new online education platform specializing in vocational skills would analyze competitors like Coursera, Udemy, and LinkedIn Learning. This analysis would assess their course catalog, pricing, instructor quality, user experience, and marketing reach. Such an analysis might reveal opportunities to differentiate through more hands-on, project-based learning with direct industry mentorship, a feature often less prevalent on larger, generalized platforms.

Marketing and Sales Strategy: Pricing

Pricing is a critical component of your marketing and sales strategy, far more than just covering costs and generating profit. It acts as a powerful communication tool, signaling value, quality, and brand positioning. Consider various pricing models, including cost-plus, value-based, competitive, penetration, and premium pricing. Each model has distinct advantages and disadvantages, dependent on your product, market, and business objectives.

For instance, a luxury watch brand might employ a premium pricing strategy to convey exclusivity and high quality. Conversely, a new software service aiming to disrupt an established market might use penetration pricing, offering a lower initial price to gain market share. Your chosen pricing strategy must be clearly justified and linked to your market analysis and competitive positioning.

Product or Service Line: Value and Protection

When detailing your product or service, consider the entire customer journey and the value delivered at each touchpoint. For physical products, this includes the unboxing experience, ease of assembly/use, and after-sales support. For services, focus on the customer experience from initial inquiry through ongoing engagement. What tangible and intangible benefits will your customers receive? A consulting firm, for example, offers tangible deliverables like reports, but also intangible benefits such as peace of mind and strategic clarity.

Intellectual property protection is also crucial. If your business relies on proprietary technology, unique designs, or a distinctive brand name, a clear patent, trademark, or copyright strategy is essential. This is particularly important when seeking investment, as it demonstrates a significant barrier to entry for competitors.

Financial Projections: Accuracy and Realism

Financial projections are often the most scrutinized section of a business plan, especially by investors. Accuracy and realism are paramount. Clearly state all assumptions underlying your financial forecasts. For example, if you project 20% year-over-year revenue growth, explain whether this is based on anticipated market growth, planned marketing spend, or customer acquisition targets. Presenting multiple scenarios (conservative, realistic, optimistic) can demonstrate a comprehensive understanding of potential outcomes and mitigate risk.

Break-even analysis is vital, indicating the point at which revenue equals costs and your business becomes profitable. For cash flow projections, consider the timing of cash inflows and outflows, as a profitable business can still fail due to a lack of liquidity. Understanding working capital requirements—the capital needed for daily operations—is another key aspect of financial planning.

Executive Summary: The Compelling Narrative

The Executive Summary should be more than just a summary; it needs to be a compelling narrative. It should tell your business's story, highlighting the opportunity, your unique solution, and the potential for significant returns. Think of it as a movie trailer for your business: engaging, concise, and impactful, designed to leave the reader wanting more.

It should touch upon key elements that will be expanded in later sections: the problem, your solution, your target market, your competitive advantage, your business model, your management team's expertise, and your financial highlights. For instance, an executive summary for a tech startup might begin by outlining the massive market disruption caused by legacy systems, introduce its innovative software solution, highlight the experienced founding team, and conclude with a clear statement of funding sought and projected ROI.

A robust financial strategy forms the cornerstone of any successful business venture. It's more than just optimistic predictions; it's about translating market insights, sales approaches, and operational blueprints into concrete numbers that highlight your venture's financial viability and potential for profit. Without a clear financial forecast, your business plan remains an abstract concept, lacking the tangible proof needed to convince investors, lenders, and even yourself of its potential. This section will equip you with the knowledge and framework to develop crucial financial projections, specifically focusing on revenue and expense forecasting, and understanding the key financial statements that will shape your financial blueprint.

Forecasting revenue is often the most critical and challenging aspect of financial projections. It demands a deep dive into your market analysis and a realistic evaluation of your sales strategy's effectiveness. The initial step involves developing a sales forecast, which should be rooted in data and logical assumptions. Start by identifying your target customer segments and estimating the number of customers you can realistically acquire within a specific timeframe. This should be informed by your market size research, customer acquisition cost (CAC) estimates, and the capacity of your sales and marketing efforts. For instance, if you've identified a niche market of 10,000 potential customers and your marketing campaign is projected to reach 20% of them, with a 5% conversion rate, this translates to 100 customers during that period.

Forecasting Revenue

To project your revenue, start by calculating the average revenue per customer. This figure is influenced by your pricing strategy and the nature of your product or service. For one-time purchases, it's the average product price. For subscription models, it's the average monthly or annual recurring revenue per subscriber. Account for variations like tiered pricing or product bundles.

- **Example (Niche Coffee Beans):** If a customer spends $50 per month on beans and you expect 100 customers in the first year, your initial projected revenue for that segment is $50 x 100 customers x 12 months = $60,000.

Build your sales forecast month-by-month for the first year, then annually for years two through five. This detailed approach provides an accurate cash flow picture and highlights seasonal trends or growth points. Retail businesses, for instance, might see higher sales during holidays, while consulting firms might peak in the first and third quarters due to budget planning.

Factor in growth assumptions:

- **Customer acquisition growth rate:** How many new customers do you anticipate?
- **Average revenue per customer increase:** Will upselling or new products boost individual customer spending?

These growth rates should be clearly stated and justified.

- **Example (Coffee Business):** If you project acquiring 150 customers in year two and 200 in year three, and the average purchase value increases to $55, these changes directly impact your revenue projections.

Consider multiple revenue streams. If your business offers complementary services or different product lines with varying price points and sales volumes, forecast each stream separately before aggregating them for your total revenue projection.

- **Example (Software Company):** Revenue streams could include initial software licenses, recurring subscription fees, implementation services, and ongoing support contracts. Each requires a distinct forecast, considering factors like market adoption rates, churn rates, and service team capacity.

Forecasting Expenses

The expense side of your financial projections is equally crucial, requiring meticulous identification and estimation of all business costs. These fall into two broad categories: Cost of Goods Sold (COGS) or Cost of Services (COS), and Operating Expenses (OpEx).

Cost of Goods Sold (COGS) / Cost of Services (COS): These are direct costs related to producing or delivering your product or service.

- **Manufacturing:** Raw materials, direct labor, manufacturing overhead.
- **Service:** Direct labor costs of employees delivering the service, or software licenses used for service delivery.
- **Example (Coffee Bean Business):** COGS includes the cost of green coffee beans, roasting, packaging materials, and shipping to the customer. If beans cost $5/pound, roasting/packaging $1/pound, and shipping $2/pound, and a customer buys 1 pound/month, COGS per customer per month is $8.

Operating Expenses (OpEx): These are day-to-day business costs not directly tied to production.

- **Examples:** Salaries for administrative and sales staff, rent, utilities, marketing and advertising, insurance, legal and accounting fees, office supplies, and depreciation.

Categorize these expenses properly:

- **Fixed Costs:** Relatively constant regardless of sales volume (e.g., rent, salaries).
- **Variable Costs:** Fluctuate with sales volume (e.g., sales commissions, some marketing expenses).

- **Semi-Variable Costs:** Have both fixed and variable components (e.g., utilities).

When projecting operating expenses, consider every potential cost.

- **Retail Store:** Rent, utilities, property taxes, insurance, salaries for sales associates and managers, POS system fees, security, and marketing.
- **Online Business:** Website hosting, e-commerce platform fees, digital marketing spend, customer support software, and salaries for remote employees.

An itemized list of anticipated expenses is often helpful.

- **Example (Coffee Business):** OpEx would include salaries for marketing and customer service staff, website development and maintenance, online advertising, payment processing fees, and potentially rent for a small office. Projected monthly marketing spend of $500 and a customer service salary of $3,000 per month are examples.

A common pitfall is underestimating expenses. Always build in a contingency fund or buffer for unexpected costs. Factor in inflation and potential increases in key expenses like rent or raw material costs over the projection period.

- **Example:** Projecting a 3% annual increase in employee salaries and a 5% annual increase in coffee bean costs due to market fluctuations should be included in projections for years two, three, and beyond.

Constructing the core financial statements requires accurate revenue and expense forecasts. The Income Statement, or Profit and Loss statement, provides a historical overview of financial performance. It calculates gross profit by subtracting the Cost of Goods Sold (COGS)/Cost of Sales (COS) from total revenue. Operating expenses are then deducted to arrive at operating income (EBIT – Earnings Before Interest and Taxes). Finally, interest expenses and taxes are subtracted to determine net income, or profit.

For a coffee business, year one might look like this:

- **Revenue:** $60,000
- **COGS:** $24,000 ($8 per customer per month for 100 customers)
- **Gross Profit:** $36,000

- **Operating Expenses:** $30,000 (e.g., $3,000/month customer service salary + $500/month marketing + $2,000/month for website/software/other)
- **Operating Income:** $6,000
- **Net Income:** $6,000 (assuming no interest or taxes in year one)

The Balance Sheet offers a snapshot of your company's financial position at a specific point in time, adhering to the fundamental accounting equation: Assets = Liabilities + Equity.

- **Assets:** What your company owns (e.g., cash, accounts receivable, inventory, equipment, buildings).
- **Liabilities:** What your company owes to others (e.g., accounts payable, loans, deferred revenue).
- **Equity:** The owners' stake in the company.

A new business's balance sheet would reflect initial owner investments and loans, alongside assets purchased with that capital. Over time, cash, inventory, and accounts receivable/payable will fluctuate.

For example, if a coffee business starts with $10,000 in owner equity and a $5,000 loan, and purchases $2,000 in inventory and $1,000 in office equipment, the initial balance sheet would show:

- **Assets:** $3,000 (equipment) + $2,000 (inventory) + initial cash (calculated to balance the equation)
- **Liabilities:** $5,000 (loan)
- **Equity:** $10,000

The Cash Flow Statement is crucial for operational success, particularly for startups, as it tracks the actual movement of cash. Profitability on the income statement doesn't always equate to cash in the bank. This statement reconciles net income to actual cash generated and used, categorized into three activities:

- **Operating Activities:** Cash from normal business operations.
- **Investing Activities:** Cash from buying or selling long-term assets (e.g., equipment).
- **Financing Activities:** Cash from debt and equity transactions (e.g., loans, stock issuance).

Even with a $6,000 net income in year one, a coffee business's cash flow could differ. If $60,000 in sales only resulted in $55,000 cash collected (due to accounts receivable), operating cash flow would be lower. Conversely, buying $3,000 of inventory on credit (accounts payable) wouldn't immediately impact cash flow but would affect the balance sheet. The cash flow statement reveals available cash for bills, growth, and effective business management, making monthly projections vital for startups to prevent running out of cash.

When developing financial projections, clearly articulate all assumptions:

- **Revenue:** Specify customer acquisition rates, average transaction values, and churn rates.
- **Expenses:** Detail expected costs for labor, materials, marketing, rent, utilities, and other overhead.
- **Changes:** Explain significant increases in sales (e.g., marketing initiatives, sales team expansion) or decreases in expenses (e.g., renegotiated contracts, improved energy efficiency).

Transparency in assumptions builds credibility.

A break-even analysis is also beneficial, determining the point where total revenue equals total costs, meaning no profit or loss.

- **Break-Even Point (in Units):** Fixed Costs / (Sales Price Per Unit – Variable Cost Per Unit)

- **Break-Even Point (in Sales Dollars):** Fixed Costs / Gross Profit Margin

Understanding this point helps set realistic sales targets. For the coffee business, if monthly fixed costs (salaries, rent, website) are $3,000 and the gross profit per pound of coffee is $7 (selling price $10, COGS $3), the break-even point is approximately 429 pounds of coffee per month.

Finally, conduct sensitivity analysis to test how changes in key assumptions impact projections. By modeling scenarios like a 10% lower customer acquisition rate or a 5% increase in COGS, you can identify risks and develop contingency plans. Presenting "worst-case," "most likely," and "best-case" scenarios demonstrates a thorough understanding and proactive approach. Financial projections are dynamic and should be regularly reviewed and updated to guide the business toward sustainable financial health and growth.

Securing startup capital is a critical and often challenging step for entrepreneurs. It fuels the transformation of ideas into tangible operations. While a strong business plan and financial projections are foundational, acquiring funds requires a strategic approach, understanding available options, and convincingly articulating your venture's potential. This section explores various startup funding options, providing a roadmap for entrepreneurs to navigate this crucial phase.

Personal savings are often the first and most accessible funding source, demonstrating a deep commitment to your venture and signaling dedication to external investors. This includes money from salaries, investments, or personal asset sales. The main advantage is retaining full control and ownership without immediate external reporting or equity dilution. However, it's vital to balance commitment with personal financial security. Using a portion of savings to cover initial operating expenses, with a clear plan for its use, showcases responsible financial stewardship. For instance, an entrepreneur starting an artisanal bakery might use significant savings for equipment, commercial kitchen rent, and initial raw materials, signaling full commitment to future lenders or investors.

Startup Funding Avenues: A Comprehensive Guide

Securing funding is a critical step for any startup. This guide explores various traditional and emerging financing options, from institutional loans to community-driven crowdfunding, along with key considerations for each.

1. Loans from Financial Institutions

Traditional loans from banks, credit unions, and small business lenders remain a widely used method. To qualify, you'll need:

- A robust business plan.
- Detailed financial projections.
- A clear understanding of your creditworthiness.

Lenders require a realistic repayment plan, often with collateral or personal guarantees, and will scrutinize your cash flow.

Advantages:

- You retain full ownership and control of your company.
- Interest paid on the loan is a tax-deductible business expense.

Challenges:

- Fixed repayment obligations, irrespective of business performance.
- Difficult for early-stage businesses with unproven revenue or limited credit history.

Enhancing Your Chances: Demonstrate a strong market need, a viable business model, and a clear path to profitability. For example, a tech startup seeking to scale a new product could secure a term loan for R&D, manufacturing, and marketing if they present a compelling case for future revenue generation.

2. Angel Investors

Angel investors are high-net-worth individuals who invest their personal funds in early-stage companies in exchange for equity.

Benefits:

- Financial backing.
- Valuable industry experience, mentorship, and a network of contacts.
- Higher risk tolerance compared to traditional lenders.

Attracting Angels: Present a compelling pitch highlighting your unique value proposition, market opportunity, scalability, and team expertise. Angels expect significant returns (multiple times their investment within a few years) and look for a clear path to substantial growth and an exit strategy (e.g., acquisition or IPO). A concise and persuasive pitch deck is essential. A biotech startup with a groundbreaking drug, for instance, might seek angel investment for clinical trials, emphasizing scientific rationale, market size, and a strong management team.

3. Venture Capital (VC) Firms

VC firms are professional investors managing pooled capital from institutional investors, pension funds, and wealthy individuals. They typically invest larger sums in companies with demonstrated traction or proven business models.

What VCs Look For:

- Businesses with the potential to become market leaders.
- Substantial returns, usually within a 5-10 year timeframe.
- Significant equity stake and often board seats, actively participating in strategic direction.

The Pitch Process: Rigorous due diligence is conducted on your market, technology, financials, team, and competitive landscape. Your business plan and financial projections must be exceptionally well-researched and defensible. A company developing innovative software with a rapidly expanding user base might attract VC to fuel aggressive expansion, hire talent, and invest in sales and marketing. VCs will seek evidence of scalability, a defensible competitive advantage, and a strong management team.

4. Crowdfunding

Crowdfunding has emerged as a powerful, democratized way to raise capital, especially for consumer-facing products or businesses with strong community appeal. Platforms include Kickstarter and Indiegogo.

Models:

- **Reward-based:** Backers receive a product or perk.
- **Donation-based:** Typically for social causes.
- **Equity crowdfunding:** Backers receive a small ownership stake.

Advantages:

- Fundraising and market validation.
- Customer base building and generating buzz.

Challenges:

- Requires significant marketing effort to reach critical mass.
- Immense pressure to deliver on promises to early supporters.

Keys to Success: Thorough campaign planning, realistic funding goals, and compelling marketing materials. An eco-friendly consumer product company could use crowdfunding for initial production, offering early bird discounts and exclusive bundles, thereby building a loyal community of early adopters.

5. Other Funding Avenues

- **Government Grants and Loans:** Available from federal, state, and local agencies, often targeting specific industries, R&D, or underserved communities. These can be highly advantageous (no repayment or equity dilution) but involve stringent application processes and eligibility criteria.
- **Incubators and Accelerators:** Offer a blend of funding, mentorship, and resources to early-stage startups, often in exchange for a small equity stake. They are designed to rapidly grow businesses and prepare them for larger funding rounds.

Securing External Funding: A Meticulous Process

Obtaining external funding demands thorough preparation. The cornerstone of this process is a compelling pitch, which condenses your business plan into an engaging narrative. This narrative should clearly articulate the problem you address, your unique solution, the market opportunity, your business model, your team's capabilities, and your financial projections.

Crafting Your Pitch Deck

An effective pitch deck, typically 10-15 slides, is crucial. It should comprehensively cover:

- The problem your business solves
- Your proposed solution
- The size and opportunity within your target market
- Detailed information about your product or service
- Your business model
- Your marketing and sales strategies
- Your management team's expertise
- Your financial projections
- The amount of funding requested
- A clear plan for how the funds will be utilized

Mastering Your Pitch and Understanding Investor Expectations

Rehearsing your pitch is paramount; you must deliver it confidently and be prepared to answer questions thoroughly and honestly. Crucially, understand that different investors have varying expectations:

- **Angel Investors:** Often prioritize the team and the disruptive potential of the idea.
- **Venture Capitalists (VCs):** Scrutinize scalability, potential for market dominance, and a clear exit strategy.
- **Lenders:** Primarily focus on your ability to repay the debt.

Always research potential investors to align with their investment thesis and target companies.

Effective Fund Management

Once secured, managing funding effectively is as vital as raising it. This entails:

- **Disciplined Budgeting:** Strict adherence to financial plans.
- **Transparent Financial Reporting:** Clear and consistent communication of financial status.

- **Strategic Capital Allocation:** Directing funds towards growth initiatives that align with your business plan.
- **Open Communication with Investors:** Proactive updates, even on challenges, build trust and facilitate collaborative problem-solving.

Mismanagement can quickly derail promising ventures, leading to cash flow issues and a loss of investor confidence. Therefore, rigorous financial oversight and a clear understanding of your burn rate (the rate at which capital is spent before generating positive cash flow) are indispensable.

Illustrative Funding Scenarios

SaaS Startup:

- **Initial Capital:** Founders' savings for a Minimum Viable Product (MVP).
- **Angel Investment (Post-MVP Traction):** Used for product refinement based on user feedback, hiring a small sales and marketing team, and covering operational expenses for 12-18 months. The pitch emphasizes recurring revenue, Customer Acquisition Cost (CAC) vs. Customer Lifetime Value (CLV), and the large addressable market.

- **Series A Funding (Post-Significant Growth):** Larger investment from VCs to fuel aggressive scaling, including expanding the sales force, investing in product development, and increasing marketing spend. The VC pitch focuses on market leadership, defensible competitive advantages, and a clear path to a substantial exit (e.g., acquisition or IPO).

Physical Product Business (e.g., Sustainable Fashion Brand):

- **Initial Capital:** Personal savings for design, ethical material sourcing, and prototype creation.
- **Crowdfunding Campaign:** Pre-selling the first collection to generate capital and gather market feedback.
- **Small Business Loan or Angel Investment (Post-Successful Crowdfunding):** Capital for larger-scale manufacturing, e-commerce platform development, and marketing/PR to build brand awareness. The pitch highlights sustainability, growing consumer demand for ethical products, and potential for brand loyalty.

The Non-Linear Path to Startup Capital

Securing startup capital is rarely a linear process. It often involves combining different funding sources at various stages of a business's lifecycle. Each option presents unique advantages, disadvantages, and requirements. By thoroughly understanding these options, meticulously preparing your business case, and strategically approaching potential funders, entrepreneurs can significantly increase their chances of securing the financial runway needed to transform innovative ideas into thriving enterprises.

The key is to align your funding strategy with your business goals, understand the expectations of each funding source, and demonstrate a clear vision for how the capital will be deployed to achieve sustainable growth and profitability.

The Strategic Importance of Pricing

Understanding how to price your products and services is a cornerstone of financial planning. Pricing is not merely about covering costs; it's a strategic decision that directly impacts revenue, profitability, market perception, and ultimately, your venture's long-term success. Having established the groundwork for securing capital, we now pivot to generating revenue and managing finances effectively, beginning with a robust pricing strategy. This section will guide you through various pricing approaches, helping you determine optimal price points that align with your business goals, market realities, and the inherent value you deliver to your customers.

Developing a robust pricing strategy begins with a comprehensive understanding of your cost structure. Before considering customer willingness to pay or competitor pricing, you must precisely know the cost of producing and delivering your product or service. This requires meticulous tracking of both direct and indirect costs.

Direct Costs are directly attributable to the creation of your product or service. Examples include:

- **Physical Products:** Raw materials, components, and direct manufacturing labor.
- **Service-Based Businesses:** Labor hours spent on service delivery or direct software licenses used for services.

Indirect Costs (Overhead) support business operations but aren't directly tied to a specific product or service. These can include:

- Rent for office/production facilities
- Utilities
- Administrative staff salaries

- Marketing and sales expenses
- Insurance
- Equipment depreciation

Pricing Strategies

1. Cost-Plus Pricing

This common method calculates the total cost of production/delivery and adds a predetermined markup percentage to determine the selling price. For instance, a $10 widget with a 50% markup would sell for $15 ($10 + ($10 * 0.50)).

- **Advantages:** Relatively simple to implement, ensures cost coverage and profit margin (assuming sales volume).
- **Limitations:**
    - Ignores customer demand or willingness to pay, potentially leaving money on the table or leading to unsold inventory.
    - Assumes efficient and optimized costs, which may not always be true.
    - Sole reliance on this method can be a missed opportunity.

2. Value-Based Pricing

This more sophisticated approach focuses on the perceived value your product or service offers the customer. It asks: "How much is this solution worth to the customer?"

- **Implementation:** Requires deep understanding of your target market's needs, pain points, and the benefits they derive from your offering. Market research (surveys, focus groups, interviews, competitor analysis) is crucial to quantify this value.
- **Examples:**
    - A software solution automating a complex manual process might be priced based on substantial labor savings it provides, rather than just development costs.
    - Luxury handbags are priced based on prestige, craftsmanship, and exclusivity, not just material costs.
    - Consultants charging significant fees for delivering millions in revenue understand the value they provide far exceeds their direct costs.
- **Challenge:** Accurately quantifying and effectively communicating that value to potential buyers.

3. Competitive Pricing

This strategy sets prices based on what competitors charge for similar offerings, acknowledging market dynamics. Various approaches include:

- **Price Matching:** Setting prices at par with key competitors to attract price-sensitive customers. Requires close monitoring of competitor pricing.
- **Premium Pricing:** Pricing higher than competitors, often used when your offering has superior features, quality, brand recognition, or customer service. Signals higher value and exclusivity (e.g., Apple iPhones).
- **Penetration Pricing:** Setting a lower price (sometimes below cost) to quickly gain market share and attract a large customer base. Typically a short-term strategy for new products or market entry, with prices gradually increasing later (e.g., early streaming services).
- **Skimming Pricing:** Setting a high initial price for new, unique, or technologically advanced products, then gradually lowering it over time. Captures value from early adopters and then attracts more price-sensitive customers as the market matures (common in electronics).
- **Crucial Considerations:**

- Simply matching competitor prices without considering your own costs or unique value can be detrimental.
- Analyze competitors' value propositions: Is their lower price due to lower quality, poorer customer service, or a less established brand? Understanding these nuances is vital.

Successful pricing strategies often combine various approaches. A common and effective method is value-plus pricing. This strategy merges an understanding of customer value with a consideration of costs. To implement value-plus pricing, first identify your product or service's perceived value. Then, ensure your price covers all costs, provides a healthy profit margin, and remains appealing to your target market.

For example, a freelance web designer would calculate the time and resources (costs) required to build a website. They would also research competitor pricing and, importantly, understand the value a well-designed website brings to a client's business (e.g., increased leads, improved brand image). Based on this information, they would set a competitive price that reflects the delivered value and ensures profitability.

Psychological pricing is another crucial consideration, appealing to consumers on an emotional or subconscious level. Common tactics include:

- **Charm Pricing (or Odd Pricing):** Ending prices with .99 or .95 (e.g., $19.99 instead of $20.00) to create the perception of a lower price and a bargain. Consumers often focus on the first digit, making $19.99 seem significantly cheaper than $20.00.
- **Prestige Pricing:** Setting artificially high prices to convey quality, luxury, and exclusivity. This is often used for high-end goods or services where brand image is paramount.
- **Bundle Pricing:** Offering a package of products or services at a lower price than if purchased individually. This can increase sales volume and introduce customers to a wider range of offerings. For instance, a software company might bundle its core product with an add-on module at a discounted price.
- **Price Anchoring:** Presenting a higher-priced item first to make subsequent lower-priced items appear more affordable by comparison, establishing a reference point in the consumer's mind. Showcasing a premium package before a standard package can make the standard package seem like a better deal.

When determining pricing, understanding the price elasticity of demand is essential. This economic concept measures how much demand for a product or service changes in response to a price change. Products with high price elasticity are very sensitive to price changes; a small price increase can lead to a significant drop in demand. This often applies to non-essential goods or products with many close substitutes. Conversely, products with low price elasticity are not significantly affected by price changes; demand remains relatively stable even if prices increase. This is typically true for essential goods, unique products with no close substitutes, or products for which consumers are very brand loyal. Understanding price elasticity helps predict how pricing strategy changes might affect sales volume and overall revenue.

For startups, especially in digital environments, dynamic pricing can be a valuable consideration. This involves adjusting prices in real-time based on factors like demand, time of day, customer segment, or inventory levels. Ride-sharing services like Uber and Lyft use surge pricing, increasing fares during high demand. Airlines and hotels have long employed dynamic pricing to maximize revenue by adjusting prices based on booking patterns and demand forecasts. While effective, dynamic pricing requires sophisticated technology and careful management to avoid alienating customers who might perceive it as unfair.

Pricing services is often more complex due to their intangible and labor-intensive nature. Common service pricing models include:

- **Hourly Billing:** Charging a fixed rate per hour of service. While straightforward, it can be difficult to estimate accurately and may not reflect the true value delivered if a service is completed efficiently. It can also incentivize inefficiency.
- **Project-Based (or Fixed-Price) Billing:** Quoting a single price for the entire project or service. This provides predictability for the client and requires the service provider to accurately estimate time and resources. A clear scope of work and a process for handling changes are crucial. This model aligns with value-based pricing, as the price reflects the perceived outcome rather than hours spent.
- **Retainer Agreements:** Charging clients a recurring fee for ongoing access to services or a set amount of work each month. This provides predictable revenue for the service provider and ensures ongoing support for the client.
- **Performance-Based Pricing:** Tying a portion of the fee to achieved results. For example,

a marketing consultant might charge a base fee plus a percentage of increased sales revenue generated by their campaign. This model aligns the interests of the service provider and the client but requires clear performance metrics.

Pricing is not static and should be reviewed and adjusted periodically as your business evolves, market conditions change, costs fluctuate, and your understanding of customer value deepens. Regularly analyze sales data, customer feedback, and competitor actions to identify optimization opportunities. Consider A/B testing different price points to determine the best performers.

Key Considerations for Setting Your Prices:

1. **Know Your Customer:** Understand your target audience's needs, budgets, and price sensitivity.
2. **Understand Your Value Proposition:** Identify what makes your product or service unique, the benefits you offer, and how it solves a problem or creates value.
3. **Analyze Your Costs:** Accurately calculate all direct and indirect costs to ensure your pricing covers these and allows for a sustainable profit margin.

4. **Research Your Competition:** Determine what similar businesses charge and how your offering compares in terms of features, quality, and benefits.
5. **Choose the Right Pricing Model:** Select a strategy that aligns with your business goals, market position, and the nature of your product or service.
6. **Communicate Your Value:** Clearly articulate the benefits and value of your offering to justify your price through effective marketing and sales messaging.
7. **Monitor and Adapt:** Regularly review your pricing strategy and be prepared to make adjustments based on market feedback, sales performance, and changes in costs or the competitive landscape.

For example, a small-batch coffee roaster might start by calculating the cost of green beans, roasting labor, packaging, and overhead (cost-plus pricing). Knowing their target market values quality, ethical sourcing, and unique flavor profiles, they might then employ value-based pricing, positioning themselves as a premium brand. They would research other specialty coffee roasters and perhaps price their beans slightly higher, supported by marketing that highlights their artisanal process, direct trade relationships, and distinctive tasting notes. They might also offer a subscription service with a slight discount (bundle pricing) to encourage recurring revenue and customer loyalty.

Pricing is an ongoing process that requires a combination of analytical rigor, market insight, and strategic thinking. By applying these principles diligently, entrepreneurs can establish pricing strategies that ensure financial viability, reinforce perceived value, and strengthen their market position, thereby laying a solid foundation for profitable growth. Your price signals the quality and value of your offerings, making it essential for building a sustainable and successful business.

A well-defined pricing strategy drives revenue, but robust budgeting and financial management are crucial to translate that revenue into sustained success. This isn't about being overly restrictive, but rather instilling discipline, foresight, and a clear understanding of your financial landscape. Your budget acts as a roadmap for spending and investment decisions, while ongoing financial management navigates, constantly checking your position against the map and making necessary course corrections. Without these, even promising ventures can falter due to poor resource allocation or an inability to adapt to changing economic conditions.

The cornerstone of financial management is a comprehensive operating budget, a detailed plan for anticipated revenues and expenses over a specific period, usually a fiscal year, broken down monthly or quarterly. It begins with a realistic sales projection, informed by your pricing strategy and sales forecasts, which then dictates your affordable operational capacity. Subsequently, you meticulously list all anticipated expenses, categorized as follows:

- **Cost of Goods Sold (COGS):** Directly related to the production or acquisition of products. For manufacturers, this includes raw materials, direct labor, and manufacturing overhead. For retailers, it's the inventory purchase price.
- **Operating Expenses (OpEx):** All day-to-day business costs excluding COGS. This broad category includes salaries and wages (beyond direct labor), rent, utilities, marketing and advertising, insurance, professional fees (legal, accounting), software subscriptions, office supplies, and other necessary overhead. It's crucial to be exhaustive, as minor expenses can accumulate significantly.

When constructing your budget, consider **zero-based budgeting** versus **incremental budgeting**. Incremental budgeting adjusts the previous period's budget by a percentage for inflation or growth, which can perpetuate inefficiencies. Zero-based budgeting, however, demands justification for every expense, forcing a critical re-evaluation of each cost center and encouraging strategic resource allocation. For example, a zero-based approach to marketing would ask: what are our marketing goals, what activities will achieve them, and what is the precise cost? This often leads to optimized spending and identifies areas for cost reduction or reallocation to higher-impact initiatives.

Beyond the operating budget, a **cash flow forecast** is equally vital. While a budget outlines profitability, a cash flow forecast tracks the actual movement of money into and out of your business. This is critical because a profitable business can fail if it lacks cash to meet short-term obligations like payroll or supplier payments. This forecast should map expected cash inflows (from sales, loan proceeds, or investments) against expected cash outflows (for expenses, loan repayments, and capital expenditures). A positive cash flow forecast indicates sufficient liquid assets for immediate needs, while a negative forecast signals a potential cash crunch requiring proactive solutions, such as securing a line of credit or accelerating collections.

For instance, a seasonal landscaping company's operating budget might show annual profitability, but its cash flow forecast would highlight a significant winter deficit when revenue is minimal, but expenses like equipment maintenance, insurance, and office rent continue. Recognizing this in advance allows the owner to arrange a line of credit or plan alternative off-season revenue streams, preventing a liquidity crisis even with profitable contracts lined up for spring.

Effective financial management hinges on consistent monitoring of financial performance. This involves comparing actual results against budgets and forecasts using key performance indicators (KPIs).

Key Performance Indicators (KPIs) for Monitoring:

- **Profitability Metrics:**
    - **Gross Profit Margin:** (Revenue - Cost of Goods Sold) / Revenue – Indicates the profitability of core products.
    - **Operating Profit Margin:** Operating Income / Revenue – Shows profitability after all operating expenses (OpEx).

    - **Net Profit Margin:** Net Income / Revenue – Reveals ultimate profitability after all expenses, interest, and taxes.
- **Liquidity Ratios:**
    - **Current Ratio:** Current Assets / Current Liabilities – Assesses the ability to meet short-term debts.
- **Leverage Ratios:**
    - **Debt-to-Equity Ratio:** Measures the proportion of debt financing relative to equity.

Analyzing Variances:

A critical aspect of monitoring is analyzing variances—the differences between budgeted and actual figures. If revenue falls short or expenses exceed the budget, it's crucial to investigate the root causes (e.g., pricing issues, lower sales volume, increased competition, unexpected supplier price increases). This analysis provides actionable insights for adjusting strategies and informs future budgeting and operational decisions.

Data-Driven Financial Decisions:

Moving beyond intuition, data-driven financial decisions are paramount. By meticulously collecting and analyzing financial data, businesses can make informed choices. For instance, if data shows a product with a higher profit margin and faster sales cycle, allocating more marketing resources to it makes strategic sense. Conversely, data might support discontinuing underperforming product lines.

Example: SaaS Company Decisions:

A SaaS company can use data to make informed decisions about pricing tiers by tracking customer acquisition costs (CAC) and lifetime value (LTV). If the highest tier has a significantly higher LTV relative to its CAC, investing more in acquiring customers for that tier is a sound strategy. Similarly, analyzing churn rates in specific tiers can pinpoint areas for product or customer support improvement.

Reinvestment for Growth:

Sound financial management prioritizes reinvestment. A portion of profits should be allocated for growth and innovation, such as investing in new equipment, R&D, expanding the team, enhancing marketing, or technology upgrades. These strategic investments should be explicitly accounted for in the budget and financial management system to prevent stagnation and maintain competitiveness.

Managing Economic Fluctuations and Ensuring Resilience:

Robust financial management is crucial for navigating economic downturns, supply chain disruptions, shifts in consumer behavior, and regulatory changes. Businesses with a solid budget, healthy cash reserves, and a clear understanding of their financial levers are more resilient. Diversified revenue streams, lean operational costs, and contingency funds (often a percentage of operating expenses) provide a crucial buffer during challenging times.

Financial Discipline:

Financial discipline is the bedrock of effective management, requiring adherence to the budget, scrutiny of deviations, and informed decisions for any divergence. It involves resisting impulse spending and ensuring all expenditures align with strategic objectives. Cultivating a culture of financial awareness through regular training reinforces cost control and efficient resource utilization.

Accurate and Up-to-Date Financial Records:

Meticulous record-keeping of all transactions (sales receipts, invoices, expense reports, payroll data) is fundamental. These records are essential for budgeting, performance monitoring, tax compliance, audits, and future financing. Accounting software streamlines this process, ensuring accuracy and providing real-time insights, making it easier to prepare financial statements (income statement, balance sheet, cash flow statement) for assessing business health.

Scenario Planning for Startups and Growing Businesses:

Scenario planning is an invaluable tool, involving the creation of multiple budget and cash flow forecasts based on best-case, worst-case, and most-likely future outcomes. By modeling scenarios (e.g., lower sales, increased supplier prices), businesses can anticipate challenges and develop contingency plans proactively. This enhances adaptability and survival during unexpected events, such as a manufacturing firm planning for equipment breakdown or identifying backup partners in advance.

Effective pricing and budgeting operate in a continuous feedback loop. Your pricing strategy dictates your revenue, forming the bedrock of your budget.

Conversely, your budget and financial performance actively inform your pricing decisions. For instance, if your budgeted cost structure is higher than anticipated, you may need to adjust pricing to ensure profitability. Conversely, if sales consistently exceed projections and you have excess capacity, you might explore strategies to boost volume, such as lowering prices or investing in promotions. This iterative approach ensures your financial plan remains relevant and effective.

Consider a consultancy firm that initially set prices based on industry averages and perceived value. Through rigorous financial management, they discovered higher-than-expected overhead costs, including sophisticated project management software, extensive professional development, and a high-quality office environment. Their budget revealed that current pricing, while competitive, yielded only a slim profit margin. This data prompted a revision of their pricing structure, perhaps by introducing premium service packages or slightly increasing hourly rates, coupled with clear communication of the added value and expertise provided to clients. This budget-driven adjustment was vital for long-term sustainability and the ability to reinvest in their core strengths.

Debt management is another critical aspect of sustainable financial management. While debt can facilitate growth through capital expenditure loans or lines of credit for working capital, it requires prudent management. This involves not only meeting repayment schedules but also understanding the impact of interest costs on profitability. Excessive debt makes a business vulnerable to interest rate fluctuations and economic downturns, as a larger portion of revenue is committed to debt servicing. Therefore, your budget should meticulously account for all debt obligations, and your financial management should include strategies for debt reduction or refinancing when favorable opportunities arise. The objective is to use debt strategically to enhance returns, not to burden the business with an unsustainable load.

Ultimately, sustainable budgeting and financial management aim to create a financially resilient organization. This means building a business that can not only survive but thrive through diverse economic conditions, adapt to market changes, and consistently pursue its growth objectives. It demands a commitment to accuracy, a proactive mindset, and a willingness to allow financial data to guide strategic decisions. By embracing these principles, your financial plan transforms from a static document into a dynamic, living system that actively contributes to the enduring success of your enterprise. This rigorous approach to financial management is not merely about tracking numbers; it's about building a robust, adaptable, and ultimately, a sustainable business capable of achieving its long-term vision.

FIVE

LEGAL STRUCTURES AND COMPLIANCE ESSENTIALS

Choosing the Right Legal Structure for Your Business

The legal framework of your business is as crucial to its long-term success as financial management or a strong pricing strategy. Your choice of legal structure impacts everything from personal liability and tax obligations to your ability to attract investors and the administrative burden you face. This guide will demystify these options, helping you select the structure that best aligns with your entrepreneurial goals and risk tolerance. It's a strategic decision, not a one-size-fits-all solution, and should evolve with your business's stage, growth, and your personal financial comfort.

Sole Proprietorship

The simplest and most common structure for individuals starting out, especially freelancers or solo entrepreneurs, is the Sole Proprietorship. In this setup, there's no legal distinction between you and your business—you are the business.

Advantages:

- **Ease of Establishment:** Minimal regulatory hurdles, often requiring only local business licenses and permits, and perhaps a "doing business as" (DBA) name registration.
- **Tax Simplicity:** Profits are taxed directly as your personal income, avoiding corporate tax complexities and potential double taxation.
- **Minimal Administration:** Fewer separate tax returns, no board meetings, and basic record-keeping requirements.

Disadvantages:

- **Unlimited Personal Liability:** This is the most significant drawback. Your personal assets (home, savings, car) are not protected from business debts or lawsuits. For example, if a freelance graphic designer operating as a sole proprietor is sued for breach of contract, their personal savings or even their house could be at risk. Similarly, a defaulted business loan could lead to lenders pursuing personal assets. This lack of protection is a critical consideration for businesses with higher risks or frequent public interaction.

While easy to start, many entrepreneurs outgrow this structure as their business expands and risk exposure increases.Partnership

Moving up in complexity and offering more protection than a sole proprietorship, a Partnership involves two or more individuals who agree to share business profits or losses. Like a sole proprietorship, there's generally no legal distinction between the owners and the business itself.General Partnership (GP)

The most common type of partnership, a GP, involves all partners sharing in operational responsibilities and liabilities.

Key Characteristics:

- **Shared Liability:** Each partner is personally liable for the business's debts and obligations, and crucially, for the actions of other partners. If one partner incurs debt or commits an act leading to a lawsuit, all partners can be held liable. For instance, in a law or dental practice, one partner's error or mismanagement could make the other partners personally responsible for the financial fallout.

- **Pass-Through Taxation:** Profits and losses flow through to individual partners' tax returns, similar to a sole proprietorship.
- **Pooled Resources:** A significant advantage is the ability to combine capital, expertise, and skills, potentially accelerating growth.

Challenges:

- **Disagreements:** Potential for disputes among partners.
- **Unlimited Liability:** Remains a major drawback, similar to a sole proprietorship.

To mitigate risks, partners should establish a **Partnership Agreement**, outlining profit/loss distribution, roles, responsibilities, dispute resolution, and procedures for new partners or dissolution.Variations of Partnerships: Limited Protection

To address the unlimited liability of general partnerships, two variations exist:

- **Limited Partnership (LP):** An LP requires at least one general partner (who manages the business and has unlimited liability) and one or more limited partners. Limited partners' liability is capped at their investment, and they typically have no management control. LPs are often used for investment or real estate ventures.
- **Limited Liability Partnership (LLP):** LLPs offer some liability protection to all partners, particularly from the professional malpractice or negligence of other partners. They are commonly favored by professional service firms (e.g., law, accounting, architectural firms). In an LLP, a partner is generally not personally liable for the wrongful acts of other partners or employees not under their direct supervision, though they remain liable for their own misconduct and general business debts.

Both LPs and LLPs generally maintain a pass-through taxation arrangement, with profits and losses allocated to individual partners.

Limited Liability Company (LLC)

An LLC offers a significant upgrade in liability protection compared to sole proprietorships or partnerships, though it comes with increased administrative complexity. This hybrid structure combines the pass-through taxation of simpler business forms with the limited liability of a corporation. This means that the personal assets of LLC members (owners) are shielded from business debts and lawsuits. Creditors can only pursue the assets of the LLC itself, providing crucial peace of mind and protecting your personal financial well-being. For example, if your retail store LLC faces a lawsuit from an injured customer, your personal savings, home, and other assets would typically be protected, with the LLC being solely liable for any judgment.

Taxation Flexibility: By default, a single-member LLC is taxed as a sole proprietorship, and a multi-member LLC as a partnership, with profits and losses passing through to members' personal income tax returns. However, an LLC can elect to be taxed as a C-corporation or S-corporation, offering strategic tax advantages depending on profitability and the owners' overall tax situation. This flexibility allows tax treatment to adapt as the business grows.

Administrative Requirements: Forming an LLC involves filing articles of organization with the state and usually includes ongoing requirements like annual reports and fees. An Operating Agreement is highly recommended for multi-member LLCs (though not always legally required). This internal document defines ownership, management, profit/loss distribution, and procedures for adding/removing members, ensuring clarity and preventing disputes. The blend of liability protection and tax flexibility makes the LLC a popular choice for small to medium-sized businesses.

Corporations

Corporations are distinct legal entities, entirely separate from their owners (shareholders), offering the strongest form of liability protection. Shareholders are generally not personally liable for corporate debts or actions, with their risk limited to their investment in the company's stock. This "corporate veil" safeguards personal assets from business liabilities, making it ideal for businesses with high risk exposure or those planning to raise substantial capital. For instance, in a large manufacturing corporation facing product liability claims or environmental cleanup costs, the personal assets of its shareholders are shielded.

Types of Corporations and Taxation:

- **C-corporation:** This standard corporate structure is taxed as a separate entity, meaning the corporation pays income tax on its profits. If profits are distributed to shareholders as dividends, those dividends are taxed again at the individual shareholder level (known as double taxation), which can be a significant drawback. However, C-corps are attractive for attracting venture capital due to their familiar structure and ability to issue different classes of stock. They also offer greater flexibility in employee fringe benefits and can retain earnings for reinvestment without immediate personal tax consequences for shareholders.

- **S-corporation:** An S-corp is a tax election available to eligible corporations (and LLCs) that allows profits and losses to pass directly to owners' personal income, avoiding the double taxation of C-corps. To qualify, a business must meet criteria such as having no more than 100 U.S. citizen/resident shareholders and only one class of stock. While offering pass-through taxation, S-corps come with stricter operational rules and ownership limitations compared to C-corps or LLCs.

Administrative Intensity: Forming a corporation is the most complex and administratively intensive business structure. It requires filing articles of incorporation, establishing a board of directors, issuing stock, holding regular board and shareholder meetings, and maintaining detailed corporate records (minutes, bylaws, etc.). Significant ongoing compliance requirements include annual reports, franchise taxes, and rigorous record-keeping. This formality is often appealing to investors, signaling a mature and well-governed business, and corporations are better positioned for raising capital through stock sales (privately and through IPOs).

1. Liability Protection: Assess your business's risk exposure. For significant personal asset protection, especially for businesses interacting with the public, handling substantial capital, or operating in litigious sectors, an LLC or corporation is generally preferred over a sole proprietorship or partnership.

2. Taxation: Consider how your business profits will be taxed. Sole proprietorships and partnerships offer straightforward pass-through taxation. LLCs provide flexibility in tax treatment. C-corporations face double taxation but are attractive for reinvestment and investors, while S-corporations offer pass-through taxation with certain limitations. Analyze your projected profitability and its impact on your personal income.

3. Administrative Complexity and Cost: Determine your willingness to dedicate time and resources to legal and administrative compliance. Sole proprietorships are the simplest and most cost-effective to establish and maintain. Partnerships are slightly more complex due to required agreements. LLCs involve more formal setup and ongoing filings. Corporations are the most complex and costly to both establish and maintain.

4. Fundraising and Investment: If you plan to seek external investment, particularly from venture capitalists or angel investors, consider that investors typically favor corporations, specifically C-corporations, due to their established legal framework, stock options, and familiar governance structures. If significant external funding is a future goal, a corporate structure may be a necessary consideration sooner rather than later.

5. Ownership Structure and Future Growth: Evaluate the number of owners and your vision for the business's evolution. For multiple owners or anticipated significant growth and ownership changes, flexible structures like LLCs or corporations are more suitable.

For instance, a freelance web designer starting with minimal risk might begin as a sole proprietor. As their client base grows and they hire employees, transitioning to an LLC would protect personal assets from potential employment-related lawsuits or contractual disputes. If this business later seeks venture capital to expand services and develop proprietary software, converting to a C-corporation would likely be a strategic move to attract investors.

The choice of legal structure is a fundamental decision that underpins your business's legal, financial, and operational framework. It requires careful consideration of current needs and future aspirations. Consulting legal and tax professionals is highly recommended to ensure you select the optimal balance of protection, flexibility, and efficiency for your unique business venture, thereby providing a stable and compliant foundation for entrepreneurial success.-----Once the most suitable legal structure for your enterprise—be it a sole proprietorship, partnership, LLC, or corporation—has been determined, the next crucial phase involves formally establishing your business and ensuring compliance with all applicable laws and regulations. This transition from concept to a legally recognized entity necessitates navigating various administrative processes, primarily focused on business registration and securing necessary licenses and permits. While specifics vary significantly by location, industry, and chosen legal structure, understanding the fundamental steps and their rationale is paramount for a smooth and compliant launch. This section will guide you through these essential bureaucratic hurdles, empowering you to build a solid legal foundation for your venture.

Obtaining an Employer Identification Number (EIN):

The foundational step for most businesses, especially those intending to hire employees or operate as anything other than a sole proprietorship without employees, is obtaining an Employer Identification Number (EIN) from the Internal Revenue Service (IRS). Also known as a Federal Tax Identification Number, the EIN serves as your business's Social Security number. It is used for tax purposes, including filing business tax returns, opening business bank accounts, and applying for business licenses. The process of obtaining an EIN is free and can be completed online via the IRS website, typically taking only a few minutes. You will need to provide information such as your business's legal name, address, and structure. While sole proprietors without employees may not strictly require an EIN, obtaining one is beneficial. It helps separate business and personal finances, crucial for clear accounting and simplifying the opening of a business bank account, which is strongly advised for all entrepreneurs. For example, a freelance photographer operating as a sole proprietor might initially use their Social Security number for transactions. However, as their business grows, attracting larger clients and potentially hiring an assistant, securing an EIN becomes necessary, lending professionalism and facilitating payroll and tax filings once employees are onboard.

Business Name Registration:

Beyond the federal EIN requirement, you must address business name registration. If your business operates under a name different from your legal name (for sole proprietorships and partnerships) or your officially registered entity name (for LLCs and corporations), you will likely need to file a "Doing Business As" (DBA), also known as a fictitious name or trade name registration. This filing is typically done at the state or county level. For instance, if Jane Doe, a consultant, operates as "Innovative Solutions," she would need to file a DBA to inform the public and government agencies that she owns the business operating under that trade name. DBA filing requirements vary by jurisdiction; some states have statewide registries, while others require county-level filings. Consult your local county clerk's office or your state's Secretary of State website for specific procedures and fees. Failure to register a DBA when required can lead to penalties and legal complications, including the inability to enforce contracts or open bank accounts under the fictitious name. Similarly, if forming an LLC or corporation, the entity itself must be registered with the state. This usually involves filing Articles of Organization for an LLC or Articles of Incorporation for a corporation with the Secretary of State's office in your primary state of business. These documents formally create your legal business entity and typically include the business name, registered agent (a person or entity designated to receive legal documents), and principal business address. Filing fees can range from a nominal amount to several hundred dollars, depending on the state.

Licenses and Permits:

Securing licenses and permits is arguably the most complex and diverse aspect of business registration, as requirements are layered across federal, state, and local levels and are heavily influenced by your specific industry. At the federal level, certain industries are regulated by federal agencies and require specific licenses or permits. For example, businesses involved in agriculture, alcohol and tobacco, firearms and explosives, aviation, broadcasting, fish and wildlife, commercial fisheries, mining and drilling, nuclear energy, and transportation often fall under federal oversight. Agencies like the Food and Drug Administration (FDA), the Federal Communications Commission (FCC), and the Department of Transportation (DOT) issue critical permits and licenses for operation in these sectors. For instance, a startup producing artisanal cheese would need to comply with FDA regulations and potentially state-level food safety certifications. A company planning to launch a podcast and broadcast content might require FCC licenses for certain types of transmission.

Navigating the Labyrinth of Business Licenses and Permits

Establishing and operating a legitimate business requires a thorough understanding and adherence to a complex web of licensing and permit requirements at federal, state, and local levels. These regulations are not one-time hurdles; many necessitate ongoing renewal and meticulous record-keeping to ensure continuous compliance.

State-Level Requirements

At the state level, businesses will encounter a variety of mandatory licenses and permits. These often include:

- **General Business Licenses:** A fundamental prerequisite for any commercial activity within a state.
- **Professional Licenses:** Required for professions demanding specialized knowledge (e.g., doctors, lawyers, accountants, electricians, contractors). These typically involve meeting educational qualifications, passing examinations, and adhering to continuing education. Operating without proper licensure can lead to severe penalties, including fines, business closure, and legal action. State licensing boards, often man-

aged by the Secretary of State or a similar office, serve as central points for business registration and information.

- **Sales Tax Permits:** Essential for businesses selling tangible goods or taxable services. Businesses must register with their state's department of revenue or taxation to collect and remit sales tax.
- **Environmental Permits:** Necessary for businesses whose operations might impact the environment (e.g., manufacturers, construction companies, businesses handling hazardous materials).
- **Health Permits:** Frequently mandated for businesses in the food service industry (e.g., restaurants, caterers, food manufacturers) to ensure public health and safety standards.

Local-Level Requirements

City and county governments impose an equally significant array of licensing and permit requirements, including:

- **General Business Licenses/Occupational Licenses:** Required by the specific city or county in which the business operates.
- **Zoning Permits:** Crucial for brick-and-mortar establishments, ensuring the business's

location complies with local land-use regulations and is zoned for commercial activity. Special use permits or rezoning may be required for operations in non-commercial zones.

- **Building Permits:** Necessary for any new construction or significant renovations to business premises.
- **Health and Safety Permits:** Often mandated by local authorities, particularly for businesses dealing with food, public accommodation, or specific services.
- **Fire Department Permits:** May be required for businesses posing fire risks or having specific occupancy loads.

A Systematic Approach to Compliance

Effectively navigating these intricate regulations demands a systematic approach:

1. **Thorough Research:** Begin by researching requirements at all three governmental levels (federal, state, and local) relevant to your business's location and industry. State government websites (e.g., Secretary of State, business development agencies) are excellent starting points, often offering online resources and checklists for new businesses. Local government websites for your city and county are

equally vital for identifying local ordinances and permits.

2. **Professional Guidance:** Consider utilizing online business license compliance services or consulting with a business attorney or specialized licensing consultant. These professionals can identify necessary permits, guide you through application processes, and ensure timely submission, preventing costly delays or penalties.

    - **Example:** A small bakery might require a federal EIN, a state reseller's permit (for tax-free supply purchases), a state food handler's permit for employees, a local business license, a city health department permit for its kitchen, and potentially a zoning permit for a new location. Each requires specific applications, fees, and adherence to various regulations.

3. **Ongoing Compliance:** Licenses and permits are often not one-time acquisitions; many require periodic renewal (annually or biennially). Failing to renew can lead to expiration, rendering your business non-compliant and subject to penalties. Maintain detailed records of all obtained licenses and permits, including expiration dates and renewal procedures.

This proactive approach to managing regulatory obligations mitigates stress and expense, allowing businesses to focus on growth. The effort invested in thorough registration and meticulous adherence to licensing requirements forms the bedrock of a legitimate and sustainable enterprise, ensuring legal operations and protection from disruptions. It also signals to customers, partners, and regulators a commitment to operating with integrity, laying a strong foundation for future growth and trust.

The Indispensable Role of Contracts and Agreements

Beyond initial registrations and permits, the ongoing health and resilience of any enterprise are profoundly influenced by its ability to manage relationships and obligations through clearly defined legal instruments: contracts and agreements. These documents are crucial for:

- **Outlining Engagement Terms:** Clearly defining the scope and conditions of business interactions.
- **Defining Responsibilities:** Specifying the roles and duties of all parties involved.
- **Mitigating Risks:** Reducing the potential for misunderstandings, disputes, and costly le-

gal battles that can derail progress and threaten solvency.

By proactively safeguarding business interests through well-structured contracts, ventures can ensure stability and focus on innovation and growth.

A contract is a legally enforceable agreement between two or more parties, signifying a mutual commitment to specific actions or abstentions. For entrepreneurs, proficiency in contract negotiation and management is as vital as developing a compelling product. Contracts serve several critical functions: they clarify expectations, minimize misunderstandings, establish responsibilities, provide a framework for dispute resolution, and offer legal recourse for non-compliance. Essentially, each contract acts as a shield, protecting your business from unforeseen challenges and fostering dealings based on respect and legal clarity. Without adequate agreements, a business can be exposed to significant financial and operational risks.

Entrepreneurs encounter a diverse range of contracts due to the varied relationships and transactions inherent in business operations. Understanding these types is crucial for effective leveraging.Types of Business Contracts

- **Client and Customer Agreements:** These fundamental contracts (also known as service agreements or customer contracts) define the relationship between your business and those who purchase your products or services. They are essential for setting clear expectations regarding the scope of work, deliverables, timelines, payment terms, intellectual property (IP) rights, confidentiality, and termination clauses. For example, a consulting firm's client agreement would detail advisory services, hours allocated, billing rates, payment schedules, and handling of proprietary client information. A Software-as-a-Service (SaaS) provider's customer agreement would include terms of service, a Service Level Agreement (SLA) for uptime guarantees, data privacy policies, and subscription renewal terms. A well-drafted client agreement protects revenue, defines service boundaries, and provides a clear roadmap for the client relationship, preempting disputes by explicitly stating terms and payment conditions.
- **Partnership Agreements:** Crucial for businesses formed by multiple individuals, these documents govern the internal workings of the partnership. They detail decision-making processes, profit/loss sharing, capital contributions, individual roles and responsibilities, dis-

pute resolution mechanisms, and terms for a partner's departure, expulsion, or partnership dissolution. For instance, in a tech startup, a robust partnership agreement would specify roles (e.g., Partner A for product development, Partner B for sales), equity division, salary determination, and procedures if a partner exits or becomes incapacitated, ensuring business continuity. Without such an agreement, state partnership laws, which may not align with the partners' intentions, will govern these aspects, potentially leading to damaging disputes.

- **Vendor and Supplier Contracts:** These agreements establish the terms for procuring essential resources like raw materials, equipment, and services from vendors and suppliers. Key elements typically include goods/services specifications, quality standards, delivery schedules, pricing, payment terms, warranties, indemnification clauses (protecting your business from vendor-caused harm), and termination rights. For a restaurant, a produce supplier contract would detail freshness standards, delivery days, and payment. For a manufacturer, a parts supplier contract would specify material composition, tolerance levels, and penalties for defects or late deliveries. These contracts ensure supply chain reliability, quality, prevent operational disruptions, and provide leverage if a vendor fails to meet terms.

- **Employment Contracts and Independent Contractor Agreements:** These distinct agreements govern how you engage with your team.

    - **Employment Contracts:** Used for full-time or part-time employees, these outline job responsibilities, compensation, benefits, working hours, grounds for termination, and confidentiality obligations. An executive's employment contract would detail salary, stock options, bonus structure, vacation time, and termination notice periods.
    - **Independent Contractor Agreements:** Used for individuals or entities hired for specific projects without becoming employees. These must clearly define the independent nature of the relationship, specifying project scope, deliverables, payment, IP ownership of the work product, and the contractor's responsibility for their own taxes and benefits. Misclassifying workers can lead to significant legal and financial penalties. For example, a marketing agency hiring a freelance graphic designer would specify the pro-

ject, deadline, payment, and confirm the designer is not an employee and uses their own equipment.

- **Non-Disclosure Agreements (NDAs):** Also known as confidentiality agreements, NDAs are paramount for protecting proprietary information when sharing sensitive business details with third parties (e.g., investors, partners, employees, contractors). An NDA legally binds the recipient not to disclose or misuse the information. A startup seeking venture capital funding might use an NDA when presenting business plans or proprietary technology. Similarly, NDAs ensure key employees understand their confidentiality obligations even after leaving the company.
- **Lease Agreements:** Critical for businesses operating from a physical location, commercial lease agreements outline the terms for renting office space, retail storefronts, or industrial facilities. Key provisions include lease duration, rent, maintenance responsibilities (landlord vs. tenant), permitted use, insurance requirements, and renewal/termination options. A carefully reviewed lease can prevent unexpected costs or disputes.
- **Intellectual Property (IP) Agreements:** Vital for businesses with unique creations (inventions, brands, creative works), IP agreements

include licensing agreements (allowing others to use IP under specific terms) or assignments (transferring IP ownership). A software company's license agreement would define customer software usage and restrictions. An inventor's licensing agreement with a manufacturer would outline royalty payments and manufacturing rights. Protecting IP ensures capitalization on innovations and prevents unauthorized use.

Essential Elements of a Legally Sound Contract

Beyond understanding contract types, knowing what makes a contract legally sound and effective is crucial. Most business agreements should include several essential clauses for comprehensive protection and clarity:

- **Offer and Acceptance:** A valid contract requires a clear offer from one party and unequivocal acceptance from the other, forming mutual agreement.
- **Consideration:** This refers to the value exchanged between parties—the "bargained-for exchange." It can be money, goods, services, or a promise to act or refrain from acting.

- **Legality of Purpose:** The contract's objective must be legal. Agreements for illegal acts are void and unenforceable.
- **Capacity of Parties:** All parties must have the legal capacity to enter a contract (e.g., legal age, sound mind, not under duress).
- **Specific Terms and Conditions:** This is the core of the contract, detailing rights and obligations precisely and unambiguously.

    - **Scope of Work/Deliverables:** Clearly defines the goods or services provided, including quantities, specifications, and quality standards.
    - **Payment Terms:** Details payment amount, schedule, method, provisions for late payments, and interest on overdue amounts.
    - **Term and Termination:** Specifies the agreement's duration and conditions for termination by either party, including notice periods or termination for breach/convenience.
    - **Confidentiality:** Outlines obligations to protect sensitive information.
    - **Intellectual Property Rights:** Clearly states ownership of IP created or transferred.

- **Warranties and Disclaimers:** Warranties promise quality/performance; disclaimers limit or exclude certain warranties.
- **Indemnification:** Requires one party to compensate the other for losses due to specific actions or failures.
- **Limitation of Liability:** Caps the recoverable damages in case of a breach or claim, often a heavily negotiated point.
- **Governing Law and Dispute Resolution:** Specifies the jurisdiction's laws that govern the contract and how disputes will be resolved (negotiation, mediation, arbitration, or litigation).
- **Force Majeure:** Addresses unforeseen events (e.g., natural disasters) that may prevent performance, outlining how obligations are affected.
- **Entire Agreement Clause (or Integration Clause):** States that the written contract is the complete and final understanding, superseding prior agreements.

Contracts: A Strategic Imperative

Approaching contract creation and execution with a strategic mindset is crucial. It's not just about filling out forms; it involves thoughtful negotiation and a deep understanding of each clause's implications.

Negotiation Strategies: Effective negotiation is vital for securing favorable terms. This requires thorough preparation, including understanding your own needs, your bottom line, and the other party's likely position. Aim for a "win-win" scenario where both parties feel their interests are reasonably met, fostering stronger, long-lasting business relationships. Be ready to compromise on less critical points to achieve your primary goals. Always ask questions if anything is unclear, and ensure all agreed-upon changes are documented and incorporated into the final contract. Remember, negotiation is a conversation, not a confrontation.

Seeking Professional Advice: While understanding these principles is essential, it's highly recommended that all significant contracts be drafted or reviewed by a qualified attorney specializing in business law. An attorney can ensure your contracts are legally sound, enforceable, and tailored to your specific business needs and industry regulations. They can identify potential pitfalls, advise on industry-specific clauses, and help you negotiate terms that best protect your interests. The upfront cost of legal review can save your business immeasurable expense and headaches later on. For instance, a poorly drafted vendor contract leading to a significant supply chain disruption, costing tens of thousands in lost revenue, could have been prevented by a few hundred dollars spent on an attorney's review.

Record Keeping: Meticulous record-keeping of all executed contracts is essential. Maintain a centralized, organized system for storing signed agreements. This allows for easy access when needed, helps track important dates (like renewal or expiration), and ensures compliance. Digital storage solutions are often efficient and secure.

Understanding Contractual Obligations: Once a contract is signed, diligently understanding and fulfilling your obligations is imperative. Proactive management of your contractual commitments demonstrates reliability and builds trust, which is invaluable in business. Conversely, failing to meet your end of the bargain can lead to breach of contract claims, financial penalties, damage to your reputation, and potentially, the termination of valuable business relationships.

In essence, contracts and agreements are not merely legal necessities; they are strategic tools that underpin your business operations. They define relationships, manage expectations, allocate risk, and ultimately provide critical protection for your entrepreneurial endeavors. By investing the time and resources to understand, negotiate, and properly document your agreements, you build a more robust, resilient, and legally secure business, setting the stage for sustained growth and success.Intellectual Property: Your Business's Creative Armor

In the intricate tapestry of building and sustaining a business, intellectual property (IP) stands as one of the most valuable and often intangible assets an entrepreneur possesses. While contracts form the legal framework for your operational relationships, intellectual property protection is the digital and creative armor that shields your brand, innovations, and unique business processes from exploitation. Without a robust strategy for safeguarding your IP, even the most groundbreaking ideas can be swiftly diluted, copied, or stolen, eroding your competitive advantage and potentially jeopardizing your entire venture. This section delves into the critical aspects of identifying, protecting, and enforcing your intellectual property rights, ensuring your brand and innovations remain yours to leverage and grow.

At its core, intellectual property refers to creations of the mind. For entrepreneurs, this can manifest in numerous ways: your company's distinct name and logo (your brand), the unique design of your product, the creative expression in your marketing materials, proprietary software code, confidential business processes, and even distinctive sounds or scents associated with your brand. Understanding the different types of IP is the first step toward effective protection.

Trademarks: Trademarks are arguably the most visible form of IP for many businesses. A trademark is any word, phrase, symbol, design, or combination thereof that identifies and distinguishes the source of goods or services of one party from those of others. Examples include the Apple logo, the distinctive sound of Netflix's intro, or the name "Coca-Cola." These are all trademarks consumers instantly recognize and associate with specific products and companies. For an entrepreneur, your business name, logo, and even your tagline can serve as powerful trademarks. Registering your trademark provides significant legal advantages, including the exclusive right to use your mark in connection with registered goods and services, the ability to sue infringers in federal court, and the presumption of ownership and validity. The process typically involves filing an application with the relevant national IP office, such as the United States Patent and Trademark Office (USPTO). This application requires a clear description of the mark, the goods or services it will be used with, and often a specimen showing how the mark is actually used in commerce. The examination process ensures the mark is not confusingly similar to existing registered marks and meets other legal requirements. While common law rights can be established through use, federal registration offers a much stronger level of protection and nationwide rights. Consider a new artisanal coffee shop, "The Daily Grind," with a distinctive steaming coffee cup logo. Registering "The Daily Grind" as a trademark for café services and the logo as a trademark for café services would prevent other coffee shops from opening with similar names or logos in a way that could confuse consumers. This protection is vital for building brand loyalty and ensuring your marketing efforts build equity in your brand, not someone else's.

Copyright: Copyright, on the other hand, protects original works of authorship fixed in any tangible medium of expression. This includes literary works, music, dramatic works, pictorial, graphic, and sculptural works, motion pictures, sound recordings, and architectural works. For an entrepreneur, copyright can protect website content, blog posts, marketing copy, software code, product manuals, videos, photographs, and even the creative design elements of your packaging. Unlike trademarks, copyright protection automatically vests in the author at the moment the work is created and fixed in a tangible form. However, registration with the U.S. Copyright Office provides significant benefits, including the ability to sue for infringement, the ability to recover statutory damages and attorney's fees in infringement cases (which can be much more substantial than actual damages), and the creation of a public record of your copyright. Imagine a software company that has developed a proprietary customer relationship management (CRM) system. The code for this software is protected by copyright. Furthermore, the user manuals, marketing brochures, and tutorial videos created to support the CRM are also protected by copyright. Registering these works provides strong legal standing should a competitor attempt to copy and distribute the software or its supporting materials. Without registration, pursuing legal action for copyright infringement becomes considerably more difficult and costly, potentially limiting the remedies available.

Patents: Patents are designed to protect inventions. There are three main types of patents: utility patents, design patents, and plant patents. Utility patents protect the way an invention works or is used—essentially, the functional aspects of an invention. This is the most common type of patent and can cover new and useful processes, machines, articles of manufacture, or compositions of matter, or any new and useful improvement thereof. For example, a new type of energy-efficient engine or a novel algorithm for data processing would likely be protected by a utility patent. Design patents, conversely, protect the ornamental design of an article of manufacture—how it looks rather than how it works. If your product has a unique and aesthetically pleasing appearance that is not purely functional, a design patent might be appropriate. Think of the distinctive shape of a Dyson vacuum cleaner or the aesthetic design of a smartphone. Plant patents protect new varieties of asexually reproduced plants. Obtaining a patent is a complex and often lengthy process, involving a thorough examination by a patent office. It requires demonstrating that the invention is novel, non-obvious, and useful. Once granted, a patent gives the owner the right to exclude others from making, using, offering for sale, or selling the invention in the country where the patent was granted, and from importing the invention into that country. For a startup developing a groundbreaking medical device, securing utility patents for its novel mechanism and design patents for its ergonomic casing would be crucial. This exclusivity allows the company to recoup its research and development costs and build a market position before competitors can replicate their innovation. Without patent protection, competitors could immediately copy the device, undermining the startup's market advantage and profitability.

Trade Secrets: Trade secrets represent another vital category of IP, particularly for businesses with unique processes, formulas, or proprietary information that provides a competitive edge. Unlike patents, trade secrets are not publicly disclosed. Protection is maintained as long as the information remains confidential and provides a competitive advantage. Examples include the formula for Coca-Cola, Google's search algorithm, or a company's confidential customer list. Protection for trade secrets relies on reasonable efforts to maintain secrecy, such as using non-disclosure agreements (NDAs) with employees and business partners, implementing security measures for sensitive data, and limiting access to confidential information on a need-to-know basis. While there is no registration process for trade secrets, legal recourse is available if a trade secret is misappropriated through improper means, such as theft, bribery, or breach of an NDA. For a food manufacturing company, the precise recipe for its best-selling sauce would be a trade secret. Strict internal protocols, including access controls to the recipe document, secure storage, and mandatory NDAs for all employees who might come into contact with the information, are essential to maintaining this protection. If a competitor somehow obtained the recipe through illicit means and started producing a similar sauce, the company could take legal action based on trade secret misappropriation.

Identifying and Protecting Your IP: Identifying your IP assets is the foundational step in this protection strategy. This involves a comprehensive audit of your business to recognize what constitutes valuable intellectual property. Examine every aspect of your operations: your brand identity (name, logo, slogans), your products (design, functionality, underlying technology), your marketing and sales materials (website copy, advertisements, videos), your internal processes (proprietary software, manufacturing techniques), and any unique data you collect or generate. Engaging with your team, including product development, marketing, and operations departments, can help uncover hidden IP assets. For instance, an engineer's innovative solution to a technical problem in product assembly might be patentable, while a graphic designer's unique visual style for your social media campaigns could be protected by copyright.

Once identified, the next critical step is the registration of your IP where applicable. For trademarks and copyrights, registration offers significant legal advantages beyond basic protection. For patents, registration is a prerequisite to legal enforcement. The registration process can be complex and time-consuming, often requiring the expertise of specialized attorneys or IP agents. They can help navigate the application requirements, conduct necessary searches to ensure your IP is unique, and respond to any objections or challenges from the examining authorities. For example, a trademark attorney will conduct a thorough "knockout search" to see if similar marks are already registered or in use, significantly increasing the chances of successful registration. Similarly, a patent attorney will perform a prior art search to determine the novelty and non-obviousness of an invention, a critical hurdle in the patent application process. Failing to properly prepare and file these applications can lead to rejection, costly delays, or even the loss of the opportunity to protect your IP.

Enforcing Your IP Rights: Enforcing your IP rights is as crucial as obtaining protection in the first place.

Vigilant monitoring is crucial to detect and address intellectual property (IP) infringement, even after registration. This involves actively watching online marketplaces, competitor activities, and general market trends for unauthorized use of your trademarks, copyrights, or patented inventions. Tools like Google Alerts for brand and product names, regular online marketplace searches, and specialized IP monitoring services can help identify potential infringements.

Upon detection, a strategic response is essential. Often, a cease and desist letter from an attorney can resolve the issue without litigation. This formal letter notifies the infringing party of their violation and demands an immediate halt to the activity. If this fails, or in cases of significant damage, legal action may be necessary. This could involve filing a lawsuit seeking an injunction (a court order to stop the infringement) and damages to compensate for losses.

Consider an e-commerce business selling handmade jewelry that finds a competitor selling identical designs under a similar brand name. After direct attempts to resolve fail, the business owner hires an attorney who sends a strong cease and desist letter, citing trademark and copyright infringement. If the competitor doesn't comply, a lawsuit might be filed to seek an injunction to stop sales and damages for lost profits and reputational harm. Proactive enforcement is vital for protecting revenue and brand integrity.

Beyond formal registration and enforcement, other strategies can strengthen IP protection. Implementing robust internal policies and employee training is critical. Educating staff on confidentiality, proper IP use, and handling sensitive information can prevent accidental leaks or misuse. Clear employment and contractor agreements with strong IP clauses, stating that all IP created during employment or under contract belongs to the company, are also essential. For example, if an employee develops a new software feature, the employment agreement should clearly assign ownership to the company. Additionally, judicious use of Non-Disclosure Agreements (NDAs) with external parties (investors, collaborators, suppliers) creates legal obligations of confidentiality, safeguarding trade secrets and proprietary information.

Licensing agreements offer a strategic way to leverage IP while retaining control. For patented technology or copyrighted creative work, you can grant another party a license to use it in exchange for royalties or fees. A well-drafted licensing agreement precisely defines the license's scope, territory, duration, royalty rates, and quality control standards. For instance, a graphic designer creating a unique font could license its use to various companies for a fee, generating ongoing revenue while ensuring appropriate usage.

In summary, intellectual property is fundamental to a sustainable and competitive business. It demands proactive identification, strategic protection through registration and contracts, and diligent enforcement. By understanding and actively safeguarding trademarks, copyrights, patents, and trade secrets, businesses build stronger, more defensible brands, protect innovations, and ensure the exclusive ownership of their creations. This is a critical element for long-term entrepreneurial success. The effort invested in IP protection is not merely a legal formality; it is an investment in the future of your business, ensuring that your unique market contributions are recognized, respected, and rewarded.

Navigating the financial landscape of entrepreneurship inevitably leads to the crucial, yet often daunting, aspect of understanding and fulfilling tax obligations. This is more than a procedural hurdle; it's a fundamental pillar of legal operation, financial integrity, and long-term business sustainability. Ignoring or misunderstanding tax responsibilities can quickly turn a promising venture into a costly legal and financial quagmire, laden with penalties, interest, and reputational damage that are exceedingly difficult to overcome. Therefore, a proactive and informed approach to taxation is not optional; it is an essential component of responsible entrepreneurship, as critical as developing a strong business plan or securing adequate funding.

At its most basic level, every business entity, regardless of its chosen legal structure, will face various tax liabilities. The specific types and rates of these taxes depend on your business structure (as previously discussed), revenue, expenses, location, and the nature of your operations. However, several core tax categories are almost universally applicable to businesses in most jurisdictions. Foremost among these is income tax, levied on your business's profits. For sole proprietorships and partnerships, business income typically passes through to the owners' personal tax returns and is taxed at individual rates. Corporations, conversely, are separate legal entities, taxed on their profits at the corporate rate; dividends paid to shareholders are then taxed again at the individual level (known as "double taxation," though specific tax laws can mitigate this). Understanding your gross revenue, deductible business expenses, and ultimately your net profit is paramount for accurately calculating your income tax liability. Meticulous record-keeping of all financial transactions forms the bedrock of this calculation. Every invoice, receipt, bank statement, and payroll record contributes to an accurate financial picture that underpins your tax filings. Without this detailed trail, you leave yourself vulnerable to audits and disputes with tax authorities.

Beyond income tax, businesses must also consider sales tax or Value-Added Tax (VAT), which varies based on location and the goods or services sold. Sales tax is collected from the consumer at the point of sale and then remitted to the government. For businesses selling across state lines or internationally, understanding "nexus" rules—which dictate when a sufficient presence requires sales tax collection—is crucial. E-commerce businesses, in particular, must stay updated on these regulations to avoid significant penalties and liabilities from incorrect collection and remittance. In regions with a VAT system, businesses charge VAT on sales and may reclaim VAT paid on purchases. It's important to remember that sales tax and VAT are liabilities collected on behalf of the government, not operational expenses.

Employment taxes are another critical compliance area once a business hires employees. Employers are responsible for withholding federal and state income taxes, Social Security, and Medicare taxes from employee wages and remitting these amounts to tax authorities. Additionally, employers pay their share of Social Security and Medicare taxes (employer taxes) and typically federal and state unemployment taxes. Calculating and remitting employment taxes requires understanding wage bases, tax rates, and specific filing deadlines, which differ from income and sales taxes. Errors or misclassifying employees as independent contractors can lead to severe penalties, back taxes, and interest. Correct worker classification and diligent compliance with employment tax obligations are essential.

Businesses may also be subject to other specific taxes depending on their industry and location. These can include excise taxes (e.g., on gasoline, tobacco, alcohol), property taxes on real estate, or specialized industry taxes and licensing fees. Even minor overlooked taxes can lead to compliance issues, so staying informed about all potential tax liabilities is vital.

Key Pillars of Tax Compliance:

- **Accurate Record-Keeping:** This goes beyond just receipts; it involves maintaining a clear, auditable trail of all financial activity. This includes meticulously recording income, categorizing expenses, tracking asset purchases and depreciation, managing inventory, and maintaining precise payroll records. A robust accounting system is indispensable, ensuring records are detailed enough to substantiate all tax return claims (e.g., business travel, equipment purchases).
- **Understanding Tax Deadlines:** Tax authorities impose strict deadlines for filing returns and making payments. These are legal requirements, not suggestions. Estimated income tax payments are often quarterly, and employment taxes have monthly or semi-monthly remittance schedules. Missing deadlines trig-

gers automatic penalties and interest. A tax calendar or accounting software can help ensure timely filings and payments, and proactive document gathering prevents last-minute errors.

- **Seeking Professional Advice:** Given the complexities and consequences of non-compliance, professional guidance from qualified accountants or tax advisors is a strategic necessity for most entrepreneurs. They can assist with:

    - Choosing a tax-advantageous legal structure.
    - Setting up accurate accounting systems.
    - Developing tax planning strategies to legally minimize tax burdens (e.g., maximizing deductions, utilizing tax credits).
    - Accurately preparing and filing tax returns.
    - Navigating tax audits to achieve favorable outcomes.

    When selecting a professional, look for expertise in your industry and business size, and certifications like CPA or Enrolled Agent (EA).

Ongoing Commitment to Compliance:

Tax compliance is an ongoing commitment requiring a diligent, informed, and organized approach throughout a business's life. By understanding tax obligations, maintaining impeccable records, respecting deadlines, and leveraging professional expertise, businesses avoid costly penalties and build financial credibility with lenders, investors, and customers. This commitment reflects professionalism and dedication to a legitimate and sustainable enterprise, ensuring long-term health and stability, allowing focus on growth and innovation.

The interconnectedness of business functions with tax obligations highlights the need for a holistic approach. Marketing and sales strategies directly impact sales tax liability (e.g., pricing, discounts, returns). Hiring decisions affect employment tax responsibilities. Understanding these connections enables more integrated and effective business planning, preventing unexpected compliance burdens (e.g., researching sales tax on digital services for new offerings).

Furthermore, tax laws are not static; they evolve with economic changes, policy shifts, and technological advancements. Tax authorities regularly update regulations, reporting requirements, and tax rates. Entrepreneurs must stay abreast of these changes, or ensure their tax advisor does, through news updates, industry webinars, or regular consultations. For example, recent court rulings have significantly changed how sales tax applies to online transactions, expanding states' rights to collect from out-of-state sellers, meaning previously compliant businesses might now face new obligations.

A fundamental distinction for every entrepreneur is between "tax avoidance" and "tax evasion." Tax avoidance involves legally using the tax system to lower tax liability through legitimate deductions, credits, and planning. Tax evasion, conversely, is the illegal act of misrepresenting or concealing income to avoid taxes, which is a criminal offense with severe penalties. A reputable tax advisor will always guide businesses toward legal tax avoidance strategies, ensuring compliance while minimizing tax burdens. Accurate accounting records are crucial for defending against accusations of evasion, providing proof of legitimate business activities and tax calculations.

Diligent, foresightful, and accurate handling of tax obligations is not merely about avoiding penalties; it's about building a sound, compliant, and ethical business. This financial stewardship protects assets, preserves reputation, and contributes to economic governance. Tax compliance is a vital, albeit often hidden, operational function that underpins a business's viability and growth.

Tax compliance extends beyond just filing returns; it requires embedding tax awareness into daily operations through internal processes. This includes training sales staff on proper invoicing and sales tax calculation, ensuring all employee expense claims are documented and approved, and clearly separating business from personal expenses, especially for sole proprietors. For businesses with employees, regular training for payroll staff on current withholding tables and employment tax regulations is essential. Implementing automated systems, such as accounting software for sales tax or payroll software for withholdings, can significantly reduce human error.

Consider a small consulting firm managing projects with varied billing structures, travel expenses, and subcontractors in different states. Without a systematic method to track revenue and expenses per project and apply correct sales tax rules, the firm could easily mismanage sales tax collection. Furthermore, if the firm hires freelance consultants, it must properly classify them as independent contractors, issue appropriate tax forms (W-9s and 1099s), and adhere to reporting requirements to avoid penalties for incorrect withholding or reporting.

For rapidly scaling businesses, tax obligations grow exponentially, increasing scrutiny from tax authorities. What was manageable with a simple spreadsheet initially can become overwhelming as transactions, employees, and locations multiply. This highlights the critical need for professional accounting and tax services. Investing early in a good accounting system and a qualified tax advisor can prevent significant headaches and financial penalties, allowing entrepreneurs to focus on strategic growth instead of administrative tasks.

Understanding tax obligations also begins with the initial business setup. The chosen business structure profoundly impacts taxation. A sole proprietorship has different reporting requirements than a partnership, LLC, C-corporation, or S-corporation. For instance, an S-corporation offers pass-through taxation and limited liability, allowing owners to receive a "reasonable salary" subject to employment taxes, with remaining profits distributed as dividends not subject to self-employment tax. While potentially advantageous, this comes with stricter operational requirements and IRS scrutiny over salary reasonableness. An LLC offers flexibility, allowing it to be taxed as a sole proprietorship, partnership, or corporation, enabling entrepreneurs to tailor their tax structure to their circumstances and growth plans. Understanding these options and their tax consequences is crucial for financial success.

Ultimately, the business owner bears the responsibility for ensuring all taxes are paid accurately and on time. While accountants and tax advisors are invaluable, they do not absolve the owner of this ultimate obligation. Active engagement, robust financial management, and professional guidance form the bedrock of responsible and successful entrepreneurship.

SIX

MARKETING AND SALES STRATEGIES

Sustainable growth for any business hinges on its ability to effectively engage and convert its target audience, not just on product or service innovation. A comprehensive marketing strategy is crucial, serving as a meticulously crafted roadmap that guides a business towards its goals, ensuring every marketing effort is purposeful, measurable, and aligned with financial and operational realities. Developing such a strategy requires a deep understanding of the business's core identity, unique value proposition, and the dynamic market landscape.

The foundation of any strong marketing strategy lies in clearly articulated marketing objectives. These objectives must be intrinsically linked to the broader business plan and financial projections. Marketing success can be measured by various aims, such as increasing brand awareness, generating qualified leads, driving sales volume, improving customer retention, or establishing thought leadership. These objectives must be SMART: Specific, Measurable, Achievable, Relevant, and Time-bound. For example, instead of a vague "increase sales," a SMART objective would be "increase online sales by 15% in the next fiscal quarter by optimizing our e-commerce platform and implementing targeted digital advertising campaigns." This specificity enables focused planning and provides a clear benchmark for progress.

Once objectives are set, identifying Key Performance Indicators (KPIs) is essential for tracking progress. KPIs are quantifiable metrics that reflect the performance of marketing activities in relation to objectives. For brand awareness, KPIs might include website traffic, social media engagement (likes, shares, comments), brand mentions, and search engine rankings. Lead generation can be measured by form submissions, demo requests, or inquiries. Sales-focused KPIs include conversion rates, customer acquisition cost (CAC), and customer lifetime value (CLV). Tracking these KPIs provides invaluable insights into what's working, what isn't, and where adjustments are needed. It's vital that KPIs are not mere vanity metrics; they must directly correlate with the business's strategic goals. For instance, a high number of social media followers is only positive if those followers convert into paying customers or engaged leads; otherwise, the marketing effort may be misdirected.

The heart of any marketing strategy is the selection of appropriate marketing channels to communicate with the target audience. This selection is guided by a deep understanding of the ideal customer, including their demographics, psychographics, online behavior, media consumption habits, and where they are most likely to encounter and engage with the brand. A diverse marketing mix, integrating various approaches, often proves most effective in creating a cohesive and impactful presence.

A strong marketing strategy integrates various digital and traditional channels, including Search Engine Optimization (SEO), content marketing, social media marketing, Pay-Per-Click (PPC) advertising, and email marketing. Public relations (PR) and traditional advertising also play crucial roles.

Key Marketing Channels:

- **Search Engine Optimization (SEO):** Optimizing website content, structure, and technical aspects to rank highly in search engine results for relevant keywords.

- **Content Marketing:** Creating and distributing valuable, relevant, and consistent content (e.g., blog posts, articles, e-books, videos) to attract and engage a defined audience, establishing authority and trust.
- **Social Media Marketing:** Leveraging platforms like Facebook, Instagram, LinkedIn, Twitter, and TikTok to connect with customers, build community, share content, and run targeted advertising.
- **Pay-Per-Click (PPC) Advertising:** Running highly targeted campaigns on platforms like Google Ads, where you pay for each click, offering immediate visibility and controlled spending.
- **Email Marketing:** Building an email list to nurture leads, foster customer loyalty, and drive repeat business through newsletters, promotions, and personalized communications.
- **Public Relations (PR):** Building and maintaining a positive public image, managing brand reputation, and securing media coverage through press releases, influencer engagement, and crisis communication.
- **Traditional Advertising:** Utilizing channels such as print advertising, radio and television commercials, direct mail, and billboards. The effectiveness of these channels depends on the target audience and industry.

Strategic Considerations for Effective Marketing:

- **Integration:** Consistent messaging across all platforms is vital to reinforce brand identity and value proposition. Content should be repurposed across channels for maximum reach and impact. This unified approach strengthens recall and guides customers through their journey.
- **Continuous Adaptation:** Marketing strategy is an iterative process requiring ongoing monitoring, analysis, and adjustments. Regular performance reviews, informed by Key Performance Indicators (KPIs), help identify effective channels and campaigns, allowing for resource reallocation and optimized approaches (e.g., A/B testing).
- **Buyer Personas:** Developing semi-fictional representations of ideal customers, based on market research and data, is fundamental. Personas delve into motivations, goals, challenges, and preferred communication channels, enabling the creation of resonating messages and targeted channel selection.
- **Customer Journey Mapping:** Understanding the entire customer experience, from initial awareness to loyal advocacy, is crucial. Mapping this journey identifies key touch-

points where marketing interventions can be most impactful, guiding strategies for awareness, consideration, decision, and post-purchase engagement.

A crucial element of strategic development is budget allocation. Marketing endeavors necessitate investment, and it's imperative to distribute your budget judiciously, aligning expenditure with your objectives and the anticipated ROI of each channel or tactic. This demands careful deliberation of costs linked to various marketing activities, such as advertising expenses, content generation, software subscriptions, and staffing. A deep understanding of your Customer Acquisition Cost (CAC) is paramount. If your CAC surpasses your Customer Lifetime Value (CLV), your marketing initiatives, while potentially generating sales, are unsustainable. Therefore, the ongoing pursuit involves optimizing campaigns to lower CAC and elevate CLV.

Furthermore, a proactive marketing strategy foresees market trends and competitive actions. Staying informed about competitor activities, emerging marketing technologies, and shifts in consumer behavior is vital for preserving a competitive advantage. This could entail competitor analysis, subscribing to industry publications, attending conferences, and cultivating a culture of continuous learning within your marketing team. For instance, if a competitor finds success with a new influencer marketing campaign, it's worthwhile to investigate if a similar approach, perhaps with different influencers or a unique angle, could benefit your business.

The role of data analytics in refining and executing a marketing strategy cannot be overstated. Every digital marketing activity generates data, from website visits and click-through rates to conversion metrics and social media engagement. Employing analytics tools such as Google Analytics, social media insights, and CRM data furnishes the quantitative evidence needed to comprehend campaign performance. This data-driven approach transforms marketing from speculation to informed decision-making. It facilitates the identification of bottlenecks in the customer journey, the optimization of ad spend for maximum impact, and the continuous enhancement of marketing messages and targeting. For example, analyzing website traffic sources can reveal which channels are most effective at driving qualified leads, allowing for increased focus on those efforts. Similarly, tracking conversion rates by traffic source can pinpoint which channels attract customers most likely to make a purchase.

For sustainable growth, a marketing strategy must also address customer retention and advocacy. Acquiring new customers is frequently more costly than retaining existing ones. Consequently, strategies to foster loyalty, encourage repeat purchases, and transform satisfied customers into brand advocates are critical. This may involve implementing customer loyalty programs, offering exceptional post-sale support, soliciting and acting on feedback, and creating avenues for customers to share positive experiences through testimonials or user-generated content. Loyal customers who actively endorse your brand become a powerful and cost-effective marketing force in themselves.

Finally, legal and ethical marketing considerations must be integrated into the strategy. This includes adherence to data privacy regulations (like GDPR or CCPA), ensuring advertising claims are truthful and non-misleading, and respecting intellectual property rights. Building audience trust is fundamental, and any marketing activity that erodes this trust, whether intentional or due to oversight, can severely impact your brand's reputation and long-term viability. Transparent communication, ethical data handling, and a commitment to delivering genuine value are not merely good practices; they are essential components of a sustainable and responsible marketing strategy. This comprehensive approach, integrating clear objectives, measurable KPIs, targeted channel selection, continuous optimization, and ethical considerations, forms the robust framework necessary for driving sustainable growth and achieving enduring success in the marketplace.

Navigating the digital landscape is no longer optional; it is a fundamental requirement for businesses aiming for sustainable growth. At the core of this digital presence are three interconnected pillars: Search Engine Optimization (SEO), Search Engine Marketing (SEM), and Social Media Marketing. Collectively, these disciplines form a powerful engine for increasing visibility, attracting qualified traffic, and fostering meaningful engagement with your target audience. Understanding and effectively implementing strategies within these areas is paramount to building a robust online presence that directly contributes to your business objectives.

Search Engine Optimization (SEO) is the art and science of enhancing your website's visibility in organic (non-paid) search engine results. When potential customers actively search for products, services, or solutions your business offers, SEO ensures your business appears prominently at the top of these search results. This organic visibility is invaluable because it signals relevance and authority to users. A high ranking on search engines like Google not only drives significant amounts of targeted traffic to your website but also builds trust and credibility. Users are more inclined to click on and engage with sites that appear higher in search results, perceiving them as more authoritative and trustworthy.

The SEO process is multifaceted, involving several key components. Firstly, keyword research is foundational. This entails identifying the terms and phrases your target audience uses when searching for what you offer. Tools such as Google Keyword Planner, Ahrefs, or SEMrush can help uncover high-volume, relevant keywords that align with user intent. Understanding the search queries your potential customers are typing into search engines enables you to tailor your website content and optimize it to match their needs. It's not solely about identifying popular keywords, but also about understanding the intent behind those keywords – are users looking to learn, compare, or buy? This insight is crucial for creating content that truly satisfies the user's search query.

Once keywords are identified, on-page optimization becomes critical. This involves optimizing individual web pages to rank higher and attract more relevant traffic in search engines. Key on-page elements include crafting compelling and keyword-rich title tags and meta descriptions, which are the snippets of text that appear in search engine results. The content itself must be high-quality, informative, and naturally incorporate target keywords. Header tags

(H1, H2, H3, etc.) are used to structure content, making it easier for both search engines and users to understand the hierarchy of information. Image optimization, including using descriptive alt text for images, also contributes to both SEO and accessibility. Furthermore, ensuring your website has a clear, logical structure and internal linking strategy aids search engine crawlers in navigating your site and understanding the relationship between different pages.

Beyond the content itself, technical SEO addresses your website's underlying infrastructure. This includes ensuring your website loads quickly, is mobile-friendly (responsive design), and has a secure HTTPS connection. Site speed is a significant ranking factor, as users expect fast-loading pages. Mobile-friendliness is crucial, given the prevalence of mobile search; Google, in particular, prioritizes mobile-first indexing, meaning it primarily utilizes the mobile version of your content for ranking. Crawlability and indexability are also vital; this means ensuring that search engine bots can easily access and understand your website's content. This involves having a well-structured XML sitemap and a clear robots.txt file. Schema markup, a type of code that helps search engines understand the context of your content (e.g., reviews, recipes, events), can also lead to rich snippets in search results, further enhancing visibility and click-through rates.

Off-page optimization, primarily through link building, is another cornerstone of SEO. This involves acquiring high-quality backlinks from other reputable websites to your own. Backlinks act as "votes of confidence" from other sites, signaling to search engines that your content is valuable and trustworthy. Earning these links naturally through creating exceptional content, engaging in public relations, or forging partnerships is far more effective and sustainable than manipulative tactics. The quality of the linking domain, the relevance of the linked content, and the anchor text used all contribute to the impact of a backlink. Building a strong backlink profile is a long-term endeavor that requires consistent effort and a focus on earning the trust of other websites.

Finally, content marketing is inextricably linked to SEO. Creating valuable, informative, and engaging content that addresses your target audience's questions and pain points is the fuel that drives SEO success. Blog posts, articles, guides, infographics, and videos that are well-researched and shareable not only attract organic traffic but also naturally earn backlinks and social shares, further boosting your search engine rankings. The goal is to establish your website as a go-to resource in your industry.

While SEO focuses on organic visibility, Search Engine Marketing (SEM) encompasses both SEO and paid advertising strategies aimed at increasing website traffic and visibility on search engine results pages (SERPs). The most common form of SEM is Pay-Per-Click (PPC) advertising, typically through platforms like Google Ads. PPC campaigns allow businesses to place advertisements at the top or bottom of search results for specific keywords. The advertiser pays a fee each time their ad is clicked, hence "pay-per-click."

The power of SEM, particularly PPC, lies in its ability to deliver immediate and highly targeted traffic. Unlike SEO, which can take months to show significant results, PPC campaigns can be launched and generate traffic almost instantaneously. This makes it an excellent tool for short-term campaigns, product launches, or when immediate lead generation is a priority. The targeting capabilities of PPC platforms are incredibly sophisticated. Advertisers can target users based on keywords they search for, their geographical location, demographics, interests, time of day, and even the device they are using. This precision ensures that your advertising budget is spent reaching an audience most likely to be interested in your offerings.

A successful PPC campaign begins with thorough keyword research, similar to SEO, but with a focus on commercial intent. You want to bid on keywords that indicate a user is ready to make a purchase or take a desired action. Negative keywords are also crucial; these are terms that you don't want your ads to appear for, helping to filter out irrelevant clicks and wasted ad spend. For instance, if you sell new cars, you'd want to add "used cars" or "car repair" as negative keywords.

SEM: The Art and Science of Paid Search

Search Engine Marketing (SEM) is a critical component of digital marketing, focusing on paid strategies to increase website visibility on search engine results pages (SERPs). It encompasses various elements, each playing a vital role in campaign success.

Ad Copywriting: Crafting Compelling Messages

Effective ad copywriting is an art form within SEM. Given limited character space, every word must count. Ads need to be compelling, clearly communicate the value proposition, and include a strong call to action (CTA). Attention-grabbing headlines and descriptions that highlight benefits and unique selling propositions are crucial. Utilizing ad extensions (sitelinks, callout, or location extensions) can significantly improve visibility and provide more information to users directly in search results, increasing click-through rates.

Landing Page Optimization: Maximizing Conversions

The landing page, where users are directed after clicking an ad, is paramount for SEM success. It must be highly relevant to the ad copy and keywords, offer a seamless user experience, and have a clear conversion goal. Users expect to land on a page featuring the specific product or service advertised, not a generic homepage. A well-optimized landing page directly impacts conversion rates and, consequently, return on investment (ROI).

Quality Score: Influencing Position and Cost

Quality Score, a metric used by platforms like Google Ads, significantly impacts an ad's position and cost. It reflects the quality of your ads, keywords, and landing pages. Higher Quality Scores lead to lower costs and better ad positions. Factors influencing Quality Score include expected click-through rate (CTR), ad relevance, and landing page experience. Continuous monitoring and improvement of these elements are essential for maximizing PPC performance.

Budget Management and Bidding Strategies: Controlling Spend and Optimizing Outcomes

Effective budget management and strategic bidding are central to SEM. Advertisers can set daily or campaign budgets to control spending. Bidding strategies range from manual (setting a maximum cost per click) to automated, which optimize for clicks, conversions, or impression share. Understanding the target cost per acquisition (CPA) is vital for setting appropriate bids and ensuring profitability.

Regular Performance Analysis: Driving Continuous Improvement

Regular performance analysis is non-negotiable in SEM. Tracking metrics like impressions, clicks, CTR, conversion rate, CPA, and ROI for each keyword, ad group, and campaign is crucial. This data identifies what's working and what isn't, allowing for campaign optimization through bid adjustments, keyword refinement, ad copy improvements, and landing page enhancements. A/B testing different ad variations or landing page layouts can reveal the most effective approaches.

Social Media Marketing: Building Relationships and Engagement

While SEO and SEM drive traffic, Social Media Marketing is crucial for building relationships, fostering community, and engaging with your audience on a personal level. Platforms like Facebook, Instagram, LinkedIn, Twitter, TikTok, and Pinterest offer unique opportunities to connect with customers, build brand loyalty, and drive sales. The key is to select platforms where your target audience is most active and tailor your strategy to each platform's nuances.

Defining Objectives: Guiding Your Social Media Strategy

A strong social media presence begins with clearly defined objectives that align with overall marketing goals. Whether aiming to increase brand awareness, drive website traffic, generate leads, provide customer support, or build a community, each objective dictates content creation and engagement strategies.

Content Creation: The Heart of Social Media

Content creation is central to social media marketing. This involves developing a content calendar outlining post types, frequency, and platforms. Content can be diverse: engaging text, eye-catching images, informative videos, live streams, stories, and user-generated content. Successful social media content is often authentic, valuable, and shareable, resonating with the audience's interests rather than being purely promotional. Storytelling is particularly powerful for emotional connection.

Engagement and Community Management: Fostering Dialogue

Engagement and community management are critical for fostering relationships. Simply broadcasting messages is insufficient; interaction is key. This includes promptly responding to comments and messages, asking questions, running polls, and participating in relevant conversations. Building a loyal community creates brand advocates and provides valuable feedback, establishing a two-way dialogue.

Social Media Advertising: Reaching Targeted Audiences

Social media advertising offers powerful tools for reaching wider and more targeted audiences. Platforms like Facebook Ads and Instagram Ads allow for granular targeting based on demographics, interests, behaviors, and custom audiences. These paid campaigns promote content, drive website traffic, generate leads, or encourage purchases. Understanding effective ad creatives, compelling ad copy, and budget management is essential for maximizing social media advertising ROI. Retargeting, showing ads to users who previously interacted with your brand, is particularly effective for driving conversions.

Influencer Marketing: Leveraging Trust and Reach

Influencer marketing involves partnering with individuals who have significant following and influence within your niche to promote products or services. When done authentically and with careful selection of influencers whose audience aligns with your target market, it can effectively build brand awareness and trust. Transparency, with clear disclosure of sponsored content, is crucial.

Analytics and Monitoring: Informing Strategy

Analytics and monitoring are vital for understanding social media performance. Most platforms offer built-in dashboards providing insights into audience demographics, content reach, engagement rates, and follower growth. Tracking key metrics reveals what content resonates, which platforms are most effective, and where efforts yield the best results. This data should inform ongoing strategy, allowing for refinement and effective resource allocation. Data analysis can answer questions like whether video posts get more engagement than static images or if LinkedIn content drives more qualified leads than Facebook.

The Synergistic Effect: Integrating Digital Marketing Components

The integration of SEO, SEM, and social media marketing creates a powerful synergistic effect. Strong social media engagement can indirectly boost SEO by driving website traffic and increasing brand mentions and social signals. Conversely, well-optimized SEO content can be effectively promoted on social media. SEM campaigns drive immediate traffic and conversions, while also providing valuable data about keywords and ad performance that can inform SEO strategies. A truly comprehensive digital marketing strategy leverages all three components in a coordinated manner, ensuring a consistent brand message across all touchpoints and maximizing reach and impact. Mastering these digital fundamentals allows businesses to effectively navigate the online landscape, attract ideal customers, and build a strong foundation for sustainable growth. This integrated approach ensures marketing efforts work together to amplify messages and achieve business objectives in the competitive digital marketplace.

Content marketing centers on delivering value. It's a strategic method focused on creating and sharing valuable, relevant, and consistent content to draw in and keep a specific audience, ultimately leading to profitable customer actions. Unlike traditional advertising, which interrupts, content marketing engages potential customers by offering solutions, answering questions, and providing relevant insights. The goal is to become a trusted industry resource, build relationships, and foster loyalty. This shift from interruption to attraction is key for sustainable customer growth in today's competitive market.

Effective content marketing hinges on a deep understanding of your audience, extending beyond basic demographics to psychographics. This includes their pain points, aspirations, challenges, daily routines, and the questions they're asking. What keeps them up at night? What are their goals? What information do they seek when researching solutions that your product or service offers? Customer surveys, interviews, social media listening, and website search queries can provide crucial insights. Developing detailed buyer personas—fictional representations of ideal customers based on this research—humanizes your audience and ensures content creation is audience-centric. By addressing specific needs, you build trust and establish yourself as a knowledgeable and helpful entity.

The variety of content types is vast, and a multi-format approach is often best. Blog posts remain powerful for in-depth topic exploration, providing detailed information, and targeting SEO keywords, establishing thought leadership and being easily shareable. Video content has surged in popularity, offering dynamic engagement through tutorials, product demonstrations, behind-the-scenes glimpses, expert interviews, and customer testimonials. Podcasts are increasingly relevant for deep dives, allowing consumption while multitasking. Webinars and online courses provide structured education and are strong lead generation tools. Infographics visually present complex data, making it digestible and shareable. Ebooks and whitepapers are ideal for lead capture, offering comprehensive guides in exchange for contact information. Case studies showcase successful outcomes and provide social proof of your offerings' benefits.

Content marketing success isn't just about creating content, but creating *valuable* content. It must be informative, educational, entertaining, or inspiring, solving a problem, answering a question, or offering a fresh perspective. Consistency is vital; sporadic efforts won't build momentum or engagement. A content calendar is essential to map out topics, formats, keywords, responsibilities, and publication dates. A consistent schedule ensures your audience anticipates new content, keeping your brand top-of-mind and reinforcing reliability and authority.

Distribution is as crucial as creation. Simply publishing on your website is often insufficient. A robust distribution strategy involves leveraging various channels. Social media platforms are ideal for sharing posts, videos, and infographics, tailored to each platform's format and audience. Email marketing is powerful, allowing direct communication with interested individuals, sharing new content, and nurturing relationships. Segmenting email lists by interests and engagement delivers personalized content. Paid promotion via social media ads or search engine marketing can amplify reach. Collaborating with influencers or other businesses can expose your content to new audiences, and syndicating content on relevant third-party platforms extends reach and builds SEO-beneficial backlinks.

Measuring content marketing impact is crucial for optimization and demonstrating ROI. Track metrics beyond just website traffic. Engagement metrics like time on page, bounce rate, shares, likes, and comments reveal how well content resonates. Lead generation metrics, such as ebook downloads or webinar registrations, directly measure content's ability to attract potential customers. Conversion rates, tracking how many content consumers become paying customers, are the ultimate success measure. Tools like Google Analytics, social media analytics, and marketing automation platforms provide the necessary data. Analyzing this data refines your strategy, identifies effective formats and channels, and continually improves your approach. A/B testing headlines, calls to action, or formats optimizes performance.

Content marketing is a long-term strategy that builds brand equity and deep customer relationships. By consistently providing value, you position your business as an indispensable resource. This approach nurtures leads through the sales funnel, from awareness to consideration and conversion. When challenges or questions arise, potential customers turn to trusted brands for insightful information, significantly reducing sales friction. Satisfied customers who receive valuable content are more likely to become repeat buyers and brand advocates, spreading positive word-of-mouth for sustainable growth. This creates a virtuous cycle where great content attracts, educates, and retains customers, driving ongoing business success. Investing in content marketing is an investment in building a strong, enduring brand that resonates meaningfully with its audience.

Consider a software company specializing in project management tools. Instead of solely running ads, they could create a blog series on "Best Practices for Remote Team Collaboration." This might cover communication strategies, virtual team-building tools, overcoming remote work challenges, and setting up productive virtual meetings. They could then offer a downloadable ebook, "The Ultimate Guide to Seamless Remote Project Management," compiling these articles with exclusive insights. This ebook would be promoted via social media, email newsletters, and paid ads targeting project managers. Upon download, individuals enter a lead nurturing sequence, receiving follow-up emails with related video tutorials on software features or case studies of successful remote teams using their platform. This educational approach builds trust, demonstrates expertise, and naturally guides potential customers to recognize the software's value. The content isn't just selling; it's helping the audience achieve their goals, making the eventual sale a logical next step. This strategy also provides ample SEO opportunities, as people searching for remote work solutions will find the company's informative content.

Sustainable fashion brands offer an excellent example of effective content marketing. Their strategy often involves educating consumers on ethical sourcing, the environmental impact of fast fashion, and the benefits of durable, high-quality clothing. They might achieve this through a documentary series that explores their supply chain, showcases artisans, and highlights eco-friendly practices.

A brand's podcast could feature sustainability experts, fashion designers, and environmental activists. Blog content might include styling tips for versatile wardrobes, natural fabric care guides, and behind-the-scenes glimpses of the design process. Social media campaigns could leverage customer testimonials to emphasize product longevity and ethical value, encouraging user-generated content.

By consistently delivering content aligned with their brand values and educating their audience, these brands attract like-minded consumers, fostering loyalty and community. This audience is often willing to pay a premium for products that reflect their values, and content marketing effectively communicates these values to build a discerning customer base. The content, in essence, becomes a testament to their mission rather than just a product promotion.

The long-term value of content marketing lies in its compounding effect. As high-quality, relevant content accumulates, it creates a growing library of resources. This repository attracts new audiences via search engines and social shares, while also serving existing customers, reinforcing their engagement with the brand. This builds a sustainable pipeline.

Designing this customer journey requires a deep understanding of the ideal customer's psychology at each stage. What questions do they ask when initially aware of a problem? What information do they need when comparing solutions? What hesitations arise before a purchase? By anticipating these questions and providing timely, relevant information and offers, businesses build trust and guide customers through the sales funnel. This necessitates understanding the "why" behind their actions and providing solutions that resonate with their evolving needs and mindset, often anticipating needs before they are even fully articulated.

Lead generation is the primary objective at the top of the sales funnel. This is where content marketing strategies come into play. Creating valuable content such as blog posts, informative videos, helpful infographics, and downloadable resources like e-books or checklists attracts individuals interested in topics related to the brand's offerings. To convert these interested visitors into leads, compelling calls-to-action (CTAs) are crucial. A CTA instructs the audience on the next step, such as "Download our free guide,"

"Sign up for our webinar," or "Request a demo." Effective CTAs are clear, urgent, and relevant to the associated content. For example, a blog post on project management challenges should offer a CTA like a link to a project management template or a guide on selecting the right software.

Converting a visitor to a lead typically involves capturing contact information through opt-in forms on landing pages. These dedicated pages are designed for lead conversion with a specific offer. Landing pages must be clean, focused, and distraction-free, with a clear value proposition that aligns with the CTA. The form should be concise, asking only for essential information to reduce friction; an email address and name are often sufficient for initial lead capture. More detailed information can be gathered later. Offering an irresistible lead magnet—a high-value piece of content or special offer in exchange for contact details—is paramount for maximizing opt-in rates. This lead magnet should directly address a pressing need or offer a significant benefit to the target audience.

Once a lead is captured, the crucial phase of lead nurturing begins, differentiating the sales funnel from simple lead generation. Not all leads are ready to purchase immediately; many need time to build trust, understand the full value proposition, and overcome skepticism. Lead nurturing involves cultivating these relationships through consistent, personalized communication over time. Marketing automation and Customer Relationship Management (CRM) systems are invaluable here. A CRM acts as a central repository for lead and customer information, tracking interactions, managing communications, and segmenting the audience. Integrating CRM with a marketing automation platform allows for automated email sequences designed to guide leads through the funnel.

These nurturing sequences can be triggered by specific lead actions, such as downloading an e-book, visiting a pricing page, or attending a webinar. For instance, after a lead downloads a guide on "Improving Customer Service," automated emails could be sent: the first thanking them and offering a related article, the second introducing a case study on how a similar company used the solution, and a third offering a limited-time discount or free consultation. The key is to provide value at every step, avoiding a hard sell, which builds credibility and positions the brand as a helpful partner rather than just a vendor. This approach demonstrates empathy and understanding of their journey.

Segmentation is vital in lead nurturing. A one-size-fits-all approach is suboptimal. Segmenting leads based on demographics, interests, behavior, and funnel stage allows for tailored communication for maximum impact. For example, a lead interested in a specific product feature can receive targeted content and offers related to that feature, while a lead engaging with informational content might receive more educational material. This personalization effectively moves leads closer to a purchase decision.

Consider a software company with various subscription tiers. A lead who downloads a guide on basic features might receive nurturing emails focusing on the mid-tier plan's benefits, highlighting features of interest. Conversely, a lead who downloads a guide on advanced analytics might receive content promoting the premium tier, showcasing sophisticated functionalities. This tailored approach ensures relevance and increases conversion likelihood.

The conversion stage, or closing the sale, is the culmination of lead generation and nurturing efforts. This stage requires careful consideration of timing, offer presentation, and addressing final objections. For online businesses, this often means a clear and frictionless checkout process. For service-based businesses, it might involve a sales call or proposal. The final steps must be as easy and straightforward as possible; unnecessary complexity or friction can lead to lost sales. This could involve simplifying forms, offering multiple payment options, or providing clear pricing structures.

In direct sales conversations, active listening and understanding the prospect's specific needs and concerns are paramount. Sales representatives need the knowledge and tools to address objections effectively and reiterate the value proposition in a way that resonates with the individual. A robust CRM system is critical here, providing sales teams with a complete history of interactions, preferences, and pain points, enabling highly personalized and effective closing conversations. A sales team well-informed about a prospect's journey through the funnel is far more likely to close a deal successfully, anticipating questions, addressing concerns proactively, and tailoring their pitch to the individual's specific context.

Optimizing the sales funnel is an ongoing process of continuous monitoring, analysis, and refinement. Key metrics provide insights into where prospects might be dropping off or encountering difficulties. Common metrics to track include:

- **Visitor-to-Lead Conversion Rate:** The percentage of website visitors who become leads, indicating the effectiveness of lead generation and CTAs.

- **Lead-to-Customer Conversion Rate:** The percentage of leads who become paying customers, directly measuring the effectiveness of nurturing and closing processes.
- **Customer Acquisition Cost (CAC):** The total cost of sales and marketing efforts to acquire a new customer. Lowering this cost through funnel optimization directly impacts profitability.
- **Customer Lifetime Value (CLV):** The total revenue a business expects from a single customer account throughout their relationship. A well-optimized funnel acquires customers efficiently and cultivates loyalty, increasing CLV.
- **Drop-off Points:** Identifying specific stages where a significant number of prospects cease to progress. A high drop-off rate on a landing page might indicate a weak offer or confusing form. A high drop-off rate after a free trial might suggest issues with the trial experience or the value proposition of the paid product.

Effective sales funnel optimization relies on tools like Google Analytics, marketing automation platforms, and CRM dashboards to track key metrics. By analyzing this data, businesses can identify areas for improvement. For example, a low landing page conversion rate might lead to experimenting with different headlines, copy, CTAs, or form lengths. Similarly, a stagnant lead-to-customer conversion rate could signal a need to refine lead nurturing sequences, offer more targeted content, or provide better support during decision-making. A/B testing various funnel elements, such as email subject lines, landing page designs, or offer variations, enables data-driven decisions that optimize for audience preferences. Continuous iteration and refinement based on performance data are crucial for an effective sales funnel optimization strategy.

Consider a B2B software company offering a free trial of its project management tool. While initial sign-ups may be high, a low conversion rate from trial users to paid subscribers indicates a bottleneck in the nurturing or closing stages. To optimize, the company might implement a more robust email nurturing sequence during the trial, including tutorials, case studies, and personalized check-ins from a sales representative. They could also host dedicated webinars for trial users to demonstrate features and answer questions. Analyzing the in-app behavior of converting versus non-converting trial users can help identify features that correlate with higher conversion, allowing the company to proactively guide users toward those areas. This iterative process of monitoring, analyzing, and adjusting ensures the funnel efficiently converts prospects into paying customers.

Another example is an e-commerce store selling artisanal coffee beans. Their funnel might begin with blog posts on coffee brewing techniques and bean origins, attracting coffee enthusiasts (awareness and interest). A CTA could prompt downloading a "Perfect Pour" guide in exchange for an email address. Leads then receive a welcome email with a discount code, followed by emails highlighting different roasts, customer testimonials, or brewing tips based on website browsing data. For abandoned carts, an automated follow-up email with a reminder and incentive can be sent. Analyzing which emails drive purchases, what products are frequently bought together, and where customers drop off allows the store to refine its offerings and communication, optimizing the entire path from initial visit to repeat purchases.

A well-optimized sales funnel is a powerful engine for sustainable growth, transforming marketing efforts into predictable revenue by systematically guiding prospects through the buyer's journey. It prevents valuable leads from being lost due to poor follow-up or confusing decision-making. By prioritizing the customer experience at every touchpoint, from initial content interaction to final purchase and beyond, businesses build not only a customer base but also a loyal community. Investing in understanding and refining your sales funnel is an investment in predictable, scalable growth, ensuring every interaction contributes to tangible business results.

The transition from prospect to paying customer is a significant milestone, but it also marks a new beginning in the business-customer lifecycle. While attraction and conversion strategies are foundational, sustained growth and market presence truly depend on managing these relationships effectively. This is where Customer Relationship Management (CRM) and deliberate loyalty-building initiatives become paramount, transforming transactional engagements into enduring partnerships. A robust CRM system is more than just a database; it's the central nervous system for understanding, engaging with, and retaining your customer base. It provides a framework to track every interaction, from initial inquiry to post-purchase support, offering invaluable insights into individual customer needs, preferences, and behaviors.

Effective CRM recognizes the uniqueness of each customer, their journey, expectations, and evolving requirements. By leveraging CRM technology, businesses can move beyond generic tactics to deliver highly personalized experiences. For instance, if a customer who purchased a specific software feature contacts support, a well-implemented CRM system would instantly provide the agent with the customer's purchase history, previous support tickets, and sales interaction notes. This enables the agent to offer a contextually aware and efficient solution, making the customer feel understood and valued, and fostering immediate trust and satisfaction. This level of personalized service is a powerful differentiator in today's competitive landscape.

The data captured within a CRM system is vital for personalized communication. It allows businesses to segment their customer base not just by demographics, but also by purchasing behavior, product usage, engagement levels, and expressed preferences. This granular segmentation facilitates targeted marketing campaigns and communication strategies that resonate deeply with specific customer groups. For example, a customer consistently purchasing premium products might receive exclusive early access to new releases or invitations to special events, while a less active customer might be targeted with re-engagement campaigns highlighting new features or offering incentives. This strategic approach ensures communications are relevant and valuable, rather than intrusive, speaking the customer's language at the right time.

Beyond personalized outreach, CRM systems streamline customer service operations. By centralizing customer data and interaction history, support teams can resolve issues more efficiently. Features like ticketing systems, knowledge bases, and automated responses, integrated with CRM data, significantly reduce response times and improve first-contact resolution rates. For an online retailer, a CRM can automatically populate return forms with customer order details, shipping address, and item information, minimizing re-entry and speeding up processing. This focus on operational efficiency directly enhances the customer experience, reducing frustration and reinforcing positive brand perceptions.

Furthermore, CRM systems are crucial for proactive customer engagement. By analyzing data, businesses can anticipate potential issues or opportunities. For example, a subscription service might identify users frequently accessing help articles for a specific feature, indicating a potential usability issue or training need. The business can then proactively reach out with targeted tutorials, webinars, or personalized support, addressing the problem before it leads to dissatisfaction or churn. This proactive approach demonstrates a commitment to customer success and strengthens the customer-business bond, shifting from reactive problem-solving to proactive partnership.

Customer loyalty goes beyond repeat purchases; it's about cultivating an emotional connection and advocacy, building relationships based on trust, consistent value delivery, and mutual respect. Loyalty programs are effective, but their success depends on thoughtful design and CRM integration. A well-structured program might offer tiered rewards based on spending, engagement, or referrals. For instance, a coffee shop loyalty program could offer free drinks after a certain number of purchases, with higher tiers unlocking discounts or early access to new seasonal flavors. The CRM system tracks purchase history, identifies high-value customers for premium rewards, and sends personalized notifications about loyalty status and benefits.

Referral programs, often integrated with loyalty initiatives, are powerful growth engines that turn satisfied customers into brand ambassadors. When a CRM system tracks referrals, businesses can easily identify and reward customers who bring in new business. This incentivizes existing customers and provides valuable social proof for potential new customers influenced by peer recommendations. A technology company, for example, might offer discounts or credit to both the referrer and the referred customer when a new client signs up. The CRM system manages referral tracking, ensuring accurate and prompt reward distribution, thereby encouraging continued program participation.

Building emotional loyalty often stems from creating memorable and positive customer experiences, from initial onboarding to ongoing support and communication. A company selling high-end kitchen appliances might offer personalized installation services, cooking demonstrations for new owners, and regular check-ins to ensure optimal appliance performance. These added-value services, managed and tracked through a CRM, contribute to a feeling of being cared for and invested in, fostering a deeper connection that transcends the initial purchase.

Customer Lifetime Value (CLV) is deeply intertwined with CRM and loyalty. CLV signifies the total revenue a business anticipates from a customer throughout their entire relationship. By prioritizing customer retention and repeat business, companies can substantially boost their CLV. A CRM system that effectively tracks customer interactions and purchase history can offer sophisticated CLV analysis, pinpointing the most valuable customer segments and the most effective retention strategies. This data-driven approach enables businesses to strategically allocate resources, focusing on nurturing high-value relationships and optimizing engagement for maximum long-term return. For instance, if CLV analysis reveals that customers engaging with the company's online community exhibit a significantly higher CLV, the business can invest more in fostering that community, understanding its role in driving deeper loyalty and greater long-term value.

Furthermore, insights from CRM data can inform product development and service enhancements. By understanding customer feature usage, pain points, and requests, businesses can make data-backed decisions about future offerings. A software company, for example, might notice through CRM usage data that a particular integration is highly desired but not yet available. This insight can then be incorporated into the product roadmap, leading to the development of a feature that directly addresses customer demand, further enhancing satisfaction and loyalty. This iterative feedback loop, powered by CRM insights, is vital for continuous innovation and staying ahead of market trends.

Effective CRM also extends to managing customer feedback. Both positive and negative feedback should be captured within the CRM system, allowing for consistent tracking of common issues, identification of improvement areas, and follow-up with customers who have provided input. A business that actively listens to and acts upon customer feedback demonstrates a commitment to customer satisfaction, a cornerstone of loyalty. For instance, if multiple customers report a confusing website element, the CRM can flag this as a recurring issue, prompting a review and redesign of that section. Promptly addressing such feedback, perhaps with direct communication to those who reported it, can transform a potentially negative experience into a positive one, showcasing responsiveness and a genuine desire to improve.

In essence, CRM and loyalty-building strategies are not isolated initiatives but deeply interconnected components of a customer-centric business model. They aim to create a virtuous cycle where understanding, personalization, and value delivery lead to satisfied, loyal customers who, in turn, contribute to the sustained growth and success of the business. This necessitates a commitment not just to acquiring customers, but to nurturing these relationships, recognizing that in today's market, customer loyalty is one of the most valuable assets a business can possess.

Investing in a robust CRM system and a culture that prioritizes customer relationships yields dividends in terms of reduced churn, increased revenue, positive brand reputation, and a sustainable competitive advantage. It is a continuous process of engagement, learning, and adaptation, ensuring that the business evolves in tandem with the needs and expectations of its most valuable stakeholders: its customers. The ability to anticipate needs, proactively solve problems, and consistently exceed expectations through personalized interactions, all facilitated by a powerful CRM, truly differentiates thriving businesses from those that merely survive.

SEVEN

BUILDING FOR THE LONG TERM

Optimizing Business Processes for Sustainable Growth

To achieve sustainable growth and market leadership, businesses must meticulously refine their operational processes for peak efficiency. As companies mature from customer acquisition to ensuring long-term customer health and scalable expansion, a rigorous examination and optimization of daily activities become essential. This isn't merely about accelerating tasks but about executing them more intelligently, minimizing waste and errors, and ultimately reallocating valuable human and financial resources toward strategic objectives that generate genuine value and competitive advantage. The careful streamlining of operational workflows is not an optional enhancement; it's a fundamental requirement for any business aiming for agility, cost-effectiveness, and superior service, particularly as it scales.

The Foundation: Process Mapping

At the core of operational refinement is process mapping. Before any improvements can be made, a clear, detailed, and accurate understanding of current workflows is crucial. Process mapping visually documents each step of a business activity from start to finish. This can encompass a customer inquiry's journey through the sales funnel, the intricate steps of fulfilling a product order, or the administrative tasks involved in onboarding a new employee. Tools like flowcharts, swimlane diagrams, or sophisticated Business Process Management (BPM) software can be used to capture these sequences.

For instance, consider mapping the process of handling a customer support ticket. The map would detail every interaction: initial customer contact, ticket logging, assignment to a representative, steps for diagnosis and resolution, necessary escalations, customer communication, and final resolution and closure. By documenting each stage, identifying involved individuals or teams, and noting inputs and outputs, businesses gain unprecedented clarity into their operations. This visual representation acts as a diagnostic tool, revealing bottlenecks, redundancies, error-prone areas, and opportunities for simplification. Without this foundational understanding, optimization attempts are like performing surgery without anatomical knowledge—likely ineffective or even detrimental.

Leveraging Automation for Improvement

Once processes are mapped, the next vital step is identifying opportunities for improvement, with a strong emphasis on automation. Automation involves using technology to perform tasks previously done manually. This can range from simple email auto-responders and automated data entry to complex robotic process automation (RPA) that mimics human interaction with digital systems.

In customer service, for example, repetitive queries like "What is my order status?" or "How do I reset my password?" can be efficiently handled by chatbots or self-service portals integrated with backend systems. This offers immediate customer responses, boosting satisfaction, and frees human agents to tackle more complex issues requiring empathy and problem-solving skills. Similarly, in order fulfillment, automated inventory management systems can trigger reorder alerts when stock levels drop, ensuring popular products are always available and preventing lost sales due due to stockouts. Automated invoicing and payment processing significantly reduce administrative overhead, minimize financial record-keeping errors, and accelerate cash flow. Even in HR, automated workflows for leave requests, expense approvals, or onboarding paperwork can streamline operations, reduce paper-based processes, and ensure compliance. The key is to pinpoint tasks that are repetitive, rule-based, and time-consuming, then explore how technology can fully or semi-automate them, allowing for human oversight where necessary.

Implementing Best Practices

Adopting industry-recognized best practices across various operational domains is another cornerstone of streamlining. This involves integrating proven methods and standards effective in similar business contexts. In customer service, best practices might include establishing clear Service Level Agreements (SLAs) for response times, implementing a robust knowledge base for agents and customers, and adopting a first-contact resolution policy.

For order fulfillment, best practices could involve optimizing warehouse layouts for efficient picking and packing, utilizing barcode scanning for accuracy, and partnering with reliable shipping providers offering trackable services. In administrative tasks, best practices might include clear procedures for document management, regular data backups, and periodic audits to ensure compliance and identify inefficiencies. For example, a business that manually processes invoices each month will face delays, potential data entry errors, and a significant drain on administrative resources. By adopting best practices, such as implementing an electronic invoicing system that automatically generates invoices based on sales data, facilitates online payment processing, and integrates with accounting software, the business can achieve a far more efficient and accurate financial cycle. This not only reduces operational costs but also enhances the perception of professionalism and reliability among clients and suppliers.

Streamlining operations offers numerous benefits that directly support a business's ability to scale effectively.

Key Advantages of Streamlining:

- **Reduced Operational Costs:** By eliminating redundancies, minimizing errors, and automating manual tasks, businesses can significantly lower labor costs and reduce expenses associated with correcting mistakes and addressing customer complaints. These savings can then be strategically reinvested into growth initiatives, marketing, product development, or talent acquisition.

- **Improved Service Quality:** Efficient processes and minimized errors lead to faster, more accurate, and more consistent service, boosting customer satisfaction and fostering loyalty. This enhanced service quality can be a powerful differentiator in competitive markets. For example, an online retailer with same-day shipping due to streamlined order fulfillment will likely see higher customer satisfaction and repeat business than competitors with slower, less reliable services.
- **Time for Strategic Growth:** Streamlining frees employees from manual, repetitive, or inefficient tasks, allowing them to focus on high-value activities that drive growth. This includes developing new products, exploring new markets, building customer relationships, and strategic planning. This shift from operational minutiae to strategic advancement is vital for long-term scalability and market leadership. For instance, automating marketing campaign performance reports allows teams to analyze insights, optimize strategies, and develop innovative approaches instead of spending days on manual compilation.

Implementing and Maintaining Streamlined Operations:

Achieving these benefits requires a structured and disciplined approach, viewing it as an ongoing commitment to continuous improvement rather than a one-time fix. This may involve:

- Establishing a dedicated process improvement team or assigning responsibility for operational efficiency.
- Regularly reviewing processes and soliciting feedback from frontline employees.
- Staying informed about technological advancements.

This proactive approach ensures that as a business expands, its underlying processes can support growth without becoming a hindrance, thereby laying a robust foundation for sustained success and scalability.

Streamlining Specific Areas: Customer Service, Order Fulfillment, and Administrative Tasks

Customer Service

Customer service is the primary point of contact for customers and directly influences their perception and loyalty. Beyond standard CRM features, operational efficiency can be significantly improved through:

- **Tiered Support System:** This system categorizes inquiries by complexity and urgency. Simple, frequently asked questions can be handled by self-service options (FAQs, chatbots) or junior staff. More complex issues are then escalated to experienced agents or specialized technical teams. This optimizes resource allocation and speeds up resolution for simpler queries.
- **Robust Internal Knowledge Base:** A comprehensive internal knowledge base, containing solutions to common problems, troubleshooting guides, and product information, enables agents to quickly access accurate information. This leads to more efficient issue resolution, reduces the need for multiple contacts, ensures consistent answers, minimizes agent cognitive load, and reduces the risk of misinformation.

Order Fulfillment

For businesses dealing with physical products, order fulfillment is another critical area for streamlining. Efficiency here directly impacts customer satisfaction through delivery speed and accuracy, and indirectly affects profitability through inventory management and shipping costs. Key strategies include:

- **Optimized Warehouse Layout and Inventory Management:** This involves logically organizing stock based on product velocity (fast-moving items placed for easy access), implementing a clear labeling system, and potentially using technology like barcode scanners or RFID tags for precise inventory tracking and rapid picking. Reducing picker travel distance within the warehouse and minimizing search time for items can dramatically increase throughput.
- **Warehouse Management Systems (WMS):** For growing businesses, investing in a WMS can be transformative. A WMS can automate tasks such as receiving, put-away, picking, packing, and shipping, while also providing real-time visibility into inventory levels and order status. This level of control and automation is essential for handling increased order volumes without compromising accuracy or speed.
- **Streamlined Shipping Process:** Integrating with multiple carriers, automating shipping label and customs documentation generation, and optimizing packaging to reduce material costs and shipping weight can lead to signifi-

cant savings and faster delivery times. Negotiating favorable rates with shipping partners based on projected volume is also crucial for efficient logistics.

Administrative Tasks

Often viewed as back-office functions, administrative tasks can significantly drain resources if not properly streamlined. These include accounting, payroll, human resources, IT support, and general office management. Automation is a powerful tool in these areas:

- **Cloud-Based Software:** Cloud-based accounting software can automate invoice generation, payment tracking, and bank reconciliation. Payroll systems can automate salary calculations, tax deductions, and direct deposits, significantly reducing administrative burden and ensuring accuracy.
- **Specialized HR Software:** HR functions can benefit from applicant tracking systems, onboarding portals, and performance management software, which automate many manual processes involved in managing employees.
- **IT Support Tools:** IT support can be enhanced by ticketing systems and remote man-

agement tools that allow for efficient tracking and resolution of technical issues.

- **Integrated Digital Solutions:** The principle is to move away from manual data entry, paper-based workflows, and disconnected systems towards integrated, digital solutions. This not only saves time and reduces errors but also provides better data visibility and control. For example, implementing a central document management system ensures critical business documents are easily accessible, secure, and version-controlled, improving collaboration and reducing the risk of data loss, rather than relying on scattered network drives or physical filing cabinets.

Overarching Management: Best Practices and Project Management

The concept of "best practices" in operations extends beyond specific departments to the overarching management of projects and resources. This includes:

- **Project Management Methodologies:** Adopting methodologies like Agile or Waterfall, depending on the project's nature, ensures efficient planning, execution, and delivery.

- **Robust Communication Protocols:** Implementing clear communication protocols ensures information flows smoothly between teams and departments, preventing misunderstandings and delays. For example, launching a new product requires streamlined processes for market research, product development, manufacturing, marketing, and sales. Each stage needs to be interconnected and efficient, with clear handoffs and feedback loops.
- **Collaborative Tools and Software:** Utilizing collaborative tools and project management software can facilitate efficient management by providing a central platform for task management, communication, and progress tracking.

For any business, especially one aiming for significant growth, a strong team is fundamental. While efficient systems and streamlined processes provide the necessary structure for scalability, it's the people within these frameworks who truly energize the business and propel its progress. Building and effectively managing a team is an ongoing, strategic effort requiring careful consideration throughout every growth stage. This involves attracting individuals who possess the essential skills and align with the company's vision and culture, then cultivating an environment where they can achieve their highest potential. Neglecting this crucial aspect can quickly turn operational efficiencies into bottlenecks, as a poorly managed or unsuitable team can undermine even the most meticulously designed systems.

Recruiting the Right Talent

The initial and foundational step in building a strong team is recruiting the right talent. This process starts with a clear understanding of the roles that need to be filled, along with the specific skills, experience, and cultural attributes essential for success in those positions. It's not enough to simply find someone who can perform the tasks; the ideal candidate will also be a cultural fit, embodying the company's values and work ethic. For example, a company valuing innovation and rapid problem-solving should prioritize candidates comfortable with ambiguity and proactive in seeking solutions, even if other candidates possess more technically advanced but less adaptable skill sets.

The recruitment process itself should reflect the company's brand and values. This includes crafting compelling job descriptions that accurately represent the role and culture, using diverse channels to reach potential candidates, and implementing a structured interview process that assesses both technical proficiency and cultural alignment. This structured approach may involve multiple interview stages, skill-based assessments, and background checks to ensure candidates are not only qualified but also trustworthy and aligned with the company's long-term objectives. For instance, when hiring for a customer-facing role, interviewers might use hypothetical customer scenarios to evaluate problem-solving abilities and empathy—traits vital for customer retention and satisfaction—beyond just communication skills. Similarly, for a technical role, a practical coding challenge or case study could be more insightful than a traditional Q&A session. The ultimate goal is to create a predictive selection process that maximizes the likelihood of a successful hire.

Effective Onboarding

Once promising candidates are identified, the onboarding process becomes the next critical phase. A comprehensive and well-executed onboarding program goes beyond mere paperwork and initial introductions. It's an immersive experience designed to integrate new hires into the company's operations, culture, and team dynamics, setting them up for long-term success. This process should begin even before the employee's first day with pre-boarding activities, such as sending welcome kits, providing access to company information, and outlining the first week's schedule.

On the first day, the focus should be on making the new employee feel welcomed, valued, and equipped with the necessary tools and information to begin contributing. This typically includes a clear introduction to their team, workspace setup, and initial training sessions. As onboarding continues over the first few weeks and months, it should incorporate a structured learning plan, regular check-ins with their manager and HR, and opportunities to connect with colleagues across different departments. For example, a company selling complex software might provide new sales representatives with in-depth product training, shadowing opportunities with experienced sales professionals, and access to a library of case studies and customer testimonials, ensuring they have the knowledge and confidence to effectively engage with potential clients. Similarly, a new engineer might be assigned a mentor, given access to the company's codebase and development tools, and tasked with small, manageable coding projects to gradually acclimate them to the team's workflow and standards. A robust onboarding process significantly reduces ramp-up time for new employees, boosts their productivity, and increases their overall job satisfaction and retention rates, thereby minimizing the costs associated with employee turnover.

Continuous Improvement and Financial Impact

Furthermore, a culture of continuous improvement, often referred to as "kaizen" in some business philosophies, is vital for sustained operational efficiency. This involves empowering employees at all levels to identify and suggest improvements to existing processes. Regularly scheduled meetings where teams review workflows, discuss challenges, and brainstorm solutions can be incredibly effective. This not only leverages the practical knowledge of those performing the tasks but also fosters a sense of ownership and engagement. When employees feel their input is valued and that they can directly contribute to making their work more efficient and effective, morale and productivity tend to increase. This cultural shift is as important as any technological solution.

The financial implications of streamlining are substantial. Reduced operational costs directly impact the bottom line, increasing profitability. Improved efficiency can lead to higher throughput without a proportional increase in overhead, thus improving margins as the business scales. For instance, if a manufacturing company can increase its production output by 20% through process optimization without hiring additional staff or investing in new machinery, its cost per unit decreases significantly, making its products more competitive and its overall operations more profitable. Moreover, faster order fulfillment and improved customer service can lead to increased customer loyalty and repeat business, which are generally more profitable than acquiring new customers. Increased customer lifetime value, as discussed in previous contexts, is a direct result of efficient and positive ongoing interactions.

To truly embed efficiency, businesses should consider investing in employee training. Even the most well-designed processes and advanced technologies will falter if employees are not adequately trained on how to use them effectively. Training should not only cover the technical aspects of new systems or tools but also the underlying principles of efficiency and the importance of adhering to established best practices. This investment in human capital is crucial for ensuring that the benefits of streamlining are fully realized and sustained over time.

In summary, streamlining business processes is not a one-time project but a continuous journey of refinement and optimization. It requires a deep understanding of existing workflows through process mapping, strategic application of automation to repetitive and time-consuming tasks, and the diligent implementation of industry best practices across all operational domains. By focusing on efficiency in areas like customer service, order fulfillment, and administrative tasks, businesses can significantly reduce costs, improve service quality, and liberate valuable resources. This operational excellence is not just about making the business run more smoothly; it's about building a robust, agile, and cost-effective foundation that can support ambitious growth strategies and ensure long-term competitive advantage and profitability in an ever-evolving market landscape. The disciplined pursuit of operational efficiency is, in essence, the engine that powers scalable and sustainable business success.

Building a Thriving Work Culture

A positive and productive work culture is the foundation of any successful team. It fosters an environment where employees feel motivated, respected, and empowered. Key aspects of such a culture include:

- **Open Communication:** Transparent feedback, both given and received, is crucial for growth and understanding.
- **Clear Purpose:** Employees need to understand how their work contributes to the company's overarching goals.

- **Recognition and Appreciation:** Acknowledging good work, through formal programs or informal gestures, boosts morale and reinforces positive behaviors.
- **Continuous Learning:** Investing in professional development and growth opportunities, such as "lunch and learn" sessions or subsidies for external training, demonstrates that employee growth is valued, fostering loyalty and engagement.
- **Cross-Departmental Collaboration:** Encouraging teamwork across different departments breaks down silos and creates a more cohesive organizational spirit.

A strong culture is an invaluable asset, guiding behavior, shaping decisions, and ultimately driving performance. It attracts and retains talented individuals, making a company a desirable place to work and grow.Effective Delegation: A Key Leadership Skill

Delegation is an essential leadership skill for effective team management and scalability. It involves strategically entrusting tasks and responsibilities to team members, empowering them to take ownership and contribute to company objectives. Effective delegation goes beyond simply offloading work; it requires:

- **Identifying the Right Tasks for the Right People:** Matching tasks to individual skills and development needs.
- **Providing Clear Instructions and Context:** Ensuring team members understand the task, objectives, and any relevant background information.
- **Granting Autonomy:** Allowing team members the freedom to execute the task their way, fostering a sense of ownership.

When done correctly, delegation develops employee skills, builds confidence, and frees up leaders to focus on more strategic initiatives. For example, a marketing manager might delegate social media campaign management to a junior associate, providing clear objectives, brand guidelines, and performance metrics. This not only allows the manager to focus on strategy but also offers the associate valuable skill development and career progression.

Successful delegation relies on proper preparation, including clearly defining the task, outlining desired outcomes, specifying constraints, and establishing communication channels. Equally important is follow-up, which involves providing constructive feedback, offering support without micromanaging, and celebrating successful completion to reinforce the value of the delegated task and the employee's contribution. Conversely, poor delegation can lead to frustration, errors, and a lack of accountability.Optimizing Performance Through Management

Performance management is vital for ensuring individuals and teams operate at optimal levels. It's a continuous process, not just an annual event, involving:

- **Setting Clear Expectations:** Establishing SMART goals (Specific, Measurable, Achievable, Relevant, Time-bound) for each employee, aligned with company objectives.
- **Regular Feedback:** Conducting consistent one-on-one meetings to track progress, identify challenges, and provide ongoing coaching and support. These meetings should offer constructive feedback, both positive and developmental, helping employees understand their strengths and areas for improvement.
- **Periodic Evaluations:** Objectively tracking performance data and achievements, and delivering timely and specific feedback.

When performance falls short, prompt and constructive intervention is necessary, potentially including a performance improvement plan. Conversely, outstanding performance should be recognized and rewarded to reinforce desired behaviors and motivate continued excellence. Effective performance management drives individual growth and contributes significantly to the overall productivity and success of the team and organization.Empowering Employees Through Leadership

Leadership strategies are pivotal in empowering employees and driving business success. Effective leaders inspire, motivate, and guide their teams toward common goals through empathy, vision, and the ability to foster a collaborative environment. Different leadership styles can be effective depending on the context and team needs:

- **Transformational Leadership:** Focuses on inspiring employees to reach their full potential, fostering innovation and positive change.
- **Servant Leadership:** Prioritizes the needs of the team, empowering and supporting them to succeed.

A key aspect of employee empowerment is providing autonomy and growth opportunities. This means trusting employees to make decisions, allowing them to own their work, and providing the necessary resources and support. For example, empowering a project team by allowing them to determine the best approach to a problem fosters ownership and creative thinking.

Furthermore, effective leaders excel at conflict resolution, constructively navigating disagreements within the team to maintain focus on objectives. They also champion diversity and inclusion, recognizing the strength derived from varied perspectives and backgrounds. By cultivating a supportive and empowering leadership approach, businesses can unlock their teams' full potential, driving innovation, productivity, and sustained success.

Cultivating a Scalable Team

Building a team that scales effectively requires a proactive approach to talent management, moving beyond initial hiring to continuous development, succession planning, and flexible organizational structures. As businesses grow, roles and required skill sets evolve, necessitating investment in continuous training and development programs. This can involve cross-training, leadership opportunities, or external education. Succession planning is crucial for business continuity and leadership development; identifying and mentoring high-potential employees prevents talent gaps. A flexible organizational structure, utilizing cross-functional teams, agile methodologies, and empowered employees, ensures adaptability to changing market conditions. For instance, a growing e-commerce company might form a dedicated cross-functional team to explore new market entry strategies. This adaptability ensures the team remains agile and responsive.

The financial benefits of effective team building are substantial, contributing directly to long-term scalability and profitability. A well-managed team is a significant asset, driving innovation, improving efficiency, and enhancing customer satisfaction. Conversely, poor hiring, inadequate onboarding, or weak management can lead to high turnover, decreased productivity, increased costs, and hindered growth. Investing in talent acquisition and development is a strategic investment with significant returns. For example, a comprehensive onboarding program can increase new hire retention by 20% in the first year, reducing replacement costs. An empowered, high-performing team can achieve higher sales targets, improve operational efficiency, and build stronger customer loyalty, all leading to increased revenue and profitability. By building a high-performing team, businesses create a sustainable engine for growth, equipped with the human capital needed to navigate scaling complexities and achieve long-term objectives. The synergy between optimized processes and a skilled team is key to transitioning from a startup to a dominant market force.

Building a Resilient Supply Chain and Strong Vendor Relationships

The success of bringing a product or service to market, especially as a business scales, critically depends on the robustness of its supply chain and the strength of its vendor relationships. While internal operations are the core engine, the external network of suppliers and partners acts as the vital circulatory system, ensuring consistent and timely delivery of necessary components, raw materials, or services. Neglecting this external ecosystem can lead to vulnerabilities such as production delays, compromised quality, increased costs, and dissatisfied customers, ultimately hindering scalability. Building a resilient and responsive supply chain is an evolving strategy requiring ongoing attention, adaptation, and a commitment to fostering strong, mutually beneficial partnerships.

The foundation of an effective supply chain lies in the careful selection of vendors and suppliers. This process goes beyond simply seeking the lowest price; it involves a comprehensive evaluation of potential partners based on factors aligned with the business's strategic objectives and operational requirements. Reliability is paramount, requiring thorough vetting that may include site visits to assess manufacturing capabilities, quality control, and ethical labor practices. Financial stability is another crucial consideration, as a supplier in distress can disrupt the business. A supplier's capacity to scale with the growing business is also a key determinant; a vendor unable to expand output as demand increases will become a bottleneck. Technical expertise and innovation capabilities are also important, particularly for businesses relying on specialized components or seeking to leverage supplier innovation. For example, an electronics company might prioritize suppliers leading in miniaturization technology, or a food manufacturer might seek suppliers with sustainable sourcing practices. Beyond these tangible aspects, cultural alignment and a shared commitment to quality and customer service foster smoother collaboration and proactive problem-solving. It's about finding partners who are integral contributors to the business's success, not just transactional providers. This rigorous selection process may involve issuing a Request for Proposal (RFP) to a shortlist of vendors, clearly outlining needs, expectations, and evaluation criteria. Responses to RFPs should be meticulously reviewed for pricing, depth of understanding, proposed solutions, and demonstrated commitment to partnership.

After identifying and vetting potential vendors, the next crucial step is negotiating favorable terms.

This establishes a mutually beneficial relationship that protects your business's interests while valuing the supplier. Key negotiation areas typically include:

- **Pricing:** Go beyond simple per-unit costs to explore volume discounts, long-term contract pricing, or even cost-plus models for specialized components.
- **Payment Terms:** Balance supplier cash flow needs with your revenue cycles. Negotiating terms like Net 30, Net 60, or early payment discounts can significantly impact working capital.
- **Delivery Schedules:** Specify lead times, Minimum Order Quantities (MOQs), and penalties for late deliveries.
- **Quality Specifications:** Define these unambiguously, referencing industry standards or detailing precise tolerances and performance metrics.
- **Warranty Provisions:** Protect your business against defects or failures, outlining processes for returns, repairs, or replacements.
- **Intellectual Property (IP) Protection:** Essential for regulated industries or proprietary technology, safeguarding confidential information and innovations.

A well-negotiated contract provides a clear roadmap, minimizing ambiguity and offering a framework for dispute resolution. It's also wise to build in flexibility for evolving business needs, perhaps through review periods or agreed-upon change order processes.

Ongoing vendor relationship management is as critical as initial selection and negotiation. This involves clear communication, performance benchmarks, and regular reviews.

- **Proactive Communication:** Keep suppliers informed about demand fluctuations, new product developments, or challenges to foster an integrated and responsive supply chain.
- **Key Performance Indicators (KPIs):** Establish objective measures like on-time delivery rates, defect rates, responsiveness, and pricing adherence. Tracking and sharing these KPIs creates accountability and identifies improvement areas.
- **Performance Reviews:** Quarterly or semi-annual reviews offer a structured forum to discuss KPIs, address issues, and explore collaboration opportunities. For example, a joint effort to identify the root cause of delays can turn a problem into an improvement catalyst.

Foster a partnership recognizing that supplier success often intertwines with your own. This can involve sharing market insights, offering training, or collaborating on ventures and product development, leading to greater loyalty, innovation, and a resilient supply chain.

For scaling businesses, risk mitigation is a critical aspect of vendor management. Supply chains are vulnerable to disruptions from natural disasters, geopolitical events, economic downturns, or supplier instability. Identifying risks and developing contingency plans is essential for operational resilience.

- **Supplier Base Diversification:** Reduce single-source dependency by having at least one alternative supplier for critical components, even if used less frequently.
- **Strategic Inventory Buffers:** Build buffers for key components or finished goods, with levels depending on criticality, lead time, and inventory holding costs versus stockout risks.
- **Geographical Diversification:** Spread risk by exploring suppliers in different locations if a significant portion of your supply chain is concentrated in a disaster-prone region.
- **Contractual Risk Clauses:** Incorporate risk-sharing or force majeure provisions.

- **Regular Risk Assessments:** Continuously identify and evaluate vulnerabilities as your business and supply chain grow more complex.

This proactive approach ensures your business can navigate unexpected challenges, maintain operational continuity, and serve customers even during turbulent times.

Effective supply chain and vendor management profoundly impact a company's profitability and scalability. A well-managed supply chain can significantly reduce the cost of goods sold (COGS) through favorable pricing, optimized logistics, and minimized waste. This can be achieved by negotiating better terms, consolidating purchases, or exploring alternative sourcing. Efficient inventory management, driven by accurate forecasting and timely deliveries, reduces holding costs, minimizes obsolescence, and frees up working capital. Minimizing stockouts and ensuring timely deliveries directly impacts customer satisfaction and sales revenue, as lost sales and damaged customer loyalty are costly to recover.

Conversely, a poorly managed supply chain leads to inflated costs from expedited shipping, premium pricing for last-minute orders, increased waste from damaged or expired goods, and significant expenses from quality issues or product recalls. High inventory levels tie up capital, and stockouts result in lost revenue and customer attrition. Investing in strong vendor relationships, quality assurance, and supply chain technology (e.g., ERP or SCM systems) can provide greater visibility, improve forecasting accuracy, and automate procurement and logistics. For instance, an SCM system can track shipments in real-time, predict delays, and optimize routes, leading to substantial savings and improved delivery reliability. By treating the supply chain as a strategic enabler of growth and efficiency, businesses can unlock significant financial benefits, enhance their competitive advantage, and build a scalable operation. This focus on external partnerships and the flow of goods and services is crucial for long-term business success, complementing internal strengths.

Consider a rapidly growing direct-to-consumer apparel brand that initially sourced fabrics from a single local supplier. As demand surges, this supplier may struggle to keep pace and lack capacity for specialized, sustainable fabrics. This highlights the need to proactively identify and qualify alternative suppliers, such as overseas manufacturers specializing in organic cotton or recycled polyester with larger production capabilities. Negotiating new contracts involves not only pricing but also stringent quality control, defined shipping timelines, and robust communication protocols. Regular quality audits and an inventory management system tracking fabric availability across multiple production runs would also be necessary. A disruption at the original supplier, like a fire, would not halt production if a backup sourcing channel is established. Engaging new suppliers in discussions about future trends can lead to exclusive designs or more competitive pricing, strengthening the supply chain and reinforcing brand commitment to quality and sustainability. This strategic evolution of the supply chain is essential for maintaining growth and supporting increasing customer demand.

Another example is a technology company providing cloud-based software solutions. While their product is digital, operations often rely on third-party hardware for servers, data centers, and client-side devices, as well as external services for network infrastructure, cybersecurity monitoring, or customer support outsourcing. An initial setup might involve a single cloud provider and IT hardware vendor. As the company scales, data storage needs explode, requiring more servers and bandwidth. If the original cloud provider cannot offer competitive pricing or adequate scalability, the company faces a critical decision point. This could lead to negotiating better terms with the existing provider or a competitive bidding process involving multiple cloud infrastructure providers. The company would meticulously evaluate technical specifications, service level agreements

(SLAs) for uptime and performance, data security protocols, and pricing models of potential new partners. Similarly, if the initial hardware vendor's lead times for new server deployments become too long, the company might explore partnerships with multiple manufacturers, diversifying its critical infrastructure supply. Managing these external technology relationships requires constant vigilance, including regular performance reviews against SLAs, proactive security monitoring, and staying abreast of technological advancements. Failing to manage this external tech ecosystem effectively could lead to performance degradation, data breaches, or an inability to onboard new clients efficiently, directly impeding growth.

The complexity of supply chain management intensifies with globalization and interconnected markets. Businesses aiming for substantial scale often source materials or components from various countries, necessitating an understanding of international trade regulations, customs procedures, currency fluctuations, and diverse cultural business practices. Managing a global supply chain requires sophisticated logistics planning, including international shipping, freight forwarding, and warehousing in different regions. It also demands robust risk management strategies to account for geopolitical instability, tariffs, and potential disruptions. For example, a company manufacturing outdoor gear might source waterproof fabrics from Asia, high-strength zippers from Europe, and assemble products in a third country with lower labor costs. Each location presents unique challenges and opportunities. Negotiating with overseas suppliers might involve navigating different languages, legal frameworks, and payment methods (e.g., letters of credit). Adhering to import/export regulations is paramount to avoid costly delays or penalties. Furthermore, managing the environmental and ethical impact of a global supply chain is increasingly important for brand reputation and regulatory compliance. Companies are now expected to demonstrate responsible sourcing, fair labor practices, and a commitment to sustainability throughout their value chain. This often involves conducting due diligence on suppliers regarding their environmental policies, labor conditions, and ethical standards. Certifications from recognized organizations can help validate these practices. Implementing supply chain visibility tools, which provide real-time tracking of goods across borders, becomes invaluable for managing these complex international flows. Such visibility allows businesses to anticipate delays, identify bottlenecks, and respond proactively to issues during transit, ensuring efficient product delivery and regulatory compliance. The financial benefits of global sourcing can be significant, but they are only realized through meticulous planning, rigorous management, and a commitment to building strong, trustworthy relationships with international partners.

To succeed in today's dynamic business environment, companies must possess the ability to expand operations smoothly in response to increasing demand. As a company matures from its initial stages, where flexibility and resourcefulness are key, to a growth-oriented enterprise, its operational structure must be carefully designed to handle greater volumes without becoming inefficient or compromising its core value. This requires a deliberate and strategic approach, integrating the potential for expansion into the business model from the very beginning. The goal is to build a robust system that can accelerate without faltering, ensuring the business has the necessary infrastructure and processes to fully capitalize on opportunities.

A core component of scalability involves the strategic planning and implementation of flexible production and service delivery systems. For manufacturers, this means designing production lines that can be easily reconfigured or expanded to manage higher output. This might involve investing in modular machinery that can be added or removed as needed, or designing workflows that enable parallel processing. For instance, an electronics company might start with a single assembly line. As demand grows, they could add more lines or implement automated conveyor systems to boost throughput on existing ones. The key is to avoid creating rigid bottlenecks that become unmanageable as order volumes rise. This often requires a thorough analysis of the longest lead-time processes within the operation and proactively addressing them. Diversifying production capabilities, perhaps by partnering with contract manufacturers for specific components or finished goods during peak demand, can also be beneficial. This external capacity provides a vital buffer, allowing rapid scaling without the significant capital expenditure and lead times associated with building new internal facilities overnight. The decision between internal expansion and external partnerships will depend on factors like anticipated growth speed, available capital, and the strategic importance of maintaining complete control over production.

Similarly, for service-based businesses, scalability often relies on adaptable technology infrastructure and flexible workforce management. A software-as-a-service (SaaS) company, for example, must ensure its cloud hosting environment can dynamically scale to accommodate a growing user base and increasing data processing demands. This involves selecting cloud providers with robust auto-scaling features and carefully architecting the software to be stateless and distributed, allowing for easy addition of server instances. The architecture must be designed with future growth in mind, anticipating higher transaction volumes, increased data storage, and potential spikes in user activity. Beyond the technical infrastructure, customer support and service delivery teams must also be scalable. This can involve implementing tiered support systems, utilizing AI-powered chatbots for initial inquiries, and developing comprehensive knowledge bases to empower customers to find answers independently. As the client base expands, the internal team may need to grow, but the focus should be on building systems that facilitate efficient onboarding and training of new support staff and equipping existing staff with tools that enhance their productivity. For example, a growing online education platform might invest in a powerful learning management system (LMS) that can handle many concurrent users and provide standardized training modules for new instructors, ensuring consistent educational quality as the student population increases.

Furthermore, the financial structure of a business must be as adaptable as its operational one. Scaling frequently requires substantial capital investment in new equipment, expanded facilities, increased inventory, and a larger workforce. Businesses need to establish clear financial models that project future capital needs and identify potential funding sources. This could include reinvesting profits, securing lines of credit, or seeking equity investment. Crucially, as a business scales, its cost structure will inevitably change. Direct costs, such as raw materials and labor, will increase proportionally with output, but many indirect costs, such as overheads, marketing, and administrative expenses, will also rise. Understanding these cost dynamics and how they evolve with scale is essential for maintaining profitability. For instance, a catering company starting with small events will see its ingredient and staff costs rise significantly when taking on larger banquets. However, the cost per person might decrease due to bulk purchasing power and more efficient use of kitchen and serving staff. Strategic financial planning also involves effectively managing working capital. As sales increase, the amount of cash tied up in inventory and accounts receivable will also grow. Businesses need to implement efficient inventory management practices and optimize their invoicing and collection processes to ensure healthy cash flow that supports ongoing growth. The ability to accurately forecast revenue and expenses becomes even more critical at scale, enabling proactive financial management rather than reactive crisis mitigation.

Achieving scalability in business relies on several interconnected factors: standardized processes, a strong human element, strategic technology use, and continuous adaptation.

Standardized and Repeatable Processes:

As businesses expand, moving beyond ad-hoc methods to documented, repeatable processes is crucial. This involves detailing key operational procedures—from order fulfillment and quality control to customer onboarding and employee training—to ensure consistent execution, regardless of who performs the task. Documented processes serve multiple functions: they maintain quality and efficiency, simplify new employee training, and provide a foundation for continuous improvement. For a logistics company, this could mean detailed Standard Operating Procedures (SOPs) for handling packages, including quality checklists and exception protocols. A digital marketing agency might develop templates for client proposals, standardized campaign workflows, and consistent performance reporting metrics. The act of documenting often reveals opportunities for simplification, automation, or the elimination of redundant steps, further enhancing scalability. This systematic approach fosters a predictable framework, allowing creativity to thrive within a managed growth environment.

The Human Element:

Scalability also hinges on the evolving organizational structure and team dynamics. This requires not only increasing staff but also strategically building out management layers and specialist roles. Cultivating a culture that embraces change and continuous learning is essential, ensuring employees understand growth objectives and their role in achieving them. Leadership must excel at delegation, empowering teams, and fostering strong communication across the expanding organization. For example, a founder initially involved in all aspects of a startup must transition to a more strategic role, entrusting daily operations to capable managers. This necessitates investing in leadership development and creating clear career progression paths. The ability to attract, retain, and develop talent becomes a significant competitive advantage, driven by competitive compensation, engaging work environments, professional development opportunities, and a strong, cohesive company culture even as the workforce expands.

Strategic Use of Technology:
Leveraging technology strategically is indispensable for scalable operations. Beyond specific production and service delivery technologies, businesses need overarching systems that integrate functions and provide critical data for decision-making. Enterprise Resource Planning (ERP) systems, for instance,

integrate various business processes (finance, HR, manufacturing, supply chain) into a unified system, offering a holistic view, improving data accuracy, and streamlining workflows. Customer Relationship Management (CRM) systems manage customer interactions, sales pipelines, and marketing efforts, providing insights for growth strategies. Business Intelligence (BI) and analytics tools are vital for tracking Key Performance Indicators (KPIs), identifying trends, and making data-driven decisions. A rapidly growing retail business, for example, could use BI tools to analyze sales data across categories and locations to allocate resources effectively. Technology enables automation of repetitive tasks, improves communication, and provides actionable insights, allowing businesses to achieve more with less and make informed decisions during expansion.

Continuous Evaluation and Adaptation:

Finally, preparing for scalability is an ongoing process of evaluation and adaptation. The market is dynamic, with evolving customer needs, competitive pressures, and technological advancements. A truly scalable business anticipates these changes and proactively adjusts strategies and operations. This requires establishing internal and external feedback mechanisms and fostering a culture of continuous improvement. Regular strategic reviews, performance analyses, and competitive landscaping are essential for staying ahead. A food delivery service, for example, might constantly monitor customer feedback for expansion ideas or new cuisine offerings, while also tracking competitor pricing. The ability to pivot and adapt quickly, without losing sight of core mission and values, is a hallmark of a scalable enterprise. This agile approach ensures the business can manage current growth and is well-positioned to capitalize on future opportunities and navigate unforeseen challenges, embedding scalability as an ongoing organizational discipline.

Achieving scalability presents a unique set of challenges. Unplanned, rapid expansion can dilute quality, strain resources, and hinder communication. Sustainable growth requires a measured pace, with each expansion step supported by robust infrastructure, processes, and talent. This necessitates strategic resource allocation, prioritizing investments for long-term growth, and declining opportunities that don't align with objectives or overextend capabilities. The goal is sustainable growth, fostering a resilient and profitable enterprise that thrives over time. This demands a balanced approach, blending ambition with prudence and a deep understanding of operational strengths and limitations. It's about organic adaptation and growth, rather than artificial inflation leading to collapse.

Scaling a business is intrinsically linked to operational excellence. While building growth infrastructure is vital, its efficient and effective operation requires a strong framework for performance measurement and continuous improvement. This is an ongoing process, a continuous dialogue between operational realities and strategic aspirations. It's about establishing a feedback loop to identify successes, failures, and areas for enhancement. Without this diligent approach, even well-designed scalable systems can stagnate, leading to missed opportunities and a gradual erosion of competitive advantage.

Central to this continuous improvement cycle is the establishment of Key Performance Indicators (KPIs). These are not arbitrary but quantifiable measures reflecting critical business success factors. For manufacturing, KPIs might include units produced per hour, defect rates, or on-time delivery percentages. SaaS companies might track customer acquisition cost, churn rate, monthly recurring revenue, or customer lifetime value. Service-based businesses could focus on customer satisfaction scores, average resolution time for support tickets, or employee productivity. Critically, KPIs must align directly with overarching business objectives. If market share growth is the goal, KPIs should reflect customer acquisition and sales volume. If profitability is key, metrics like gross margin, operational efficiency, and cost per unit become more prominent. KPI selection should be a deliberate, strategic process, ensuring measurement of what truly matters for sustainable growth and profitability. Avoid tracking every possible metric; focus on the vital few that provide the clearest signal of operational health and progress towards goals.

Once KPIs are defined, the next crucial step is implementing systems for consistent tracking and reporting. Technology, such as Business Intelligence (BI) tools, analytics platforms, and sophisticated spreadsheet software, is invaluable for collecting, processing, and visualizing performance data. For instance, a retail business aiming to improve inventory turnover might use a system that automatically tracks sales data by SKU against stock levels, alerting when inventory moves too slowly or quickly. Similarly, a customer support team might use a CRM system integrated with a helpdesk platform to monitor average response times, first-contact resolution rates, and customer satisfaction scores. The objective is to create a single source of truth for performance data, easily accessible to relevant stakeholders. Dashboards offering real-time or near real-time KPI updates can powerfully keep the entire organization focused on performance. These dashboards should be designed for clarity and actionability, presenting complex data in an easily digestible format that highlights trends and deviations from targets.

Driving Growth Through Data Analysis and Continuous Improvement

To achieve scalable growth, organizations must move beyond mere data collection and cultivate a deep understanding of their performance drivers. Analyzing data from various systems is crucial for uncovering insights into underlying causes of performance, whether it's identifying machinery issues in a production line, understanding customer churn in a SaaS company, or pinpointing dissatisfaction with specific product features. This analytical phase demands a combination of quantitative skills and business acumen, encouraging a critical examination of data to identify patterns, correlations, and anomalies. Techniques like root cause analysis, Pareto analysis, and statistical process control are invaluable for pinpointing these performance drivers.

Implementing Targeted Actions for Improvement

The insights gained from rigorous data analysis are the foundation for continuous improvement. These findings enable organizations to take targeted actions that rectify inefficiencies, mitigate risks, and capitalize on opportunities. Such actions might involve process refinements, investments in new technologies, additional staff training, or adjustments to overall business strategy. For instance, if customer complaints highlight a complex e-commerce checkout, the focus should be on simplifying the user interface. Similarly, reallocating resources to marketing campaigns that demonstrate higher ROI can significantly improve effectiveness. The key is to embed these initiatives within a systematic, iterative process, where each action has measurable outcomes tracked against relevant KPIs. This creates a virtuous cycle of data-informed action, leading to improved data and further informed decisions.

Fostering a Culture of Continuous Improvement

A culture of continuous improvement is not something that can be simply mandated; it must be actively nurtured and integrated into the organization's DNA. This involves empowering employees at all levels to identify potential improvements, providing them with the necessary tools and autonomy to test and implement changes, and celebrating successes. Front-line employees, with their direct experience of daily operations, are particularly valuable sources of innovative ideas for streamlining workflows, reducing waste, and enhancing the customer experience.

Creating forums for knowledge sharing, such as team meetings, cross-functional workshops, and internal suggestion schemes, helps to disseminate best practices and encourage collaborative problem-solving. Leadership plays a critical role in setting the tone, demonstrating a commitment to learning and adaptation, and ensuring that continuous improvement is viewed as an integral part of everyone's job, not an additional burden. This includes allocating time and resources, providing constructive feedback, and recognizing and rewarding employees who actively contribute to the improvement process.

Leveraging Lean Principles and Quality Management

Implementing lean principles and quality management methodologies can significantly accelerate continuous improvement efforts, particularly in scalable operations. Lean methodologies, such as the Plan-Do-Check-Act (PDCA) cycle, offer a structured approach to problem-solving and process optimization:

- **Plan:** Define the problem or opportunity and formulate a potential solution.
- **Do:** Implement the solution, ideally on a small scale to minimize risk.

- **Check:** Measure the results against the desired outcomes.
- **Act:** Standardize successful solutions or make further adjustments based on the findings.

This cyclical approach ensures data-driven improvements and integrates learnings into future efforts. Lean thinking also emphasizes identifying and eliminating all forms of waste (e.g., overproduction, waiting time, unnecessary transportation, defects). Systematically removing these non-value-adding activities enhances efficiency, reduces costs, and improves scalability. For example, a logistics company could apply lean principles to optimize warehousing operations by analyzing goods flow to reduce forklift travel distances or improve item placement.

Proactive Quality Management and the Human Element in Continuous Improvement

Maintaining consistent quality becomes increasingly challenging yet critical as operations scale. A decline in quality can severely damage customer trust and brand reputation. To combat this, businesses should implement robust quality management systems, such as those based on ISO standards. These systems provide a structured framework for consistently meeting specified requirements by establishing clear quality standards, implementing quality control checks at various stages of production or service delivery, and creating mechanisms to address and rectify issues. Tools like Statistical Process Control (SPC) are invaluable for monitoring process variability and identifying deviations before they lead to defects (e.g., monitoring cooking temperature or fill levels in food manufacturing). The primary focus should always be on defect prevention rather than mere detection, aligning with a proactive approach to continuous improvement.

Investing in the Human Element

The continuous improvement framework must also encompass the organization's human element. This requires ongoing investment in employee training and development, ensuring staff possess the necessary skills and knowledge to perform effectively and adapt to evolving processes and technologies. Performance management systems should not only evaluate past performance but also set future development goals and provide the support needed to achieve them.

Fostering a learning culture, where employees are encouraged to seek new knowledge and share expertise, is crucial for building an adaptable and high-performing workforce. This can be achieved through mentorship programs, online learning resources, or sponsoring attendance at industry conferences. As businesses scale, efficient onboarding of new employees becomes paramount. Streamlined, standardized onboarding processes, combined with ongoing support and feedback, can significantly reduce the time it takes for new hires to become productive team members.

Incorporating External Perspectives

The feedback loop for continuous improvement should actively incorporate external perspectives. This includes gathering customer feedback through surveys, reviews, and direct interactions, as well as monitoring market trends and competitor activities. Understanding customer needs and expectations is fundamental to refining products, services, and operational processes. For instance, a software company might use user feedback to prioritize the development of new features or identify areas where the existing user interface could be improved for greater intuitiveness. Similarly, staying abreast of competitors' offerings and operational efficiencies provides valuable insights and highlights areas where a business may need to adapt or innovate. This external scanning ensures that continuous improvement efforts are informed by market realities and the evolving demands of the customer base.

Continuous Improvement: A Never-Ending Journey

Finally, it's crucial to recognize that continuous improvement is an ongoing journey, not a destination. It demands continuous vigilance, a willingness to challenge the status quo, and a commitment to iterative progress. Systems and processes effective today may need re-evaluation and adaptation as the business grows and the external environment changes. By embedding performance measurement and continuous improvement into the organization's core, businesses can build a resilient and adaptable operational engine well-equipped to navigate the complexities of scaling and achieve sustained long-term success. This transforms the ambition of growth into a tangible, measurable, and consistently refined reality. This diligent focus on optimization ensures that as the business expands, its efficiency, quality, and ability to serve customers only improve, creating a powerful and difficult-to-replicate competitive advantage.

EIGHT

FINANCIAL MANAGEMENT AND INVESTMENT STRATEGIES

For a scaling enterprise to truly master its financial trajectory, it must move beyond basic budgeting and cash flow projections. This is where Advanced Financial Planning and Analysis (FP&A) becomes essential, offering sophisticated tools and methodologies to equip entrepreneurs with a forward-looking and resilient financial strategy. While foundational financial management ensures operational continuity and funding, advanced FP&A aims to build a financial fortress capable of weathering storms, capitalizing on opportunities, and driving sustained, profitable growth. It shifts the approach from reacting to financial events to proactively shaping them.

One of the most potent tools in advanced FP&A is scenario analysis. This technique involves developing multiple plausible future financial states for the business, based on varying assumptions about key drivers. Rather than relying on a single, often optimistic, "base case" projection, scenario analysis compels a deeper consideration of potential upside and downside risks.

Consider a rapidly growing e-commerce business. A base case might project consistent 15% month-over-month revenue growth. However, a well-executed scenario analysis would also include:

- **Optimistic Scenario:** What if a major marketing campaign goes viral, leading to 25% month-over-month growth? What are the implications for inventory, staffing, and operational capacity?
- **Pessimistic Scenario:** What if a new competitor enters the market with aggressive pricing, or a key supply chain partner experiences significant disruption, resulting in only 5% growth or even a decline? How would this impact profitability, cash reserves, and debt covenants?

- **Most Likely Scenario:** A more conservative but still positive growth rate, perhaps 10%, considering a blend of known market factors.

By constructing these distinct financial narratives, entrepreneurs gain a panoramic view of their financial landscape. This facilitates the proactive identification of critical inflection points and the development of contingency plans. For instance, if the pessimistic scenario reveals a potential cash shortfall in six months, management can initiate actions like securing a line of credit, exploring cost-reduction measures, or delaying non-essential capital expenditures before a crisis hits. The process itself sharpens strategic thinking, compelling leaders to question their underlying assumptions about market demand, pricing elasticity, cost structures, and operational scalability. It transforms financial projections from mere numbers on a spreadsheet into strategic intelligence.

Complementary to scenario analysis is sensitivity testing, often referred to as "what-if" analysis. While scenario analysis presents a holistic picture of interconnected variables, sensitivity testing isolates the impact of changes in a single key variable on the overall financial outcome. For example, a software-as-a-service (SaaS) company might analyze how a 1% change in its annual customer churn rate impacts its

Net Present Value (NPV) or Internal Rate of Return (IRR) over a five-year period. Similarly, a manufacturing firm might test how a 5% increase in the cost of a critical raw material affects its gross profit margin.

The power of sensitivity testing lies in its ability to highlight the most impactful variables—those that, when changed, cause the most significant swings in profitability or cash flow. These are often the areas where management should focus its most rigorous attention, risk mitigation efforts, and operational improvement initiatives. If a sensitivity analysis shows that a 10% increase in customer acquisition cost (CAC) drastically reduces profitability, it signals that optimizing marketing spend and conversion rates should become a top priority. Conversely, if a 20% fluctuation in a minor operational cost has a negligible impact, it suggests that while efficiency is always good, this particular area might not warrant excessive management focus compared to more sensitive drivers. This focused approach ensures that resources and attention are directed where they will yield the greatest financial leverage.

The foundation of advanced FP&A is robust long-term financial forecasting. This extends beyond the typical one-year operational budget or the 18-month sales forecast. True long-term forecasting looks out three, five, or even ten years, projecting the business's financial performance under various strategic growth initiatives and market conditions. This is not about predicting the future with perfect accuracy, which is impossible, but about creating a rational, data-driven view of what the business could look like if certain strategic decisions are made and specific market trends materialize.

Long-Term Forecasting: A Cornerstone of Strategic Expansion

For companies eyeing significant expansion into new global markets, long-term forecasting is an indispensable tool. It involves meticulously projecting future revenues, marketing and operational expenses, capital investments for infrastructure or distribution, and the overall impact on profitability and cash flow over several years. This detailed projection is crucial for:

- **Capital Investment Decisions:** Justifying substantial capital outlays for new factories, acquisitions, or major product launches by demonstrating expected financial returns and payback periods.
- **Strategic Planning:** Guiding decisions on market entry, product development pipelines, R&D investments, and potential mergers or ac-

quisitions, quantifying the financial implications of various strategic paths.

- **Financing Needs:** Anticipating future funding requirements, enabling proactive engagement with lenders or investors with a well-defined growth plan and clear ability to service debt or provide investor returns.
- **Talent Acquisition:** Planning for future staffing needs by projecting revenue growth and operational complexity to forecast the required number and type of employees across the organization.

The process typically involves building integrated financial models that link the income statement, balance sheet, and cash flow statement. These models facilitate dynamic analysis, where changes in one area (e.g., increased marketing spend) automatically cascade and affect other financial elements (e.g., revenue growth, cost of goods sold, operating expenses, net income, and cash flow). This interconnectedness ensures internally consistent projections and a realistic portrayal of business activities.

Optimizing Financial Performance through Advanced FP&A

Beyond merely hitting targets, advanced financial planning focuses on actively optimizing financial performance, seeking ways to enhance efficiency and profitability. Key techniques include:

- **Working Capital Management:** Analyzing and optimizing accounts receivable, inventory, and accounts payable. For instance, reducing invoice collection periods can significantly boost cash flow without impacting sales, while efficient inventory management minimizes holding costs and prevents stockouts.
- **Cost Optimization:** Moving beyond simple cost-cutting to strategic cost management. This involves analyzing cost drivers, identifying process improvements to reduce waste or overhead, and evaluating the ROI of different expenditure categories.
- **Pricing Strategy Analysis:** Utilizing data analytics to understand customer price sensitivity, competitor pricing, and the impact of pricing changes on sales volume and profit margins, often employing techniques like conjoint analysis or elasticity modeling.
- **Capital Structure Optimization:** Evaluating the optimal blend of debt and equity financing to balance the cost of capital, financial risk, and control.

Proactive Financial Planning: A Strategic Imperative

The proactive approach fostered by advanced Financial Planning & Analysis (FP&A) is not an academic exercise but a strategic necessity for navigating business uncertainties. Economic downturns, regulatory changes, shifts in consumer behavior, or technological disruptions can significantly impact a company's financial health. Businesses engaged in meticulous scenario analysis, sensitivity testing, and long-term forecasting are far better equipped to anticipate, understand, and respond to these challenges.

For example, a business reliant on an imported raw material might use scenario planning to identify geopolitical events as a risk to supply and pricing. This foresight enables proactive measures like seeking alternative suppliers, exploring domestic sourcing, or investing in backward integration to control the supply chain. Such proactive stances, driven by advanced financial planning, can be critical for weathering crises.

Furthermore, advanced FP&A is vital for securing and managing external funding. Investors and lenders expect to see a clear vision for the company's future and a data-driven understanding of how their capital will generate returns. Detailed financial models, robust forecasts, and well-reasoned scenario analyses are essential for sophisticated financial discussions, demonstrating financial discipline, strategic foresight, and a commitment to maximizing shareholder value. Without this level of financial sophistication, companies may struggle to attract necessary investment or face less favorable terms from lenders.

Effective management of cash flow is vital for any business's survival and growth, regardless of its size or industry. While profitability on paper indicates success, the actual movement of money—cash flow—determines a business's ability to operate, meet obligations, and seize opportunities. Without sufficient liquidity, even profitable companies can face severe disruptions, leading to missed payroll, unpaid suppliers, and ultimately, business failure. Cash flow management is a strategic discipline that underpins an enterprise's very survival and growth potential, ensuring the right amount of cash is available at the right time for necessary operations.

At its core, cash flow management involves meticulously tracking, analyzing, and optimizing the inflow and outflow of cash. This process begins with understanding the business's cash conversion cycle—the time it takes to convert investments in inventory and other resources into cash flows from sales. A shorter cash conversion cycle generally indicates a healthier, more efficient business. This cycle is influenced by the time it takes to sell inventory, the period for customers to pay invoices (accounts receivable), and the time available to pay suppliers (accounts payable). Optimizing each of these elements is crucial.

Managing accounts receivable, the money owed by customers for goods or services already delivered, is a critical area. While extending credit can be a powerful sales tool, it also ties up cash. The longer customers take to pay, the longer cash is locked in, potentially hindering immediate operational needs or new investments. Therefore, implementing robust credit policies and diligent collection practices is essential. This starts with clearly defined payment terms for all customers, such as "due upon receipt," "net 15," "net 30," or "net 60," which reduces ambiguity and sets expectations.

Beyond clear terms, proactive communication and follow-up are vital. Promptly and accurately sending invoices is the first step, as many payment delays stem from administrative oversights like incorrect or lost invoices. Automated invoicing systems can significantly mitigate these issues, ensuring consistent and efficient invoice generation and dispatch. For customers nearing or past due dates, a structured follow-up process is necessary. This might include automated payment reminders before the due date, followed by a polite but firm call or email on the due date. Subsequent follow-ups should escalate in intensity based on the receivable's age and the customer's payment history.

Consider implementing early payment discounts. A small discount, such as 2% off if paid within 10 days ("2/10 net 30"), can incentivize faster payments. This discount cost should be weighed against the cost of carrying the receivable and the potential benefit of improved cash flow. This strategy can significantly accelerate cash inflows in certain industries or customer segments. Conversely, for consistently late-paying customers, imposing late payment fees or adjusting credit terms (e.g., requiring payment upon receipt for future transactions) may be necessary.

Thoroughly vetting new customers before extending credit is a crucial preventative measure. Performing credit checks, reviewing financial statements (for larger accounts), or requesting trade references helps identify potential credit risks. Establishing credit limits based on a customer's creditworthiness and payment history prevents overexposure to any single defaulting account. The goal is to balance sales desires with the need for timely payments, thereby protecting cash. Regularly reviewing the accounts receivable aging report, which categorizes outstanding invoices by their duration, is a non-negotiable part of cash flow management. This report highlights problematic invoices requiring immediate attention.

Equally important is the strategic management of accounts payable—the money your business owes to suppliers and vendors. While it may seem counter-intuitive, effective payable management can significantly improve cash flow. The objective is not to delay payments indefinitely, which can damage supplier relationships and incur penalties, but to utilize the payment terms offered by suppliers to your advantage. This means paying bills on time, but not necessarily before they are due, unless there is a compelling reason, such as an early payment discount.

Integrating advanced Financial Planning & Analysis (FP&A) into a company's operations demands a commitment to data integrity, analytical rigor, and a culture that embraces forward-looking financial insights. This often involves investing in appropriate financial planning software and ensuring the finance team possesses the necessary analytical skills. This investment is undeniably worthwhile. By moving beyond reactive financial management to proactive, sophisticated financial planning and analysis, entrepreneurs can build a more resilient, profitable, and strategically agile business. This approach better prepares them to seize opportunities and navigate inevitable challenges on the path to sustained success. This deep dive into financial foresight empowers leaders to make not just good decisions, but strategically optimal ones, anchored in a clear understanding of potential financial outcomes.

Optimizing Cash Flow Through Supplier Management

Effective cash flow management begins with a thorough understanding of your suppliers' payment terms. Many offer "net 30" terms, meaning payment is due within 30 days of the invoice date. By meticulously tracking these due dates and ensuring sufficient cash availability, you can sustain positive supplier relationships while retaining capital within your business for the maximum allowable period. This strategic approach provides crucial working capital for immediate operational needs.

Negotiating more favorable payment terms can also significantly benefit your business. A strong credit history and consistent payment record may enable you to secure extended terms, such as net 45 or net 60. This effectively prolongs the period you can hold onto cash without incurring penalties or jeopardizing supplier relationships, which is especially advantageous if your sales cycle exceeds your suppliers' payment cycles.

Prioritizing payments is another wise practice. Not all payables hold equal weight. Payments to essential suppliers or those offering substantial early payment discounts should be prioritized. Conversely, less critical expenses or those with extended payment terms can be scheduled closer to their due dates. Implementing a clear system for tracking payables, often integrated with accounting software, is vital to prevent missed payments or unnecessary early disbursements.

Optimizing Cash Flow Through Inventory Management

Inventory management presents a substantial opportunity to optimize cash flow. Excess inventory ties up significant capital that could be deployed elsewhere, incurring costs related to storage, insurance, obsolescence, and potential damage or spoilage. Conversely, insufficient inventory can lead to stockouts, resulting in lost sales, dissatisfied customers, and production delays. The key is to achieve a balanced inventory level that meets demand without accumulating excessive stock.

Implementing just-in-time (JIT) inventory principles, where feasible, can be a powerful strategy. This approach involves receiving goods from suppliers only as they are required for production or to fulfill customer demand. While a full JIT implementation can be challenging for businesses with unpredictable demand or unreliable supply chains, adopting elements of it can yield considerable benefits through close collaboration with suppliers for timely and reliable deliveries.

Utilizing inventory management software offers real-time visibility into stock levels, sales trends, and lead times. This data facilitates more accurate demand forecasting, enabling more strategic inventory ordering. Techniques such as the Economic Order Quantity (EOQ) model can help determine the optimal order quantity that minimizes total inventory costs by considering ordering and holding costs. However, EOQ models are based on assumptions and require adaptation to real-world conditions.

Another effective approach is ABC analysis, an inventory categorization method based on value and importance. 'A' items are high-value, critical inventory requiring strict control and frequent review. 'B' items are of moderate value and importance, while 'C' items are low-value, high-volume items that can be managed with simpler controls. By concentrating rigorous management efforts on 'A' items, you ensure the effective utilization of your most significant capital investments in inventory.

Regular physical inventory counts or cycle counting are essential to maintain accurate inventory records. Discrepancies between recorded and actual stock can lead to poor purchasing decisions and negatively impact cash flow. Identifying slow-moving or obsolete inventory is also crucial. These items represent tied-up cash and should be disposed of through discounts, liquidation, or write-offs, even if it means recognizing a loss, to free up capital and storage space.

Forecasting Cash Needs

Forecasting your cash needs is a proactive element of cash flow management. It involves projecting expected cash inflows and outflows over a specific period, typically monthly or quarterly, and then extending this forecast for at least 12 months. This cash flow forecast acts as a roadmap, indicating periods of surplus cash and, more importantly, potential cash deficits.

The process of creating a cash flow forecast begins with projecting all anticipated cash inflows. This includes sales revenue (broken down by payment terms and expected collection times), interest income, asset sales, or capital injections. It is crucial to be realistic, utilizing historical data, sales forecasts, and an understanding of customer payment behavior to estimate when cash from sales will actually be received.

Next, project all anticipated cash outflows, encompassing a wide range of expenses: cost of goods sold, salaries and wages, rent, utilities, marketing and advertising, loan repayments, taxes, insurance, and any capital expenditures or investments. Accuracy in timing is paramount. For instance, payroll is a predictable outflow, but seasonal sales might lead to fluctuating inventory purchases or marketing spend, which must be factored in.

Cash Flow Management: Ensuring Liquidity and Solvency

Effective cash flow management is crucial for a business's financial health, ensuring it can meet obligations and pursue growth.

Building a Cash Flow Forecast:

- Start with projected inflows and outflows to calculate net cash flow for each period.
- Add the net cash flow to your opening cash balance to determine the closing balance.

- Repeat for subsequent periods to build a comprehensive forecast.
- This forecast will identify potential cash surpluses for investment, debt reduction, or reserves, as well as potential shortfalls that require proactive planning.

Addressing Cash Shortfalls:

If a forecast indicates a potential shortfall, consider these options to prevent a crisis:

- **Accelerate Cash Inflows:** Expedite accounts receivable collection, offer early payment discounts, or actively pursue outstanding debts.
- **Reduce Cash Outflows:** Review and reduce discretionary expenses. This may involve negotiating better supplier terms, cutting non-essential travel, or delaying capital expenditures.
- **Secure Financing:** Arrange a line of credit or short-term loan *before* a shortfall occurs to ensure better terms and immediate access to funds.
- **Sell Underutilized Assets:** Liquidate non-critical assets for a one-time cash injection.

The Dynamic Nature of Forecasting:

A cash flow forecast is not static. Regular review and updates (ideally monthly) are essential to incorporate actual results and changing business conditions. This iterative process offers valuable insights into the accuracy of assumptions and the effectiveness of cash management strategies, allowing for informed adjustments to operational and financial plans.**Profitability Analysis: Understanding and Enhancing Wealth Generation**

While healthy cash flow ensures day-to-day operations, profitability analysis explores *why* your business generates wealth and how effectively revenue translates into profit. This involves a deep dive into your income statement, dissecting both revenue streams and associated costs.

Key Questions in Profitability Analysis:

True financial acumen lies in understanding the components that drive profit. Profitability analysis helps answer:

- Which products or services are the most significant profit contributors?
- Which customer segments are most valuable?
- Where are costs concentrated, and how can they be optimized?

Segmenting Financial Data for Actionable Insights:

Moving beyond a superficial understanding, segmenting financial data reveals actionable insights. Effective approaches include analyzing profitability by:

- Product line
- Service offering
- Customer segment
- Individual salesperson or branch location

Profitability by Product or Service Line:

Businesses typically offer diverse products/services, each with unique cost structures and market demand.

- Some may have high sales volume but low margins, while others have lower sales but higher margins.
- **Accurate Cost Allocation:**
    - **Direct Costs:** Directly attributable to production (e.g., raw materials, direct labor).
    - **Indirect Costs (Overhead):** More challenging to allocate (e.g., rent, utilities, marketing). Choose an allocation method that reasonably reflects resource con-

sumption (e.g., direct labor hours, machine hours, percentage of direct costs).

- **Calculating Profit:** Once costs are allocated, calculate gross profit (revenue minus cost of goods sold) and net profit (after allocating overhead) for each product/service.
- **Strategic Decisions:** This analysis can reveal hidden profit powerhouses or low-margin items absorbing disproportionate overhead. This knowledge enables strategic decisions regarding pricing, marketing focus, product development, and even discontinuation. For consistently unprofitable products, consider price increases, production cost reductions, or reallocation of resources to more profitable ventures.

Understanding profitability through customer segmentation is vital. Not all customers offer the same value to your business. Some customers are highly profitable—making frequent, high-margin purchases and paying promptly—while others may buy infrequently, demand extensive support, and pay late. To analyze this, track revenue by customer group (e.g., industry, company size, region, or individual key accounts) and allocate associated costs, including direct sales costs, customer service, targeted marketing, and administrative overhead. Customer Relationship Management (CRM) systems are excellent for data collection.

These insights can refine sales and marketing strategies. You might increase resources for high-value customer acquisition and retention, create tailored offerings for profitable segments, or reassess the cost-to-serve for less profitable groups. It's possible that a significant portion of your customer base contributes little to your bottom line, or even incurs losses, due to the resources required to serve them. In such cases, consider strategies like repricing services, adjusting support levels, or focusing marketing on more profitable segments.

A detailed examination of your expense structure is also crucial for profitability. Costs are typically categorized as fixed (constant regardless of volume, e.g., rent, salaries) or variable (fluctuating with activity, e.g., raw materials, sales commissions). Understanding cost behavior is key for accurate budgeting, forecasting, and pricing. The break-even point—where total revenue equals total costs—is a critical concept. Calculating this in units or sales dollars reveals the minimum performance needed to avoid losses. The formula for the break-even point in units is: Fixed Costs / (Sales Price Per Unit – Variable Cost Per Unit). The denominator, known as the contribution margin per unit, represents the revenue remaining after variable costs, which then contributes to covering fixed costs and generating profit. Analyzing contribution margin by product or service can identify the most effective items for covering fixed costs.

Cost control involves actively managing expenses to maximize profitability without sacrificing quality or future growth. This isn't about indiscriminate cuts, but intelligent decisions to reduce waste, improve efficiency, and ensure every dollar spent aligns with business objectives. A systematic approach often starts with a thorough review of all expense categories on your income statement, questioning their necessity, cost-effectiveness, and identifying areas for reduction or optimization.

The cost of goods sold (COGS) is often a significant area for cost control. For product-based businesses, this includes raw materials, direct labor, and manufacturing overhead. Key strategies include negotiating better supplier prices (e.g., volume discounts, alternative suppliers, long-term agreements). For in-house manufacturing, process improvements like Lean principles can reduce waste, rework, and improve material and labor efficiency. Inventory management is also critical. Excessive inventory incurs substantial costs (storage, insurance, obsolescence, tied-up capital). Optimizing inventory through better forecasting, just-in-time (JIT) systems, and effective stock rotation can significantly reduce holding costs and minimize losses from obsolete stock.

Operating expenses (overhead) are another prime area for cost control, encompassing rent, utilities, marketing, administrative salaries, and technology. For occupancy costs, explore lease renegotiations, downsizing office space, or shared office solutions. Energy efficiency measures (e.g., LED lighting, optimized HVAC) can reduce utility bills. For marketing, track the return on investment (ROI) for every campaign and channel, focusing spend on the most effective ones. Leveraging technology can automate administrative tasks, reducing manual effort and staffing needs. Cloud-based software, for instance, can be more cost-effective and scalable than on-premises systems. Regularly reviewing subscriptions, software licenses, and other recurring expenses can uncover savings opportunities by identifying underutilized resources or negotiating better terms.

Cost control can be significantly enhanced through benchmarking, which involves comparing your business's financial metrics and operational performance against industry standards or top competitors. This process helps identify areas where your costs are unusually high, prompting an investigation into the causes and potential solutions. For instance, if your marketing spend is a higher percentage of revenue than your peers, you may need to re-evaluate your marketing strategy.

Cultivating a cost-conscious culture throughout the organization is also essential. Employees at every level can contribute to cost control by identifying and suggesting cost-saving ideas, receiving training on efficient resource utilization, and having incentives aligned with cost-reduction goals. This empowers the workforce to actively participate in maintaining financial discipline, from simple actions like mindful office supply and energy use to more complex initiatives like process re-engineering.

Budgets and variance analysis are fundamental tools for both profitability analysis and cost control. A budget is a financial plan outlining expected revenues and expenses for a specific period. Variance analysis compares actual financial results to budgeted amounts, and any differences (variances) require investigation. A favorable variance means better-than-budgeted results (e.g., higher revenue, lower cost), while an unfavorable variance indicates worse-than-budgeted results (e.g., lower revenue, higher cost). For example, if raw material costs are higher than budgeted, analysis might reveal an unexpected price increase or inefficient material usage. Understanding these variances enables management to take corrective actions, such as renegotiating with suppliers or improving production processes. Regular budget reviews and performance meetings are crucial for staying on track and addressing deviations promptly.

Profitability analysis and cost control are ongoing processes requiring continuous attention and adaptation as markets, customer preferences, and economic conditions evolve. These analyses should be integrated into the regular financial reporting cycle, tracking key performance indicators (KPIs) for profitability (e.g., gross, operating, and net profit margins) and cost management (e.g., cost per unit, overhead absorption rates, budget variances). By diligently analyzing profitability and proactively controlling costs, businesses can build a strong financial foundation, enhance competitive advantage, and drive sustainable growth and value creation. This disciplined approach ensures revenue growth is always balanced with an understanding of underlying costs and margins, leading to a more robust and resilient business.

Achieving investment readiness is a critical stage for entrepreneurs seeking external capital for growth. This involves more than just a business plan; it's about meticulously aligning all aspects of your operation to present a compelling case to potential investors. External funding from angel investors, venture capitalists, or strategic corporate partners marks a pivotal transition to accelerated growth. Successfully navigating this process requires understanding investor expectations and proactively meeting them, transforming your business's internal narrative and financial presentation into a story that resonates with those looking for substantial returns.

The cornerstone of investment readiness is a thoroughly refined and dynamic business plan. This living blueprint articulates your company's vision, mission, market opportunity, strategy, and financial projections. For external funding, the plan must be persuasive, highlighting both the current state and future potential of the business. Investors will look for a clear understanding of the market landscape, including size, growth trends, and competitive positioning. Your go-to-market strategy, customer acquisition plan, differentiation, and scaling operations will be scrutinized. The plan must also clearly outline your management team's capabilities, as investors often prioritize the team behind the idea. Detailed financial forecasts, including revenue projections, expense budgets, cash flow statements, and balance sheets for a three- to five-year period, are essential. These projections must be realistic, supported by market research and operational assumptions, and demonstrate a clear path to profitability and a significant return on investment. Regularly updating your business plan is crucial for maintaining its relevance and credibility.

Investor-Grade Financials: The Foundation for Funding

Beyond a solid business plan, compelling financial statements are crucial for securing external funding. These must be more than just accurate; they need to be "investor-grade," meaning they exhibit a high level of detail, transparency, and adherence to accounting principles to build investor confidence. This often necessitates an audit or review by an independent accounting firm.

Key Financial Statements:

- **Income Statement:** Reveals historical performance.
- **Balance Sheet:** Reflects current financial health.
- **Cash Flow Statement:** Illustrates future financial viability.

Investors will meticulously scrutinize these to identify consistent revenue growth, healthy profit margins, efficient working capital management, and a sound capital structure.

Beyond the Basics: Deeper Dives for Investors:

Investors will also typically request:

- Detailed revenue breakdowns by product or service.
- Customer segmentation analysis.
- Comprehensive cost structures.
- Burn rate (the speed at which capital is spent before achieving positive cash flow).

Demonstrating strong financial discipline and a clear understanding of **unit economics** (the direct costs and revenues per unit) is paramount.

Industry-Specific Metrics:

- **SaaS Companies:** Investors focus on customer acquisition cost (CAC), lifetime value (LTV), churn rate, and monthly/annual recurring revenue (MRR/ARR).
- **Physical Product Businesses:** Key metrics include inventory turnover, cost of goods sold (COGS) analysis, and gross profit margins.

Ensuring these figures are readily available, clearly presented, and supported by robust underlying data is non-negotiable.

The Art of the Pitch Deck: Capturing Investor Attention

A compelling pitch deck is a critical tool for engaging investors in initial meetings. This visually engaging, condensed summary of your business plan should tell a persuasive story quickly and effectively, typically within 10-15 slides.

Essential Pitch Deck Components:

- **Title Slide:** Company name, logo, and contact information.
- **Problem Statement:** Clearly articulates the market pain point.
- **Solution:** Describes your product/service and its problem-solving capabilities.
- **Market Opportunity:** Quantifies the target market's size and growth potential.
- **Business Model:** Explains revenue generation.
- **Go-to-Market Strategy:** Your plan for reaching customers.
- **Competitive Analysis:** Highlights your unique advantages.
- **Team:** Showcases expertise and experience.
- **Financial Projections:** Demonstrates growth and profitability potential.

- **"Ask" Slide:** Specifies funding amount and intended use.

Each slide should be visually appealing with minimal text and strong graphics or data visualizations. A logical narrative flow is crucial for guiding investors and building a compelling case. Thoroughly rehearsing your pitch ensures a confident, clear, and passionate delivery, allowing you to anticipate and answer potential investor questions.

Understanding Valuation: The Worth of Your Business

Another critical aspect of preparing for external funding is understanding valuation methods. Investors will want to know how you determined your company's valuation—the agreed-upon worth of your business. Valuing private, especially early-stage, companies often involves a blend of art and science.

Common Valuation Methods:

- **Discounted Cash Flow (DCF):** Projects future cash flows and discounts them to present value.
- **Comparable Company Analysis:** Examines valuation multiples of similar publicly traded or recently acquired companies.

- **Precedent Transactions:** Reviews prices paid for similar companies in past mergers and acquisitions.
- **Asset-Based Valuation:** Focuses on the net value of a company's assets.

For startups, revenue or EBITDA (earnings before interest, taxes, depreciation, and amortization) multiples are frequently used to compare your company to similar market players.

As an entrepreneur, it's vital to have a defensible valuation supported by your company's performance, market potential, and comparable benchmarks. Be prepared to negotiate, as valuation directly impacts the equity you'll exchange for funding. Overvaluing can deter investors, while undervaluing means surrendering too much ownership. A realistic valuation demonstrates a strong understanding of your business's worth and market dynamics.

Achieving investment readiness involves more than just a strong business plan and financials; it also requires demonstrating robust operational readiness. This includes having solid legal documentation covering ownership, intellectual property (patents, trademarks, copyrights), and well-executed customer and supplier contracts. Investors will conduct thorough due diligence, scrutinizing all aspects of your business, and any discrepancies can jeopardize a deal. Therefore, maintaining clean, organized, and accessible corporate records is crucial. Establishing proper governance structures, like a board of directors or advisors, even if not legally mandated, signals maturity and good corporate practice.

Understanding the various types of funding and investors is essential for tailoring your preparation. Angel investors are typically high-net-worth individuals who invest smaller sums in early-stage companies, often offering mentorship. Venture capitalists (VCs) manage funds from limited partners, investing larger amounts in high-growth potential companies, usually at later stages. VCs expect significant returns and often take board seats, influencing company strategy. Strategic investors, such as corporations, might invest for reasons beyond financial returns, like gaining access to new technology or markets. Each investor type has distinct criteria, expectations, and processes. Thoroughly researching potential investors—understanding their investment thesis, target stages and sectors, and track record—will help you identify suitable partners and customize your pitch. Networking and building relationships with investors *before* actively seeking funding, through industry events, introductions, and online communities, can significantly enhance your success.

Ultimately, being investment-ready means presenting a well-managed, scalable, and profitable business with a clear future vision. This diligent process requires strategic thinking and a commitment to showcasing your company in the best possible light. By meticulously refining your business plan, ensuring impeccable financial statements, crafting a compelling pitch, understanding valuation, and addressing all legal and operational due diligence points, you significantly improve your ability to attract and secure the external capital needed for growth. This proactive approach not only prepares you for funding but also builds a stronger, more resilient business foundation for long-term success. It demonstrates to potential investors that you are a capable leader with a well-structured, high-potential venture ready for significant investment and subsequent growth.

The decision to reinvest profits is a pivotal strategic choice for entrepreneurs, reflecting confidence in the business's trajectory and a commitment to sustainable, long-term expansion. Once an enterprise moves beyond the initial precarious stages and begins generating consistent profits, the focus shifts from survival to acceleration. Reinvestment is not merely about parking capital; it's about strategically deploying resources to boost competitive advantage, drive innovation, and capture greater market share. This phase demands a nuanced understanding of where capital can yield the highest returns, not just financially, but also in strengthening the business's underlying capabilities and resilience. It necessitates a forward-thinking approach, proactively anticipating future market needs and positioning the company to meet them.

One of the most direct and impactful avenues for reinvestment is product development and innovation. The market is constantly evolving, and what customers love today may be obsolete tomorrow. Dedicating profits to research and development (R&D) allows a business to refine existing offerings, create new products or services, and explore adjacent markets. This could involve investing in advanced materials, cutting-edge software development, sophisticated design processes, or rigorous testing. For a technology company, R&D might mean funding new features, improving user experience, or developing a next-generation platform. For a manufacturing business, it could involve investing in R&D for more efficient production methods or environmentally friendly materials. R&D should be viewed not as a cost center, but as a vital engine for future revenue and differentiation. Early-stage reinvestment in product development can build strong intellectual property, establish brand loyalty, and create a defensible competitive moat, making the business more attractive to customers and potential acquirers.

Consider a software company that, after achieving profitability, reinvests a significant portion of its earnings into developing a mobile version of its core product. This expansion opens up a new user base and revenue stream, directly contributing to further growth and solidifying its market position. Similarly, a food and beverage company might reinvest in developing healthier, plant-based alternatives to existing product lines, responding to evolving consumer preferences and tapping into a growing market segment. The ultimate goal is to ensure that the product or service remains relevant, competitive, and consistently meets or exceeds customer expectations, thereby driving repeat business and attracting new customers.

Strategic Reinvestment for Business Growth

Businesses that have achieved initial success and profitability face crucial decisions regarding reinvestment to ensure sustained growth. These strategic choices are vital for long-term prosperity and can be categorized into several key areas:

1. Market Expansion:

Once a business has successfully established itself in an initial market, the natural progression for reinvestment is to explore new geographical territories or customer segments. This involves:

- **Geographic Expansion:** Opening new physical locations, establishing e-commerce presences in different regions, and adapting products or services to local tastes and requirements.
- **Customer Segment Diversification:** Developing tailored marketing campaigns to reach new demographics, building new distribution channels, and hiring local talent.

Market expansion requires thorough research into consumer behavior, competitive landscapes, regulatory environments, and logistical considerations. The rewards include a diversified revenue base, reduced reliance on a single market, and significant overall growth. For example, a domestic e-commerce retailer might reinvest profits to establish international operations, including localized websites and adapted marketing messages. Similarly, a consulting firm could target a related but previously untapped industry sector, diversifying its reach and impact. This strategic move is not merely about selling more of the same, but about extending the business's core value proposition.

2. Technology Upgrades and Infrastructure:

In today's digital age, outdated technology can impede efficiency, increase costs, and limit scalability. Reinvesting profits in technology is crucial for maintaining a competitive edge and involves:

- **Hardware and Software Enhancements:** Upgrading IT systems, implementing enterprise resource planning (ERP) systems for integrated functions, and enhancing customer relationship management (CRM) software.
- **Automation and Analytics:** Investing in advanced analytics tools for deeper data insights and automating repetitive tasks to free up human capital for strategic work.

Modernizing technology allows businesses to handle increasing workloads, process information effectively, and improve operational efficiency and productivity. A manufacturing company might invest in robotics, while a service-based business could upgrade communication platforms or cybersecurity measures. Such upgrades not only reduce operational costs but also enhance product/service quality, improve customer satisfaction, and provide a robust foundation for future growth. A logistics company, for instance, could reinvest in route optimization software and real-time tracking to improve delivery times and reduce fuel costs.

3. Talent Acquisition and Development:

People are a company's most valuable asset, and reinvesting in talent is critical for long-term success. As businesses grow, so does the need for specialized skills and a highly capable workforce. This area of reinvestment includes:

- **Hiring Top Talent:** Acquiring individuals with expertise in key areas such as marketing, finance, operations, engineering, and customer service to support effective scaling.
- **Employee Development:** Investing in existing employees through training programs, professional development opportunities, and leadership initiatives. This can include sponsoring certifications, offering advanced workshops, providing mentorship programs, or tuition reimbursement.

A skilled and motivated workforce drives innovation, productivity, and customer satisfaction. A growing e-commerce business might build an in-house digital marketing team to gain greater control over its brand messaging. A professional services firm could invest in advanced training for consultants in emerging fields, ensuring cutting-edge solutions for clients. Investing in people directly enhances the company's capacity to execute its strategy, adapt to change, and achieve its long-term vision.

4. Marketing and Brand Building:

For sustained growth, especially as a company matures, reinvestment in marketing and brand building is essential. While initial efforts focus on customer acquisition, later stages emphasize solidifying market position and attracting higher-value customers through:

- **Brand Development:** Investing in content marketing, public relations, social media engagement, influencer collaborations, and strategic advertising campaigns.
- **Customer Loyalty Programs:** Creating and enhancing programs that foster trust and emotional connections with customers, leading to increased lifetime value and reduced price sensitivity.
- **Thought Leadership:** Positioning the company as an authority in its industry through various marketing initiatives.

Building a strong brand differentiates a company from competitors. A direct-to-consumer (DTC) brand might reinvest earnings in high-quality storytelling content, sponsoring industry events, or launching sophisticated loyalty programs. These efforts contribute significantly to a company's sustained growth and market leadership.

Strategic Reinvestment for Business Growth and Stability

To achieve sustained growth and competitive advantage, businesses must strategically reinvest their profits. This involves more than just generating sales; it's about building a strong brand, optimizing operations, and fortifying financial systems.

Building a Strong Brand and Cultivating Relationships:

Effective marketing and brand building are crucial for long-term success. Reinvesting in these areas strengthens brand appeal, encourages repeat purchases, and cultivates enduring customer relationships. For instance, a B2B software company might invest in white papers, case studies, and webinars to establish itself as a thought leader, attracting qualified leads and building credibility.

Enhancing Operational Efficiency and Supply Chain Management:

Streamlining operations and supply chain management can lead to significant cost savings and improved delivery times, especially for businesses dealing with physical products. This could involve:

- **Inventory Management:** Investing in better systems to ensure popular items are in stock and minimize overstocking.
- **Supplier Relationships:** Negotiating favorable terms and diversifying the supplier base to mitigate risks.
- **Logistics Technology:** Implementing new technologies to improve quality control, reduce waste, and enhance responsiveness to market demands.

For example, a restaurant chain could reinvest in an integrated point-of-sale (POS) system that connects with inventory and ordering platforms, improving efficiency and reducing errors.

Strengthening Financial Systems and Reporting:

As a company grows, its financial complexity increases. Reinvesting in robust financial systems is essential for maintaining health, ensuring compliance, and providing accurate data for strategic decision-making. This includes:

- **Accounting Software:** Investing in enterprise-level software for advanced budgeting, forecasting, and financial analysis.
- **Financial Professionals:** Hiring experienced professionals.
- **Internal Controls:** Establishing strong internal controls.

Enhanced financial reporting offers clearer insights into profitability, cost structures, and ROI, enabling more informed capital allocation.

Timing, Scale, and Continuous Monitoring:

Crucially, the timing and scale of reinvestment deployments must be carefully considered. Not all opportunities are equal, and decisions should be guided by a thorough analysis of potential returns, risks, and alignment with strategic goals. It's often beneficial to diversify reinvestment across several key areas to mitigate risks and strengthen multiple facets of the business simultaneously.

Furthermore, the scale of reinvestment should be calibrated against the company's cash flow and profitability. While aggressive reinvestment can accelerate growth, overextending financial resources can jeopardize stability. A balanced approach, often involving phased investments and continuous performance monitoring, is usually the most prudent. Regularly reviewing the effectiveness of strategies and making adjustments based on data and market feedback is vital for optimal capital deployment, sustained growth, and competitive advantage. This iterative process of investment, measurement, and refinement is fundamental to building a resilient and thriving enterprise.

NINE

BUILDING RESILIENCE AND ADAPTING TO CHANGE

The entrepreneurial journey is rarely straightforward; it's a dynamic, often turbulent path filled with unexpected challenges, market shifts, and deep uncertainty. While strategic planning, strong financial management, and innovative product development are vital for a successful business, the entrepreneur's mindset is the fundamental basis for all these elements. Developing a resilient entrepreneurial mindset is not just beneficial, but essential for navigating inevitable difficulties and emerging stronger, more capable, and not just intact. This proactive cultivation of mental toughness enables entrepreneurs to confront adversity, learn from mistakes, and maintain progress even in difficult circumstances. It is the inner drive that sustains perseverance, fuels adaptability, and fosters unwavering belief in the ultimate vision, even when external factors challenge it.

At its core, resilience in entrepreneurship is about the ability to recover from setbacks. This doesn't mean avoiding failure—which is often an essential teacher—but rather developing the psychological and emotional tools to constructively process setbacks and re-engage with challenges with renewed energy. A key component of this mindset is embracing a growth-oriented perspective. Unlike a fixed mindset, which sees abilities and intelligence as unchangeable, a growth mindset views challenges as opportunities for learning and development. When a product launch fails, a sales target is missed, or a crucial partnership dissolves, an entrepreneur with a growth mindset doesn't see it as a personal failing. Instead, they treat it as valuable data, asking: What can I learn from this? How can I adjust my strategy? What new skills do I need? This continuous learning process drives adaptation. Many entrepreneurs have faced product recalls, intense competition, or regulatory hurdles; their ability to analyze the situation, extract lessons, and pivot their business strategy directly reflects a growth mindset. Rather than being defeated by a failed product, they might analyze consumer feedback to refine the next version, understanding that initial disappointment is a stepping stone, not a dead end. This outlook shifts focus from blame to improvement, transforming potential crises into catalysts for innovation and progress. It involves seeing oneself as continually evolving and improving, rather than already defined.

Another vital aspect of a resilient entrepreneurial mindset is developing emotional regulation and stress management. The intense pressure of entrepreneurship can lead to burnout, anxiety, and decision fatigue. Therefore, effective strategies for managing stress are crucial. This can include incorporating mindfulness practices, such as meditation or deep breathing, into daily routines. These techniques help entrepreneurs stay present, reduce rumination on past failures or future worries, and respond to challenges with greater clarity and less reactivity. Regular physical activity is also a powerful stress reliever, releasing endorphins and improving cognitive function. Beyond these personal practices, establishing healthy boundaries between work and personal life is essential. While dedication is important, sacrificing well-being for the business's sake is unsustainable. Entrepreneurs must learn to delegate, say no, and schedule guilt-free downtime. Building a supportive network of peers, mentors, and friends also provides a crucial outlet for stress and a source of encouragement. For example, an entrepreneur facing a critical funding round might experience immense pressure. By engaging in regular exercise and mindfulness, they can approach investor meetings with a calmer demeanor, articulate their vision more effectively, and negotiate better, rather than being overwhelmed by anxiety. This emotional regulation enables more rational decision-making, even under high pressure, which is critical when stakes are highest.

The Resilient Entrepreneurial Mindset

Perseverance: Beyond Stubbornness

Successful entrepreneurs demonstrate perseverance that transcends mere stubbornness. It's a tenacious commitment to a vision, coupled with the flexibility to adapt. This informed persistence, rooted in a deep belief in the value proposition, allows them to push forward despite rejections, funding issues, or superior competitor products. When a sales pitch fails, a resilient entrepreneur analyzes feedback, refines their approach, and tries again, viewing each "no" as a step closer to "yes." This iterative process is crucial in sales, product development, and strategic partnerships, distinguishing those who succeed from those who give up. The countless hours spent refining plans and prototypes require grit, an internal drive to overcome multiple setbacks, often cultivated by conquering smaller challenges early on, building confidence for larger obstacles.

Adaptive Strategies for Overcoming Setbacks

A resilient mindset is characterized by developing adaptive strategies for inevitable setbacks. The entrepreneur's response dictates whether a setback is a temporary blip or a catastrophic failure. This involves a structured problem-solving approach: acknowledging the reality without despair, gathering information, analyzing root causes, identifying solutions, and creating a decisive action plan. Experimentation and learning from results are key, whether testing marketing approaches, reconfiguring product features, or exploring alternative distribution channels. Agility and responsiveness to new information are paramount. For example, a failed marketing campaign should lead to analyzing performance metrics, hypothesizing underperformance, and adjusting specific elements before a revised launch. This methodical, adaptable approach builds a robust capacity to navigate uncertainty.

Maintaining Motivation and a Positive Outlook

Sustaining motivation and a positive outlook amidst entrepreneurship's inherent volatility is fundamental. This isn't about perpetual cheerfulness, but actively cultivating optimism and purpose. Reconnecting with the initial "why" through journaling, revisiting mission statements, or visualizing the future can be powerful motivators. Celebrating small wins—securing a client, positive feedback, or new processes—boosts morale and reinforces the value of effort. Surrounding oneself with supportive co-founders, employees, mentors, or fellow entrepreneurs creates an encouraging environment. Negative influences quickly erode motivation, making it crucial to curate social and professional circles. Engaging with positive influences, such as entrepreneurs who have overcome similar downturns, serves as a powerful antidote to discouragement.

Self-Awareness and Emotional Intelligence

The entrepreneurial mindset necessitates developing self-awareness and emotional intelligence. Understanding one's strengths, weaknesses, biases, and emotional triggers allows for effective management, enabling rational and constructive responses over fear or ego-driven reactions. Emotional intelligence—understanding and managing one's own emotions and influencing others'—is vital for effective leadership, strong team dynamics, and positive customer relationships. An entrepreneur who empathizes with their team, provides constructive feedback, and inspires confidence fosters a productive and loyal workforce. Similarly, understanding and responding to customer needs builds lasting relationships and brand loyalty. These skills are developed through feedback, self-reflection, and empathetic communication. For example, recognizing a defensive reaction to critical feedback allows an entrepreneur to practice open listening and clarifying questions, improving dialogue and product.

Proactive Risk Management

Resilience in entrepreneurship is tied to proactive risk management, moving beyond reactive crisis management. This continuous process involves identifying threats, assessing likelihood and impact, and developing mitigation strategies before issues materialize. This forward-thinking approach anticipates market shifts, technological advancements, and competitive pressures, transforming potential disruptions into manageable challenges. Examples include diversifying supplier bases to reduce reliance on a single entity or investing in robust cybersecurity measures before a breach occurs. This foresight and investment in preventative measures build an inherent buffer against unforeseen circumstances, shifting focus from firefighting to strategic preparedness, and enabling businesses to weather storms confidently. This proactive approach also extends to financial planning, ensuring adequate cash reserves and exploring funding options for flexibility during uncertainty.

Embracing and Adapting to Change

The entrepreneurial journey is characterized by constant change, making embracing and adapting to it a fundamental attribute of a resilient entrepreneur. This involves viewing change as an opportunity for innovation and growth, not a threat. Entrepreneurs who adapt quickly to shifting market dynamics, evolving customer preferences, or new technologies will thrive. This often requires letting go of outdated strategies or products and embracing new approaches. Staying informed about industry trends, seeking new information, and being open to experimentation are crucial. For example, businesses that quickly established an online presence and adapted to e-commerce prospered more than those that resisted. The entrepreneurial mindset encourages a proactive approach to change, anticipating shifts and positioning the business to capitalize on them through training, new business models, or pivoting product offerings to meet emerging demands.

Building a resilient entrepreneurial mindset is an ongoing journey, demanding continuous effort, consistent practice, and a strong dedication to personal and professional development. By cultivating a growth mindset, managing stress effectively, demonstrating unwavering perseverance, employing structured problem-solving, maintaining a positive outlook, fostering self-awareness, proactively managing risks, and embracing change, entrepreneurs can develop the inner strength needed to overcome business challenges. This internal fortitude is a crucial competitive advantage, enabling entrepreneurs to confidently and agilely navigate the complexities of the business world with an enduring spirit.

The entrepreneurial path inherently involves navigating uncertainty. While innovation and strategic vision are vital, a robust approach to risk management is essential for sustained success. This isn't about succumbing to fear, but rather systematically identifying, assessing, and mitigating potential threats that could derail promising ventures. Proactive risk management transforms potential disruptions into manageable challenges, ensuring long-term stability and business continuity, building resilience into the company's very foundation.

A cornerstone of effective risk management is the thorough identification of potential threats. This requires a critical examination of every aspect of the business, both internal and external. Financial risks are often a primary concern, encompassing everything from cash flow problems and unexpected increases in material costs to currency fluctuations or the sudden withdrawal of investments. For example, a manufacturing firm relying on imported components could face significant financial strain from new trade tariffs or unfavorable exchange rate shifts. Similarly, a startup seeking venture capital could experience a major setback if funding is delayed or canceled due to shifts in investor sentiment. This identification process necessitates scrutinizing all revenue streams, expense categories, and financial projections for vulnerabilities, including understanding debt covenants, interest rate changes, and seasonal income dips. A comprehensive financial risk audit should also consider scenarios like client payment defaults or operational disruptions leading to unforeseen costs.

Beyond financial vulnerabilities, operational risks are equally critical, encompassing issues inherent in daily business operations. These include supply chain problems, equipment failures, quality control lapses, or human error. For a food service business, a contaminated ingredient, refrigeration breakdown, or hygiene protocol failure can lead to product recalls, reputational damage, and legal liabilities. For a tech company, a server outage, data breach, or critical software bug can halt operations and alienate customers. Identifying operational risks involves mapping out every process from procurement to customer service and pinpointing potential failure points. This means asking: What if our primary supplier fails? What if key machinery breaks down? Where are the single points of failure in our IT infrastructure? For a logistics company, vehicle breakdowns, driver shortages, or accidents are significant operational concerns. Meticulous documentation and staff engagement are crucial for uncovering these threats, as is considering risks associated with scaling, where existing processes may become strained.

Market risks represent another broad category of threats stemming from changes in the external market environment that impact demand, competition, or consumer behavior. Shifts in consumer preferences can quickly render products obsolete, as seen with the rise of streaming services disrupting physical media. Intense competition can erode profit margins, especially from new entrants with disruptive technology or lower cost structures. Economic downturns can reduce consumer spending, impacting sales across sectors. Technological advancements, like artificial intelligence, can create opportunities but also threaten businesses that fail to adapt. Identifying market risks requires continuous monitoring of industry trends, competitor activities, economic indicators, and evolving consumer sentiment. This includes market research, industry conferences, and active customer engagement to understand changing needs. Retail businesses need to understand demographic shifts and new retail formats, while renewable energy companies must be aware of evolving government regulations, subsidies, and technological innovations.

Legal and regulatory risks are also significant, arising from non-compliance with laws, regulations, or contractual obligations. Failure to comply with data privacy laws like GDPR or CCPA can result in hefty fines and reputational damage. Employment law violations can lead to lawsuits and penalties. Intellectual property infringement can result in costly legal battles. Environmental regulations, zoning laws, and industry-specific compliance requirements add further complexity. Identifying these risks requires a thorough understanding of the legal landscape relevant to the business's industry and location, often necessitating consultation with legal professionals. A pharmaceutical company, for instance, must navigate complex regulatory approvals. A small online retailer needs to understand consumer protection and online sales regulations. The identification process should also include a review of all existing contracts, licenses, and permits.

Once threats are identified, the next crucial step is to assess their likelihood and potential impact. This informed estimation process helps prioritize risks. Likelihood can range from "highly improbable" to "almost certain," and impact from "negligible" to "catastrophic." For example, a natural disaster might have a low likelihood but devastating impact, while a minor inefficiency might occur frequently but have minimal impact. This assessment can be qualitative (expert judgment, historical data) or quantitative (statistical modeling, financial projections). A risk matrix, which visually plots risks by likelihood and impact, is a common tool for prioritization. High-likelihood, high-impact risks demand immediate and robust mitigation strategies, while low-likelihood, low-impact risks might be accepted or monitored with less urgency. The goal is to effectively allocate resources, focusing on threats that pose the greatest danger to the business's survival and success. For instance, a company relying on a single key supplier might assess a moderate likelihood of disruption but an extremely high impact, immediately flagging it as a critical risk requiring a mitigation plan.

Implementing and Adapting Risk Mitigation Strategies

Once risks are identified and assessed, the critical next step is to develop and implement proactive mitigation strategies. This transforms theoretical threats into concrete action plans.

Mitigating Specific Risk Types:

- **Financial Risks:** Build substantial cash reserves, diversify funding sources (e.g., multiple banks or investors), and employ hedging strategies against currency or interest rate fluctuations.
- **Operational Risks:** Develop robust contingency plans, including alternative suppliers, redundant systems, strong quality control processes, and comprehensive employee training to minimize human error. For example, a business relying on specialized machinery might secure a rapid repair service contract or invest in a backup unit.
- **Market Risks:** Diversify by expanding product lines, targeting new customer segments, or exploring new geographic markets. Agility and the ability to pivot the business model in response to changing market conditions are also crucial.
- **Legal and Regulatory Risks:** Ensure rigorous adherence to compliance standards. This

includes regular employee training on relevant laws, clear internal policies, periodic audits, and investment in legal expertise (in-house or external). Companies handling sensitive data, for instance, must implement stringent security measures and regularly update privacy policies. Contract management systems are vital for reviewing, documenting, and monitoring agreements.

Developing Comprehensive Contingency Plans:

Contingency plans are essential for high-impact events, outlining specific steps to minimize disruption and facilitate swift recovery.

- **Business Continuity Plans:** Detail procedures for resuming operations after crises like natural disasters, including alternative work sites, communication protocols, and data recovery strategies.
- **Crisis Communication Plans:** Outline how to communicate with stakeholders (employees, customers, investors, public) during a crisis to manage information flow and maintain trust.

The effectiveness of these plans depends on regular review, testing, and updating. Simulations and tabletop exercises help identify weaknesses before a real crisis, such as a retail chain conducting a simulated product recall.

Fostering a Culture of Risk Awareness:

Beyond specific strategies, cultivating a company-wide culture of risk awareness is vital.

- Empower employees at all levels to identify and report potential risks without fear.
- Encourage open communication about challenges and near misses for valuable insights.
- Provide regular training on risk management principles and company-specific mitigation strategies.

This shared responsibility fosters a resilient organization where problems are addressed collectively and proactively.

Continuous Risk Management and Adaptability:

Risk management is an ongoing, iterative process, not a one-time exercise. The business environment constantly evolves, bringing new threats and changing existing ones.

- Regularly review and update the risk management framework.
- Reassess identified risks and identify new threats.
- Refine mitigation strategies to ensure continuous improvement.

This cycle ensures the business remains adaptable and well-prepared, safeguarding long-term viability and fostering trust. It allows businesses to not just react to threats, but proactively withstand and even capitalize on them, turning adversity into opportunities for growth. This ongoing vigilance distinguishes successful, enduring businesses.

Adapting to a Shifting Entrepreneurial Landscape:

To thrive, entrepreneurs must cultivate an instinctive ability to adapt to market shifts and technological advancements. This requires a proactive, forward-looking mindset that anticipates and even shapes these evolutions. Agile businesses that can fluidly adjust strategies, operations, and offerings in response to trends secure relevance and sustained growth. The ability to pivot, embrace new technologies, and understand evolving market needs is an imperative for success.

Continuous Monitoring of Industry Dynamics:

Adaptability is built on continuous monitoring of industry dynamics. This involves a deep dive into:

- Macro-economic forces.
- Subtle shifts in consumer sentiment.
- The trajectory of technological innovation.

For example, a retail business must be acutely aware of the dominance of e-commerce, demand for personalized experiences, and impact of data analytics. Failure to adapt, such as by neglecting online sales, can lead to significant market share loss and diminished profitability. Retail giants slow to adapt to the online revolution struggled or faded. Conversely, businesses that invested in online presence, embraced data-driven personalization, and experimented with new delivery models thrived. Proactive engagement with market trends helps identify threats early and spot nascent opportunities.

Navigating the Ever-Evolving Business Landscape: The Art of Adaptation

In today's rapidly changing business environment, adaptability is paramount for sustained success. Businesses face relentless forces of change, particularly from technological advancements, which can either propel them forward or leave them behind. The key lies in understanding and embracing these shifts, fostering an innovative culture, and developing a keen sense of foresight.

Embracing Technological Innovation

The pace of innovation is unprecedented, with new tools, platforms, and methodologies emerging constantly. Artificial intelligence (AI), for instance, is revolutionizing various industries, from customer service and marketing to manufacturing and logistics. Businesses that explore AI's potential to automate processes, enhance customer experiences, or provide deeper data insights will gain a significant competitive edge. Examples include AI-powered chatbots for 24/7 customer support and AI-driven analytics for personalized marketing campaigns. Similarly, for software development companies, embracing agile methodologies and cloud computing is crucial for faster development cycles, greater scalability, and robust collaboration. Companies clinging to outdated practices risk falling behind in speed to market and responsiveness to evolving customer demands.

Cultivating a Culture of Experimentation and Learning

Beyond adopting new technologies, embracing innovation also means fostering a culture that encourages experimentation and learning from both successes and failures. Startups often have an inherent advantage due to their flexibility, allowing them to iterate and adapt more quickly than larger corporations burdened by legacy systems. However, even large organizations can cultivate this adaptive spirit by empowering employees to suggest new ideas, test unproven concepts, and learn from initiatives that don't pan out as expected. A crucial aspect of this is de-stigmatizing failure, encouraging calculated risks. For example, a food manufacturing company might allocate a small budget for its R&D team to explore novel ingredient combinations or sustainable packaging, understanding that insights gained, even without immediate product launches, can inform future strategies and foster continuous improvement.

The Power of Pivoting and Foresight

The concept of "pivoting" is central to adapting to market shifts. A pivot involves making a significant change to core elements of a business model in response to new information or market dynamics, rather than a complete overhaul. This could mean changing target customer segments, altering product offerings, shifting marketing strategies, or reconfiguring revenue models. Successful pivots are data-driven, questioning existing assumptions and being open to fundamentally different approaches, as demonstrated by Dropbox's evolution from a file-syncing service to a comprehensive productivity platform.

Furthermore, entrepreneurs must develop foresight – not just understanding current trends but anticipating future market directions. This requires engaging with industry thought leaders, participating in foresight workshops, and conducting scenario planning exercises. By exploring multiple plausible future scenarios, businesses can develop robust strategies that succeed across a range of potential outcomes. For instance, an automotive manufacturer planning for different futures (e.g., electric vehicle dominance vs. hybrid prevalence) makes the company more resilient to disruptive changes.

Global Dynamics and Sustainable Practices

The interconnectedness of the global economy also plays a crucial role in market shifts. Geopolitical events, trade policies, and international economic fluctuations can have ripple effects across industries.

Businesses reliant on global supply chains, for example, might need to diversify their supplier base to mitigate risks. Additionally, the increasing focus on sustainability and Environmental, Social, and Governance (ESG) factors is a significant market shift. Consumers and investors are increasingly demanding responsible and ethical business operations. Companies embracing sustainable practices not only meet these demands but also unlock new market opportunities and enhance brand reputation, as seen with fashion brands adopting ethical sourcing.

Building a Resilient and Agile Enterprise

Building a resilient and adaptable business requires continuous learning and a willingness to step outside of comfort zones. This means investing in employee training and development to equip the workforce with necessary skills for new technologies and evolving demands. It also involves fostering a culture of curiosity, empowering employees to explore new ideas and challenge the status quo. When employees are engaged in adaptation, they become powerful allies for sustained relevance and growth. This proactive embrace of change, driven by market understanding and a forward-thinking approach to technology, distinguishes enduring enterprises.

Adaptability extends to operational structures as well. Flexible organizational models, such as fluid, project-based teams, allow companies to reallocate resources and reconfigure teams more easily in response to changing priorities or market opportunities. For a marketing agency, this might mean forming specialized task forces to explore emerging social media platforms or AI-driven advertising tools. This ability to quickly form and dissolve teams is a powerful engine for agility.

Finally, embracing lean operational principles can help businesses reduce waste, improve efficiency, and increase their capacity to respond to market fluctuations without incurring significant overhead. A manufacturing company adopting lean principles can optimize production processes to quickly adapt to changes in product demand or introduce new variations with minimal disruption, creating a business that is not only responsive but also cost-effective in its adaptations. The entrepreneur who masters this art of adaptation will not only survive inevitable shifts but will find them to be fertile ground for innovation and expansion, ensuring their business remains a leader in its field for years to come.

Digital Transformation and Data-Driven Adaptation

In today's dynamic market, the digital transformation of business processes is not merely an option but a necessity. Businesses that lag in adopting digital tools for communication, collaboration, customer relationship management (CRM), and operational management face a significant disadvantage. Cloud-based solutions, for instance, offer unparalleled flexibility and scalability, enabling businesses to access data and applications anytime, anywhere, and to seamlessly adjust their IT infrastructure as demands evolve. This stands in stark contrast to outdated, rigid on-premise IT systems that demanded substantial capital investment and were cumbersome to modify. A sales team empowered by a robust, cloud-powered CRM system can access real-time customer data, efficiently manage leads, and collaborate effortlessly, even when working remotely. This digital empowerment fosters not just efficiency but a more connected, informed, and responsive organization.

Beyond digital tools, the effective leveraging of data analytics is paramount. Businesses capable of collecting, analyzing, and interpreting data from diverse sources—customer interactions, market trends, and operational performance—are better positioned to make informed decisions and identify growth opportunities. For an e-commerce business, understanding customer purchasing patterns, website navigation, and marketing campaign effectiveness through data analytics is crucial for optimizing the customer journey and boosting sales. The insights gleaned from data can inform every aspect from product development to marketing messaging, ensuring that all business adaptations are data-driven and strategically sound.

The Entrepreneurial Mindset: A Catalyst for Adaptation

Ultimately, the entrepreneur's mindset is the most crucial factor in navigating market shifts and technological advancements. A growth mindset, characterized by a belief in the ability to learn and improve, is indispensable. Entrepreneurs with this mindset view challenges as opportunities for growth and development, rather than insurmountable obstacles. They exhibit curiosity, embrace new ideas, and are committed to investing time and resources in acquiring new knowledge and skills. This personal dedication to learning translates into a business that is more likely to embrace change and perceive adaptation as an ongoing evolutionary process, rather than a burdensome obligation. It involves cultivating a company culture where learning is not just encouraged but deeply embedded in daily operations, where employees are provided resources and opportunities to stay current, and where leadership consistently champions innovation and change. This relentless pursuit of learning and improvement, combined with a strategic understanding of market dynamics, is the hallmark of an entrepreneur destined for long-term success in an ever-evolving world.

Building Resilience: Crisis Management and Business Continuity

The unpredictable nature of the entrepreneurial journey demands a forward-thinking approach that extends beyond growth and adaptation to include safeguarding the enterprise against unforeseen disruptions. While cultivating agility to navigate market shifts and technological advancements is critical, equally important is the establishment of comprehensive strategies for crisis management and business continuity. These two aspects—proactive adaptation and robust resilience—are intrinsically linked. A business that can anticipate and respond to evolving market needs is more likely to be prepared for the shocks that can derail even well-established operations. Conversely, a business with strong crisis management and business continuity plans will possess the stability and operational capacity to pivot and adapt more effectively when external forces demand it.

At its core, crisis management is about preparedness and a structured, coordinated response to events that threaten to disrupt normal business operations, reputation, or even the company's existence. These events can range from natural disasters (floods, earthquakes) and technological failures (cyberattacks, system outages) to human-caused incidents (workplace violence, product recalls) or economic downturns. The immediate aftermath of such an event can be chaotic, marked by uncertainty, fear, and a rapid escalation of problems. Without a predefined plan, responses can be ad-hoc, reactive, and ultimately ineffective, leading to prolonged downtime, significant financial losses, reputational damage, and, in worst-case scenarios, business failure. Therefore, a well-articulated crisis management plan serves as a vital roadmap, guiding decision-making and actions during what is typically the most stressful period for any organization.

Developing such a plan begins with a thorough risk assessment. This involves identifying potential crises, evaluating their likelihood, and understanding their potential severity. For a tech startup, critical risks might include a denial-of-service (DoS) attack or a data breach exposing sensitive customer information. For a small manufacturing firm, it could be a fire destroying a key production facility or a disruption in essential raw material supply due to geopolitical instability. Each business must conduct a rigorous analysis, considering its specific industry, operational dependencies, geographical location, and customer base. This assessment should be an ongoing process, revisited regularly to account for new emerging threats and evolving business circumstances.

Once potential crises are identified, the next crucial step is to formulate specific response strategies for each. This involves designating a crisis management team, outlining clear roles and responsibilities, and establishing communication protocols. The crisis management team should comprise key individuals from various departments—operations, communications, legal, finance, IT, and human resources—ensuring diverse expertise to address the multifaceted challenges crises present. This team must be empowered to make quick and effective decisions under pressure. Communication is arguably the most critical element of crisis management. A clear, transparent, and timely communication strategy is essential for managing internal stakeholders (employees), external stakeholders (customers, suppliers, investors, regulators), and the public. This includes having pre-approved statement templates, identifying key spokespersons, and establishing multiple communication channels that can be immediately activated. For instance, in the event of a product recall, the communication plan must detail how customers will be informed, provide clear instructions for affected products, and outline steps being taken to rectify the situation. Equally important is internal communication; employees need to be kept informed and reassured to maintain morale and ensure their safety.

A business continuity plan (BCP) is a vital complement to a crisis management plan. While crisis management addresses immediate responses, a BCP focuses on the long-term goal of maintaining essential business functions during and after disruptions, ultimately aiming for a swift return to normal operations. Essentially, a BCP comprises policies and procedures designed to ensure an organization can continue delivering products or services at acceptable, predefined levels following an incident. This involves identifying critical functions, understanding necessary resources, and developing alternative methods if primary systems or resources become unavailable.

Developing a BCP typically involves several key phases, starting with a business impact analysis (BIA). This systematic process evaluates the potential effects of an interruption to critical business operations due to a disaster, accident, or emergency. The BIA helps prioritize functions based on their criticality and the potential impact of their disruption. For example, a Software-as-a-Service (SaaS) company would identify core service delivery as a critical function with minimal downtime tolerance, while internal HR administration might have a higher tolerance for temporary disruption. Understanding these priorities guides resource allocation and the development of appropriate recovery strategies.

Based on the BIA, business continuity strategies are developed to mitigate the impact of disruptions and ensure critical operations continue. For instance, if a primary data center becomes inoperable, a strategy might involve activating a backup data center remotely or using cloud-based disaster recovery services. For businesses reliant on physical premises, this could mean alternate work sites or robust remote work capabilities. Supply chain disruptions can be addressed by diversifying suppliers, increasing critical component inventory, or identifying alternative transportation routes. The key is to have prearranged, tested solutions ready for deployment.

A crucial BCP component is the disaster recovery (DR) plan, which specifically addresses the IT infrastructure and data needed to support critical business functions. This includes strategies for data backup and restoration, system recovery, and network connectivity. Regular testing of DR plans is essential, as an untested plan is merely theoretical. Testing identifies weaknesses, validates backup systems, and trains IT personnel. Tests can range from tabletop exercises to full-scale simulations, providing invaluable lessons for refining the plan's reliability.

Beyond IT, human resources and personnel continuity are equally vital. A BCP must consider employee safety and well-being during a crisis, facilitate their return to work, and manage workforce availability if a significant portion of the team is affected. This might involve cross-training, establishing emergency communication systems, or providing support services. The human element is often the most unpredictable aspect of any crisis, and a well-considered plan can significantly mitigate the impact on the workforce and their ability to contribute to recovery efforts.

Furthermore, financial continuity must be addressed, including access to emergency funds, understanding insurance coverage, and managing cash flow during periods of disrupted revenue. Knowing insurance policies, their coverage, and how to initiate claims quickly is critical for recovery. Establishing relationships with financial institutions beforehand can streamline access to credit or emergency loans if needed.

Implementing a BCP is an ongoing process of management and refinement, requiring continuous leadership commitment, regular employee training, and periodic reviews and updates. As businesses evolve, so too must their continuity strategies, adapting to new technologies, markets, and risk landscapes. Therefore, the BCP should be integrated into the company's strategic planning and risk management frameworks, serving as a living document reflecting the business's current state and operating environment.

An effective crisis management and business continuity strategy offers a significant competitive advantage. Businesses that effectively weather disruptions are often perceived as more reliable and stable by customers and partners, maintaining trust and loyalty through service continuity and transparent communication. Moreover, developing these plans can uncover inefficiencies or vulnerabilities, leading to operational improvements beyond crisis preparedness. For example, a thorough BIA might reveal a single point of failure in a critical supply chain, prompting proactive diversification of sourcing.

Building Business Resilience: A Strategic Imperative

Building resilience through robust crisis management and business continuity planning is not just a defensive tactic; it's a strategic necessity for long-term entrepreneurial success. It means acknowledging the inherent uncertainties of the business world and proactively preparing to navigate them. By investing time and resources in identifying potential threats, developing clear response protocols, and ensuring essential operations can continue, entrepreneurs significantly increase their chances of not only surviving unexpected challenges but emerging stronger and more agile. This dual focus on adapting to anticipated changes and preparing for unforeseen disruptions forms the bedrock of a truly resilient and enduring enterprise.

Interdependencies and a Holistic View

Effective planning requires a clear understanding of internal business interdependencies and external partnerships. For instance, a retail business relies on logistics providers for deliveries; a disruption to that provider could directly impact the retailer's ability to serve customers. Therefore, continuity plans must extend to key suppliers and service providers, assessing their resilience and establishing backup arrangements or service level agreements with continuity provisions. This holistic view ensures the resilience of the entire ecosystem supporting the business.

Cultivating a Culture of Preparedness

The cultural aspect of crisis preparedness is paramount. A company culture that embraces transparency, open communication, and a shared sense of responsibility for preparedness will be far more effective in implementing and executing crisis management and business continuity plans. When employees understand the importance of these plans, feel empowered to report potential issues, and are trained on their roles during an emergency, the entire organization becomes more resilient. Leadership plays a critical role in fostering this culture by actively championing these initiatives, allocating necessary resources, and ensuring preparedness is an ongoing priority, not a mere compliance exercise. Regular drills, scenario-based training, and post-incident reviews are essential for embedding a preparedness mindset within the organizational DNA. This proactive approach transforms potential vulnerabilities into strengths, enabling businesses to face the inevitable challenges of the entrepreneurial landscape with confidence and a well-defined strategy.

Embracing Failure: A Cornerstone of Resilience

The entrepreneurial journey is rarely a straightforward ascent; it is a dynamic landscape dotted with peaks of success and valleys of disappointment. While triumphs are often celebrated, the most profound and transformative learning occurs during setbacks. Embracing failure, not as an indictment of capabilities but as an inherent and instructive part of the growth process, is a cornerstone of resilience. Every entrepreneur will encounter periods where plans falter, products miss the mark, or market assumptions prove inaccurate. These are not merely deviations; they are opportunities to recalibrate, gain critical insights, and emerge stronger, wiser, and better equipped for future challenges.

Learning from Setbacks: A Mindset of Inquiry

To truly learn from failure, a fundamental shift in perspective is required. Instead of succumbing to disappointment or assigning blame, entrepreneurs must cultivate a mindset of diligent inquiry. What specific factors contributed to the negative outcome? Was it a flaw in product design, an ineffective marketing strategy, poor financial management, or an underestimation of the competition? A rigorous and honest post-mortem analysis is paramount. This involves objectively dissecting the situation, examining every facet of decision-making, execution, and external environmental influences. It's about moving beyond emotional responses to focus on actionable intelligence.

Product Development and Financial Setbacks

Consider product development: a startup might invest significant time and resources into a product that fails to gain traction upon launch. Instead of abandoning the venture or blaming the market, the astute entrepreneur will delve into understanding why. This could involve detailed customer feedback, analyzing user behavior data, reviewing the product's features against market needs, and scrutinizing pricing and distribution. Perhaps the product was too complex or its value proposition unclear. Each identified and understood issue presents a clear pathway for improvement in future iterations or even new ventures. This iterative "build, measure, and learn" process is fundamentally about embracing and learning from the failures inherent in initial development stages.

Financial setbacks also offer invaluable lessons. A business experiencing a cash flow crisis, for instance, must confront its financial planning and management realities. This could highlight inadequate forecasting, insufficient capital reserves, poor expense control, or over-reliance on a single revenue stream. An entrepreneur who meticulously analyzes the root causes of such a crisis will gain a deeper understanding of financial discipline, the importance of diversification, and the critical need for robust financial controls. They will learn to build more realistic budgets, manage cash flow proactively, and develop contingency plans for unforeseen financial pressures. These are not just lessons for surviving a single event; they are fundamental skills that build a more financially stable and sustainable business for the long term.

The journey of entrepreneurship is a constant learning experience, with market feedback and internal dynamics serving as invaluable, albeit sometimes harsh, instructors. When a company experiences a decline in market share, it's a clear signal to critically assess customer service, product innovation, and competitive strategies. Was the competition offering a superior product, a better price, or a more engaging customer experience? Entrepreneurs who can objectively analyze these market forces, identify shortcomings, and adapt their strategies will gain a significant competitive advantage. This might involve investing in R&D for innovation, refining marketing messages to better convey value, or even restructuring the business model for greater agility.

Beyond market forces, the interpersonal aspects of a business also provide crucial lessons. Setbacks stemming from poor communication, weak leadership, or unresolved internal conflicts can be as instructive as market failures. Developing effective communication, fostering team cohesion, delegating appropriately, and managing conflict constructively are essential skills. When these areas falter and the business suffers, entrepreneurs have an opportunity to reflect on their leadership style, communication methods, and team-building approach. Building a high-performing team isn't just about hiring talent; it's about creating an environment that encourages collaboration and collective problem-solving.

The key to transforming setbacks into growth opportunities lies in consistently applying these learned lessons. It's not enough to simply pinpoint what went wrong; the real power comes from integrating that knowledge into future actions. This could mean revising a business plan, altering a product roadmap, refining a marketing message, or making significant operational changes. It demands acknowledging that the previous approach wasn't optimal and committing to a new, more informed strategy. This continuous cycle of learning, adapting, and implementing builds true entrepreneurial resilience.

Cultivating this mindset also requires self-compassion and recognizing that perfection is an unattainable goal. Every entrepreneur and their business are continuously evolving. A willingness to be vulnerable, seek advice, and openly admit mistakes fosters a supportive environment for learning and growth, both for the entrepreneur and their team. When leaders model this behavior, it encourages others to do the same, normalizing and even encouraging learning from errors, which leads to faster problem-solving and a more innovative and adaptable organization.

History is replete with examples of highly successful entrepreneurs who faced significant early failures. Thomas Edison's numerous attempts to perfect the light bulb, Walt Disney's bankruptcy with his first animation company, and Steve Jobs' ousting from Apple all demonstrate the power of perseverance driven by learning. These individuals saw their struggles not as insurmountable obstacles, but as vital steps on their journey. They analyzed their failures, adjusted their methods, and ultimately achieved extraordinary success. Their experiences highlight a crucial truth: resilience isn't the absence of failure, but the ability to learn from it and move forward with renewed purpose and insight.

Developing this capacity for learning from failure requires deliberate practice. This might involve dedicating time for reflection after major projects or business events, establishing regular review meetings focused on lessons learned, or seeking mentorship from experienced entrepreneurs who have faced similar challenges. Creating formal mechanisms to capture and share these lessons across the organization ensures that knowledge gained from one individual or team benefits the entire enterprise. This can be achieved through post-project debriefs, internal knowledge-sharing platforms, or dedicated training sessions.

The entrepreneurial ecosystem itself often facilitates this learning process. Networking events, industry conferences, and mentorship programs offer opportunities to connect with peers and learn from their experiences, including their failures. Sharing stories and insights in a supportive environment normalizes setbacks and provides practical advice for overcoming them. It's a reminder that no entrepreneur is an island, and collective learning can accelerate individual growth.

Ultimately, embracing failure as a learning opportunity isn't about actively seeking hardship; it's about developing the mental strength and strategic flexibility to navigate it when it inevitably arises. It's about understanding that each setback is a valuable data point, a crucial piece of information that, when properly analyzed and applied, leads to more informed decisions, stronger strategies, and a greater likelihood of long-term success. This continuous process of learning from mistakes is not merely a technique; it is a fundamental aspect of building a resilient and adaptable entrepreneurial spirit, transforming potential endpoints into valuable stepping stones for future achievements. By internalizing this philosophy, entrepreneurs can approach their ventures with greater confidence, knowing they possess the tools and mindset to learn from any challenges, emerging stronger and more capable with each experience. This commitment to continuous improvement, fueled by a candid assessment of what doesn't work, is the foundation upon which enduring entrepreneurial success is built. It fosters a proactive approach to challenges, shifting the focus from simply reacting to problems to actively extracting value and knowledge from them, thereby enhancing both individual growth and organizational capacity.

TEN

LONG-TERM VISION AND LEGACY

The entrepreneurial journey is a marathon, not a sprint, demanding both immediate action and a clear long-term vision. Having established a strong foundation, the focus now shifts to articulating not just what your business does today, but what it will become, its future impact, and its legacy. This section is dedicated to setting long-term goals and cultivating a compelling vision. This vision provides purpose to daily operations, anchors strategic decisions, and directs team energy. Without a clear, aspirational vision, a business risks drifting, reacting to market shifts rather than shaping them, and failing to reach its full potential.

A long-term vision is more than financial targets; it's a vivid picture of your business's future state and its impact. It answers: "What are we striving to achieve in the next five, ten, or twenty years?" This vision should be aspirational, pushing boundaries. It might involve becoming a market leader, pioneering new technology, or reshaping customer expectations. Consider Apple's vision of integrating technology seamlessly into everyday life, empowering individuals through intuitive design, which went beyond market share to change how people interacted with the world. Similarly, a vision could be rooted in sustainability, aiming to build a financially thriving business that also positively contributes to environmental and social well-being, setting a benchmark for responsible corporate citizenship.

Establishing this vision requires introspection and expansive thinking. It's about identifying your business's core purpose beyond profit. What problem are you solving? What value are you bringing to customers, your industry, and society? A powerful vision acts as a North Star, guiding every strategic decision, from product development to talent acquisition. When faced with choices, asking "Does this move us closer to our long-term vision?" provides clarity, ensuring short-term expediency doesn't derail long-term aspirations. This process should be inclusive, involving key stakeholders and team members to foster shared purpose and commitment.

Translating this vision into concrete, actionable long-term goals is the next critical step. These goals should be SMART (Specific, Measurable, Achievable, Relevant, and Time-bound), though the "Achievable" aspect for longer-term goals might be audacious. They represent significant milestones toward your overarching vision. For example, if your vision is to become the leading provider of sustainable energy solutions, goals might include achieving a certain market share within a decade, developing ground-breaking new products, or establishing a global presence. Another goal could be building a renowned brand associated with innovation and environmental responsibility, measurable through brand recognition surveys and industry awards.

Long-term goals are vital benchmarks for assessing progress and making strategic adjustments. They also guide resource allocation, ensuring that investments in time, capital, and human resources align with ultimate objectives. Consider a biotechnology startup aiming to eradicate a specific disease. Their long-term goals might include successfully navigating clinical trials, securing regulatory approval in major markets, and making treatment accessible to millions within fifteen years. Each goal demands meticulous planning, significant investment, and unwavering dedication from a skilled team.

Setting these goals requires rigorous market analysis, competitive landscaping, and an honest assessment of capabilities and resources. What market trends will shape the industry in the next decade? How do competitors differentiate themselves, and how can you do the same? What internal capabilities are needed to achieve your vision? This involves scenario planning and anticipating future challenges and opportunities. For instance, a technology company aspiring to lead in artificial intelligence would set long-term goals for R&D investment, AI talent acquisition, and strategic partnerships with research institutions, while also considering regulatory shifts and ethical implications.

Furthermore, long-term visions and goals should not be static. The business landscape constantly evolves, necessitating refinement or redefinition in response to new information, technological advancements, or unforeseen market shifts. Adaptability is crucial. The vision provides enduring purpose, while goals act as adjustable navigational points. Regularly reviewing and updating objectives ensures their relevance and actionability, keeping the business agile and responsive. This review should be a formal part of the strategic planning cycle, typically annual, but with flexibility for earlier revisions if significant changes occur internally or externally.

A well-defined long-term vision also serves as a powerful tool for leadership and team motivation. When employees understand their work's grand purpose and how their daily contributions fit into a meaningful narrative, their engagement and commitment soar. A compelling vision inspires loyalty and fosters a culture where individuals are motivated by a shared aspiration to achieve something significant, beyond just their paychecks. For example, a company focused on affordable housing might envision housing every family in need. This ultimate goal imbues the challenges of sourcing materials, navigating regulations, and managing construction with deeper significance; they are building homes and transforming lives.

This shared vision also attracts top talent. Ambitious individuals are drawn to organizations with clear direction and a mission that resonates with their values. They seek to contribute to a cause that matters. Articulating a compelling long-term future creates an irresistible magnet for the talent needed to achieve it, particularly in today's job market where professionals prioritize purpose and impact alongside career advancement and compensation.

The Power of a Long-Term Vision

A strong long-term vision is an anchor in times of uncertainty and crisis. When challenges arise, a clear understanding of your ultimate goal helps maintain focus, ensuring decisions align with your core mission and preventing short-term panic. This vision provides continuity and stability in turbulent environments. For example, during an economic downturn, a company with a strong vision for long-term growth might continue investing in R&D or strategic acquisitions, positioning itself to emerge stronger, rather than simply cutting costs. This foresight, guided by a long-term vision, can be a significant competitive advantage.Building a Lasting Legacy: Vision, Innovation, and Adaptation

Defining Your Enduring Impact:

A business's long-term vision goes beyond financial success to encompass its legacy. Consider the lasting impact you want to leave on your industry, community, and the world. This includes the values you uphold, the innovations you pioneer, the people you empower, and the positive change you facilitate. Steve Jobs's ambition to "put a dent in the universe" exemplifies a legacy-driven approach, fueling his pursuit of excellence and the creation of innovative, user-friendly products. Similarly, a company might aim to be known for its integrity and commitment to employee well-being, creating a lasting positive influence.

Operationalizing Your Vision:

To achieve this legacy, establish clear mission and vision statements. Your mission should define your company's purpose and values, while your vision paints a picture of its desired future. These are not mere formalities; they are living documents that guide strategic planning, marketing, hiring, and daily operations. For instance, a company committed to "empowering small businesses through accessible technology" might envision itself as "the indispensable digital partner for entrepreneurs worldwide." This vision would then shape their long-term goals related to product accessibility, customer support, and market reach.

Communicating and Reinforcing the Vision:

Consistent communication of your vision and long-term goals to your team is crucial. This involves ongoing dialogue through internal newsletters, all-hands meetings, team discussions, and performance reviews. Reinforce the vision and demonstrate how current efforts contribute to its realization. Celebrate milestones to maintain momentum and ensure everyone understands their role in achieving the shared future. This fosters a unified front, transforming the business from a collection of individuals into a cohesive force with a shared purpose. This strategic foresight is the foundation of lasting impact and enduring enterprises.The Lifeblood of an Enduring Enterprise: Improvement and Adaptation

Cultivating a Culture of Innovation:

For businesses to remain relevant and competitive, a relentless pursuit of improvement and a strong capacity for adaptation are essential. As you consider your business's long-term trajectory, fostering a robust culture of innovation and continuously evolving your product or service offerings becomes paramount. This isn't about chasing every trend, but about establishing a strategic framework that anticipates, embraces, and drives change within your industry. A proactive, forward-thinking approach transforms potential market disruptions into opportunities for growth and differentiation, ensuring your offerings remain valuable.

Investing in Research and Development (R&D):

A deep commitment to R&D forms the bedrock of this proactive stance. R&D should be viewed as a critical investment in the future, not a cost to be minimized. This investment can manifest in various ways: dedicated R&D departments, cross-functional teams exploring new possibilities, or strategic partnerships with academic institutions and research firms. Allocating resources—financial capital, human talent, and dedicated time—to the exploration and development of new ideas, technologies, and solutions is key. The pharmaceutical industry, with its decades-long R&D cycles for life-saving drugs, exemplifies this long-term vision. Similarly, technology giants like Google invest billions in R&D, not only to enhance existing services but also to explore new frontiers like AI, self-driving cars, and quantum computing, ensuring a pipeline of future innovations.

Agile and Customer-Centric Innovation:

Innovation isn't exclusive to large corporations with vast R&D budgets. Smaller enterprises can embrace a more agile and customer-centric approach. This often begins with a keen understanding of customer pain points and unmet needs. By actively listening to customers, analyzing their feedback, and observing their behaviors, businesses can identify opportunities for improvement and new product development. Implementing structured feedback mechanisms like surveys, user interviews, beta testing, and dedicated customer success teams is crucial. These channels serve as early warning systems and fertile ground for new ideas. For example, a SaaS company noting a recurring feature request from its users would proactively dedicate development resources to explore its feasibility. This not only enhances the product but also demonstrates customer value, fostering loyalty and a continuous feedback loop for further innovation.

For innovation to truly flourish, an internal culture that welcomes experimentation and tolerates failure is crucial. Creativity can be stifled by a fear of failure. Leaders must actively encourage employees to propose new ideas, test hypotheses, and learn from both successes and setbacks. This could involve creating "innovation labs" or "skunkworks" projects, giving teams the freedom to explore unconventional ideas without immediate commercial pressure. Pixar Animation Studios, for example, is known for its collaborative and experimental filmmaking approach, fostering an environment where artists and storytellers can freely share ideas, iterate on concepts, and offer constructive criticism. They understand that the best stories often emerge from a rigorous, iterative process that includes moments of failure and redirection. This mindset—viewing failure as a learning opportunity rather than a punitive event—is a powerful engine for continuous improvement.

Beyond internal R&D and customer feedback, staying ahead requires a proactive approach to market sensing and trend analysis. This means constantly scanning for emerging technologies, shifting consumer preferences, regulatory changes, and competitive developments. This goes beyond reading industry reports; it involves engaging with the broader ecosystem. Attend conferences, participate in industry forums, cultivate relationships with thought leaders, and monitor non-traditional sources of innovation. A fashion retailer, for instance, might look beyond traditional fashion weeks to understand broader cultural shifts, social media trends, and advancements in textile manufacturing. A food manufacturer might analyze emerging dietary trends, food science advancements, and global supply chain dynamics. This comprehensive market intelligence allows businesses to anticipate future demand and position themselves to meet it.

This proactive trend analysis should directly inform your product development roadmap. Instead of merely reacting to current demand, you should be building the products and services that customers will want or need in the future. This demands strategic foresight and the ability to connect seemingly disparate trends. Consider the evolution of personal computing: early pioneers like Apple and Microsoft didn't just build better typewriters; they envisioned how computing could transform communication, entertainment, and work. This long-term vision, fueled by an understanding of emerging technologies and potential user needs, guided their product development, leading to personal computers, graphical user interfaces, and eventually, the mobile revolution. Their ability to anticipate these shifts, rather than merely respond, cemented their market leadership for decades.

A phased approach is often most effective for product development. This could include an initial ideation phase, followed by conceptualization and feasibility studies, then prototyping and testing, and finally, refinement and launch. Each phase should have clear objectives and success criteria, with built-in mechanisms for feedback and iteration. For example, a software company developing a new application might start with a minimum viable product (MVP)—a version with just enough features to satisfy early customers and provide feedback for future development. This allows for rapid deployment, early market validation, and the ability to pivot based on real-world usage before heavily investing in a fully fleshed-out product. This agile development methodology, borrowed from software engineering, is increasingly applicable across various industries, enabling businesses to bring new offerings to market more quickly and efficiently while minimizing risk.

The concept of "disruptive innovation," popularized by Clayton Christensen, offers valuable insights for staying ahead. Disruptive innovations often begin in niche markets, providing simpler, more convenient, or more affordable alternatives to existing solutions. While initially overlooked by incumbent players, they gradually improve and eventually displace established market leaders. Businesses must vigilantly identify potential disruptive technologies or business models, even if they don't immediately threaten their core operations. Netflix is a classic example, starting with DVD rentals by mail—a seemingly niche service that evolved into a streaming giant, fundamentally disrupting the traditional video rental industry. By understanding the principles of disruptive innovation, businesses can either proactively develop their own disruptive offerings or prepare to defend against those that might emerge unexpectedly.

Furthermore, a commitment to continuous improvement extends beyond brand-new product development to encompass the ongoing enhancement of existing offerings. This involves iterative updates, feature additions, and performance optimizations that keep your products and services competitive and relevant. For physical products, this might mean incorporating new materials, improving manufacturing processes for greater efficiency or sustainability, or refining the user experience based on post-purchase feedback. For services, it could involve streamlining delivery processes, enhancing customer support, or leveraging technology to offer more personalized or value-added experiences. The automotive industry exemplifies this, with manufacturers constantly releasing updated models incorporating new safety features, improved fuel efficiency, and updated infotainment systems. This constant evolution ensures their vehicles remain desirable and competitive in a rapidly changing market.

Driving Innovation and Product Development Through Data and Collaboration

Data analytics plays a crucial role in fostering innovation and product development. By collecting and analyzing data on customer behavior, market trends, and operational performance, businesses can gain valuable insights to inform strategic decisions. Predictive analytics can forecast demand, identify emerging customer needs, and anticipate market shifts. A/B testing allows businesses to compare different versions of product features, marketing messages, or user interfaces to determine optimal performance. This data-driven approach minimizes guesswork, increasing the likelihood of successful product launches and marketing campaigns. For e-commerce businesses, analyzing browsing history, purchase patterns, and cart abandonment rates provides valuable information for personalizing recommendations, optimizing website design, and guiding new product introductions.

Cultivating partnerships and collaborations also significantly accelerates innovation. No single company possesses a monopoly on good ideas. By partnering with other businesses, research institutions, or individual innovators, companies can access new technologies, specialized expertise, and broader market insights. These collaborations can take various forms, including joint ventures, licensing agreements, co-development projects, or open innovation platforms. For example, a biotechnology startup might partner with a large pharmaceutical company to leverage manufacturing capabilities and distribution networks, accelerating market entry for new therapies. Conversely, a large tech company might collaborate with universities to fund cutting-edge research that could lead to future product innovations.

Innovating Business Models for Strategic Advantage

Innovation also extends to the business model itself. Significant advancements often arise not from improving existing products but from fundamentally changing how value is created, delivered, and captured. Subscription models, freemium offerings, platform-based businesses, and direct-to-consumer (DTC) strategies are examples of business model innovations that have reshaped entire industries. Companies like Dollar Shave Club disrupted the personal grooming market through its subscription-based delivery and direct brand messaging. Continuously evaluating and reinventing business models can unlock new revenue streams, reach new customer segments, and create a more resilient and adaptable enterprise.

A Culture of Continuous Innovation for Long-Term Success

Staying ahead of the curve is a continuous process requiring an ongoing commitment to learning, evolving, and innovating. It necessitates a culture that encourages curiosity, embraces change, and prioritizes long-term relevance. This means moving beyond a reactive stance to proactive leadership, anticipating and actively shaping the future. A relentless focus on innovation and product development ensures a business not only survives but thrives in an ever-changing world, building a sustainable legacy of value creation and market leadership. Key cornerstones of a lasting and leading organization include investing in R&D, listening to customers, fostering experimentation, analyzing market trends, and embracing new business models.

Charting a Course for Growth: Market Expansion and Diversification

The long-term vision for any enterprise involves strategically charting a course for future opportunities, not just refining current operations. Building on foundational innovation and continuous improvement, the focus shifts to tangible growth pathways: expansion into new markets and diversification of offerings. When executed thoughtfully, these strategies amplify market reach, strengthen competitive positioning, and create new revenue avenues, all while remaining aligned with the business's core mission and values.

Navigating New Market Entry

Entering new geographical markets offers significant opportunities to tap into untapped customer bases and leverage existing strengths in diverse economic and cultural landscapes. This endeavor demands meticulous planning and a nuanced understanding of the target market's unique characteristics. Before international expansion, a comprehensive market analysis is crucial, involving an in-depth examination of local consumer behavior, cultural norms, economic conditions, regulatory frameworks, political stability, and the competitive landscape. For instance, a gourmet food company might find success in Europe but would need to adapt marketing and product formulations to comply with different food safety standards and taste preferences. Similarly, a technology firm expanding into Southeast Asia would need to understand the prevalent digital infrastructure, mobile penetration rates, and preferred payment methods in each target country.

Market entry approaches vary significantly, ranging from exporting finished goods to establishing local distribution partnerships or even manufacturing facilities or subsidiaries. Each method carries distinct risks and rewards, with the optimal choice depending on the product/service, investment scale, and risk tolerance. Direct exporting offers a lower-risk entry point with minimal upfront investment, allowing businesses to test the market. However, it often relies on intermediaries, which can reduce profit margins and limit direct customer control. Conversely, establishing a local presence through a subsidiary or joint venture provides greater control and deeper market understanding but requires a more substantial financial commitment and carries higher risk.

Protecting intellectual property (trademarks, patents, and other proprietary information) in new jurisdictions is critical to prevent infringement and safeguard competitive advantage. Legal counsel specializing in international business and intellectual property law is indispensable for navigating these complexities. Furthermore, operational aspects of expansion must be carefully considered, including adapting supply chains for new logistics, ensuring compliance with local labor laws, and establishing culturally sensitive and effective customer support mechanisms. A common pitfall in international expansion is inadequate localization of marketing efforts. Successful advertising campaigns require adapting not only language but also imagery, tone, and messaging to resonate with the local audience. Building relationships with local stakeholders, including government officials, industry associations, and community leaders, can also foster goodwill and facilitate smoother entry.

Diversification expands a business's scope by introducing new products, services, or entering new industries. This strategy reduces reliance on a single revenue stream and offers a buffer against market fluctuations, opening new avenues for growth.

Types of Diversification:

- **Related Diversification:** New offerings share commonalities with existing products, services, or target markets. This approach is generally less risky as it leverages existing brand equity, customer relationships, and operational capabilities.
    - **Examples:** A software company developing project management tools might expand into collaboration software or cloud-based storage. A coffee shop chain could launch branded coffee beans, brewing equipment, or catering services, leveraging their brand and knowledge of coffee.
- **Unrelated Diversification:** Venturing into entirely new territories. While potentially offering higher rewards, this carries greater risk due to the need for new skill sets, market knowledge, and operational frameworks. Success often depends on effective management of diverse businesses and identifying non-obvious synergies.
    - **Example:** A manufacturing firm entering financial services.

Key Considerations for Diversification:

- **Brand Identity and Focus:** New ventures should not dilute the core brand or distract from the primary business. Each effort requires a clear strategic rationale aligned with the enterprise's vision and long-term sustainability.
- **Financial Capacity:** Diversification often requires significant investment in R&D, marketing, and infrastructure. A thorough financial assessment, including cost projections, revenue forecasts, and ROI analysis, is crucial.
- **Competitive Advantages:** Understand how existing competitive advantages can transfer to new contexts. Assess if these advantages are transferable or if new ones need to be developed.

    - **Example:** Strong customer service can be highly valued in a new market. A unique technological patent might require a different competitive strategy in a new geographical area.
- **Integration of New Ventures:** New products or services need effective market introduction, operational support, and smooth integration of new teams. A "launch and learn" approach with continuous monitoring and adaptation is advisable.

Strategic Partnerships:

Partnerships offer another potent avenue for expansion, allowing access to new resources, expertise, and markets without the full burden of independent development. These collaborations can take various forms:

- **Joint Ventures:** Two or more companies pool resources to create a new entity for a specific objective (e.g., entering a new market, developing a new product). This is effective when companies have complementary strengths.
    - **Example:** A technology company with new software partners with a telecommunications provider to bundle and market its offering.
- **Licensing Agreements:** A company grants another entity the right to use its intellectual property (e.g., patents, trademarks) in exchange for royalties or fees. This monetizes innovation without direct market entry or manufacturing.
    - **Example:** A company licenses a unique manufacturing process to manufacturers in other regions.
- **Strategic Alliances:** More informal collaborations where companies work together towards a common goal without a separate legal

entity. This can involve sharing marketing resources, co-developing technologies, or joint advocacy.

- **Co-branding:** Two or more brands are featured on a single product or service, leveraging multiple brands to attract a wider audience.
    - **Example:** An athletic shoe brand collaborates with an apparel designer for a limited-edition collection.

Managing Strategic Partnerships:

- **Due Diligence:** Thoroughly assess potential partners' financial stability, reputation, strategic alignment, and cultural compatibility. A misaligned partnership can be detrimental.
- **Clear Agreements:** Comprehensive agreements defining roles, responsibilities, ownership, profit-sharing, and exit strategies are crucial and should be drafted by legal professionals.
- **Ongoing Management:** Regular communication, transparent reporting, and a commitment to mutual benefit are key to fostering strong relationships and ensuring both parties achieve their desired outcomes.
- **Broader Collaborations:** Partnerships can extend beyond commercial entities to include

academic institutions, research organizations, or government bodies. These can provide access to cutting-edge research, talent, specialized facilities, funding, and help navigate regulatory environments.

The ability to identify and cultivate strategic partnerships is a hallmark of forward-thinking enterprises. By combining internal strengths with external capabilities through well-managed collaborations, businesses can unlock new levels of growth, innovation, and market influence, solidifying their long-term vision and building a robust legacy.

Lasting entrepreneurial success extends beyond immediate growth and profit; it's about building an enduring brand and a meaningful business legacy. This involves deliberately shaping an organization's identity and influence to transcend fleeting trends, creating value that resonates with customers, employees, the industry, and the wider community. A legacy is the result of principled action, consistent dedication to purpose, and an unwavering commitment to a long-term vision.

At its core, a lasting brand is a promise—a consistent embodiment of an enterprise's values, unique selling proposition, and the experience it delivers. Building this requires articulating the fundamental principles that guide the business, such as integrity, innovation, customer-centricity, or sustainability. When these values are actively lived by every member of the organization, the brand gains authenticity and trustworthiness, which are crucial for a strong legacy. Companies that have endured for decades or centuries often owe their longevity to an unshakeable commitment to these core principles, maintaining a reputation for reliability and purpose.

The internal environment is equally vital. A positive and empowering company culture drives consistent brand delivery and fosters a shared purpose. This means creating an environment where employees feel valued, respected, and motivated, promoting open communication, professional development, and a healthy work-life balance. Engaged employees become powerful brand ambassadors, upholding standards and innovating. A culture that prioritizes learning and adaptability ensures the enterprise can withstand challenges and emerge stronger. Investing in internal talent and fostering a cohesive team directly contributes to the business's longevity, reducing turnover and attracting top talent.

Beyond internal operations, a legacy is built through contributions to the surrounding ecosystem. This can include pioneering innovations, philanthropic efforts, or products and services that genuinely improve lives. For example, a company investing in R&D leaves a legacy of progress, while one prioritizing sustainable practices builds a legacy of stewardship. This broader impact requires looking beyond short-term profits to consider the long-term consequences and benefits, asking not just "how much did we make?" but "what did we create?" and "who did we help?"

Establishing a framework for the future is a hallmark of legacy building. This includes succession planning for leadership, knowledge, and vision transfer. It also involves developing robust systems that adapt to market changes and technological advancements, and cultivating a culture of continuous learning. A legacy is dynamic and requires nurturing, perhaps through an advisory board or leadership development programs, and a governance structure that safeguards long-term interests and core values.

Enduring value creation is central to this undertaking. What lasting value does the enterprise offer to its customers, employees, and society? This could be a product solving a persistent problem, a service enhancing quality of life, or an experience bringing joy. Focusing on intrinsic value anchors the brand and ensures its relevance. Exceptional customer service builds a loyal customer base, while championing ethical sourcing contributes to a more equitable marketplace, building a legacy of social responsibility. This multifaceted approach ensures the enterprise is not just a commercial entity but a force for good.

Finally, the brand's narrative profoundly shapes its legacy. How the story, values, and impact are communicated influences perception and remembrance. Compelling, authentic, and consistent storytelling across all platforms highlights the journey, mission, and positive changes, resonating deeply with stakeholders. Sharing the "why" behind the business, such as a founder's personal journey or challenges overcome, creates an emotional connection and deeper appreciation for the brand's history and purpose, becoming an integral part of its enduring identity.

Building a lasting brand and business legacy is an ongoing, intentional process. It demands a clear vision, adherence to core values, a commitment to creating genuine value, and a dedication to fostering a positive internal culture and meaningful external impact. The goal is to create an enterprise that is not only profitable but also purposeful, leaving a positive and indelible mark on the world. This forward-looking perspective and commitment to enduring influence differentiate fleeting success from true, lasting achievement, transforming a business from a mere economic entity into an institution of lasting significance.

The culmination of an entrepreneurial journey, while often focused on growth and market dominance, must also include careful consideration of the future. Building a legacy isn't solely about present achievements; it's crucially about ensuring the sustained vitality and impact of the enterprise beyond the founder's direct involvement. This forward-thinking approach requires robust exit strategies and succession planning, meticulously preparing for the eventual transition of ownership and leadership. These are not last-minute administrative tasks but integral components of a comprehensive long-term vision designed to preserve and enhance the value created over years of dedication and innovation.

When contemplating the future of your enterprise, several distinct pathways for divestment or transfer of ownership emerge, each with its own advantages, challenges, and implications for your desired legacy.Common Exit Strategies

- **Sale to a Third Party:** This is a common route, taking various forms such as a strategic acquisition by a larger competitor, a complementary business, a private equity buyout, or even an acquisition by employees through a management buyout (MBO) or an employee stock ownership plan (ESOP).

- **Strategic sale:** Often leverages synergies, potentially leading to an integrated and expanded future for the company's products, services, and workforce.
- **Private equity firms:** Typically seek to optimize operations and financial performance, often with a clear exit strategy within a defined timeframe.
- **MBO or ESOP:** Particularly appealing for maintaining company culture and rewarding instrumental employees.

Regardless of the buyer type, a well-executed sale requires meticulous preparation, including thorough financial audits, legal due diligence, and a clear articulation of the company's value proposition and growth potential. This process demands a deep understanding of the market, potential buyers, and negotiation strategies to ensure the best possible outcome, both financially and in terms of the enterprise's future trajectory.

- **Family Succession:** The transition of the business to the next generation is deeply personal and can be profoundly rewarding, but it also presents unique complexities. For businesses with strong family involvement, this can be a natural and emotionally resonant progression. However, it requires careful planning to ensure successors are not only willing but genuinely capable. This involves:

- Identifying and mentoring potential successors early on.
- Providing comprehensive training, exposure to all facets of the business, and opportunities to develop leadership skills.
- Assessing their aptitude, passion, and commitment, and fostering a clear understanding of responsibilities and challenges.

Beyond individual readiness, succession planning also addresses estate planning, ownership structures, and potential family dynamics to prevent disputes and ensure a smooth, equitable transfer of control. Establishing a clear governance structure, such as a family council or a board of directors with independent members, can provide objective guidance and facilitate difficult conversations. In this scenario, the legacy is intertwined with the continuation of family values and commitment to the enterprise.

- **Initial Public Offering (IPO):** Taking the company public is another distinct exit strategy, capable of unlocking significant capital for expansion and providing liquidity for early investors and employees. An IPO transforms a privately held company into a publicly traded entity, subject to rigorous regulatory oversight and public scrutiny. This process requires substantial preparation, including:

- Establishing robust financial reporting systems.
- Building a strong management team with public company experience.
- Developing a compelling investor relations strategy.

While an IPO offers immense growth opportunities and a clear exit for some stakeholders, it fundamentally changes the nature of the business, shifting focus from private ownership to shareholder value and public market expectations. The legacy here is often defined by the company's sustained performance on public markets and its ability to adapt to the demands of public investors, requiring a new level of transparency, accountability, and strategic communication.

Beyond the common exit strategies, a management-led buyout (MBO) or an employee stock ownership plan (ESOP) offer alternative approaches. An MBO allows senior management, often with external financial backing, to purchase the business. This is ideal for founders who trust their leadership team and want to preserve the company's existing direction. Conversely, an ESOP establishes a trust fund holding company stock for employees. This not only offers an exit route for the owner but also cultivates employee ownership and aligns their interests with the company's long-term success. Both MBOs and ESOPs demand meticulous financial and legal planning but can effectively perpetuate company culture and reward dedicated employees.

Succession planning is fundamentally linked to preserving a company's legacy. It ensures that the founding vision, values, and operational excellence are passed on to future leaders. This process goes beyond merely finding a successor; it involves a deliberate strategy for knowledge transfer, cultural reinforcement, and establishing a robust governance framework. A key component is defining clear succession criteria, ensuring that leaders possess both the necessary skills and a commitment to the organization's core principles. This can be achieved through formal mentorship programs, cross-functional training, and executive development initiatives.

Furthermore, succession planning must account for non-human assets, including intellectual property, brand reputation, operational systems, and strategic relationships. These tangible and intangible assets represent the company's collective efforts and are crucial for its ongoing success. A comprehensive succession plan will detail how these assets will be protected, managed, and utilized by future leadership. This involves documenting critical processes, safeguarding proprietary information, and maintaining key customer and supplier relationships to ensure a smooth transition, allowing the enterprise to continue operating effectively, adapt to new challenges, and seize future opportunities.

The timing of succession planning is also critical; it should be an ongoing process integrated into the business's strategic planning, ideally commencing years, even decades, before the actual transition. This timeframe allows for the identification and development of potential successors, preparing the business for sale or transfer, and addressing any potential obstacles. Early planning also provides flexibility to adjust the strategy as circumstances or successor capabilities evolve. A rushed or poorly executed succession can imperil the entire enterprise, leading to financial instability, loss of key personnel, and damage to the established legacy.

The financial implications of exit strategies and succession planning are significant. A well-executed plan maximizes the business's value, ensuring the founder reaps the financial rewards of their entrepreneurial endeavors. This entails optimizing the company's financial health, maintaining clear and transparent financial records, and understanding its market valuation. Tax implications are also a vital consideration; engaging financial and legal experts early can help structure the transaction in a tax-efficient manner, preserving more of the created value. For family businesses, careful estate planning and tax advice are paramount for a smooth and cost-effective transfer of wealth and ownership.

Ultimately, the most effective exit strategies and succession plans are those that align with the founder's overarching vision for their legacy. By answering fundamental questions about the company's future, its beneficiaries, and its enduring values, founders can make informed decisions. This ensures their entrepreneurial journey culminates in a lasting and meaningful impact, transitioning from active creation to thoughtful stewardship. The goal is for the enterprise to remain a vibrant force, a testament to the founder's vision and hard work, securing the future impact of what has been so diligently built. This final stage of the entrepreneurial lifecycle is not an end, but a deliberate and strategic pivot to ensure the enduring relevance and positive influence of the enterprise.

www.ingramcontent.com/pod-product-compliance
Lightning Source LLC
LaVergne TN
LVHW100248210926
848480LV00003B/858
* 9 7 9 8 3 4 9 6 4 7 0 5 5 *